THE EUCHOLOGION UNVEILED

An Explanation of Byzantine Liturgical Practice II

The Orthodox Liturgy Series

The Orthodox Liturgy series provides an insightful, accessible, and lucid interpretation of the theology, meaning, and function of the liturgical life of the Orthodox Church.

Paul Meyendorff
Series Editor

BOOK 1
The Anointing of the Sick
by Paul Meyendorff

BOOK 2
Byzantine Liturgical Reform
by Thomas Pott

BOOK 3
The Typikon Decoded
by Archimandrite Job Getcha

BOOK 4
The Euchologion Unveiled
by Archbishop Job Getcha

BOOK 4 OF THE ORTHODOX LITURGY SERIES

The Euchologion Unveiled

An Explanation of
Byzantine Liturgical Practice II

Archbishop Job Getcha

ST VLADIMIR'S SEMINARY PRESS
YONKERS, NEW YORK
2021

Library of Congress Cataloging-in-Publication Data

Names: Getcha, Job, Archbishop, author.
Title: The Euchologion unveiled / Archbishop Job Getcha.
Description: Yonkers, NY : St. Vladimirs Seminary Press, 2018. | Series: The Orthodox liturgy
  series ; book 4 | Includes bibliographical references.
Identifiers: LCCN 2018030111 (print) | LCCN 2018032353 (ebook) | ISBN 9780881416367 |
  ISBN 9780881416350 (alk. paper)
Subjects: LCSH: Orthodox Eastern Church--Euchologion--History and criticism.
Classification: LCC BX375.E75 (ebook) | LCC BX375.E75 G47 2018 (print) |
  DDC 264/.019--dc23
LC record available at https://lccn.loc.gov/2018030111

COPYRIGHT © 2021
ST VLADIMIR'S SEMINARY PRESS
575 Scarsdale Road, Yonkers, NY 10707
1-800-204-2665
www.svspress.com

ISBN 978–088141–635–0 (paper)
ISBN 978–088141–235–3 (electronic)

Scripture quotations from the King James Version, unless otherwise noted.

Translations of most liturgical texts quoted in this volume are drawn from the
appropriate services (sometimes slightly edited) in *The Great Book of Needs*,
Expanded and Supplemented, translated from Church Slavonic with notes by
St Tikhon's Monastery, four vols. (South Canaan, PA: St Tikhon's Seminary
Press, 1998–99); items found only in manuscripts are presented, without
comment, in the author's own translations.

Translations of texts of the Divine Liturgy are drawn from the *Hieratikon*, vol. 2
(South Canaan, PA: St Tikhon's Monastery Press, 2018).

PRINTED IN THE UNITED STATES OF AMERICA

Contents

Abbreviations

ANF   The Ante-Nicene Fathers: Translations of the Fathers down to AD 325. 10 vols. Alexander Roberts, James Donaldson, and A. Cleveland Coxe, eds. Buffalo, NY: Christian Literature Company, 1885–1896, many reprints.

Barberini   *L'Euchologio Barberini gr. 336*. Second, revised edition. Stefano Parenti and Elena Velkovska, eds. Rome: Edizioni liturgiche, 2000.

BEL   Bibliotheca Ephemerides Liturgicae

CCSL   Corpus Christianorum Series Latina. Turnhout, Belgium: BREPOLS, 1954–.

DACL   *Dictionnaire d'Archéologie Chrétienne et de Liturgie*. Ed. Fernand Cabrol and Henri Leclercq. Paris: Letouzey et Ane. Vol. 1, 1907; Vol. 2, 1910, 1925; Vol. 4, 1920.

Egeria, *Diary*   *Egeria: Diary of a Pilgrimage*, ed. Johannes Quasten, Walter J. Burghardt, and Thomas Comerford Lawler, eds. George E. Gingras, trans. Ancient Christian Writers vol. 38. New York; Mahwah, NJ: The Newman Press, 1970.

EO   *Échos d'Orient*. Paris: L'Institut Français d'Etudes Byzantines, 1897–1946.

GBN   *Great Book of Needs Expanded and Supplemented*. Translated from Church Slavonic with notes by St Tikhon's Monastery. Four vols. South Canaan, PA: St Tikhon's Seminary Press, 1998–99. [English translation of the Slavonic *Trebnik*.]

Goar   Jacobus Goar. *Euchologion sive Rituale Graecorum*. Venice: Typographia Bartholomaei Javarina, 1730.

OCA   Orientalia Christiana Analecta. Open series. Rome: Pontificium Institutum Orientalium Studiorum, 1935–.

OCP   *Orientalia Christiana Periodica*. Continuing journal. Rome:
            Pontificium Institutum Orientalium Studiorium, 1935–.

PG   J. P. Migne. Patrologia Graeca series secunda. 161 Volumes.
            Paris, 1857–66.

Philokalia *The Philokalia: The Complete Text*. Compiled by St Nikodi-
            mos of the Holy Mountain and St Makarios of Corinth.
            Translated from the Greek and edited by G. E. H. Palmer,
            Philip Sherrard, and Kallistos Ware. Four vols., fifth in
            preparation.1979 London and Boston: Faber and Faber,
            1979–1995.

PPS   Popular Patristics Series. Open series. Crestwood and Yon-
            kers, NY: St Vladimir's Seminary Press, 1977–.

REB   *Revue d'Études byzantines*. Continuing journal. Louvain:
            Peeters, for L'Institut Catholique de Paris, 1946–.

SC   Sources chrétiennes. 600 vols in an open series. Paris: Les
            Éditions du Cerf.

SVTQ   *St Vladimir's Theological Quarterly*. Continuing journal.
            Crestwood and Yonkers, NY: St Vladimir's Seminary Press,
            1952–.

Euchologion Manuscripts

Alexandria 104	14th c.
Barberini gr. 336	8th c.
Dionysiou 450	1408
Dionysiou 99	14th c.
Grottaferrata Γ. β. 1 (alias *Euchologion of Bessarion*)	13th c.
Grottaferrata Γ. β. 10	10th–11th c.
Metochion of the Holy Sepulcher in Constantinople 8 (182)	15th c.
Paris Coislin 213	1027
Patmos 105	13th c.
Patmos 690	15th c.
Patmos 691	15th–16th c.
*Sinai gr. 957**	9th or 10th c.
*Sinai gr. 958**	10th c.
*Sinai gr. 963**	12th c.
Sinai gr. 971	13th–14th c.
*Sinai gr. 973**	12th c.
Sinai gr. 974	16th c.
*Sinai gr. 980**	15th c.
Sinai gr. 981	14th c.
Sinai gr. 990	14th c.

Sinai gr. 991	14th c.
Sinai gr. 1006	15th c.
St Panteleimon 604	15th c.
St Sabbas 369	15th c.
St Sabbas 568	16th–17th c.

*Manuscripts so marked have been digitized by the Library of Congress and may be viewed on the Library's website at *https://www.loc.gov/collections/manuscripts-in-st-catherines-monastery-mount-sinai/about-this-collection/* (Accessed May 14, 2020).

Illustrations

by Megan Elizabeth Gilbert

Tables

Foreword

At the Divine Liturgy, during the Great Entrance, the deacon and the priest carry the diskos and the chalice, which are covered by veils, as the chanters sing the Cherubic hymn, which emphasizes that we are entering into a mystery:

> Let us, who mystically represent the Cherubim
> and who sing the thrice-holy hymn to the life-giving Trinity,
> now lay aside all earthly cares,
> that we may receive the King of all
> who comes invisibly upborne by the angelic hosts.

The term *mystery* (in Greek μυστήριον) refers to something secret, to something that is not comprehensible, to something that is not immediately accessible to our human senses. For this reason, this term has been chosen by Christianity to refer to sacramental actions of the Church. As Saint Symeon of Thessalonica puts it, "the mysteries are performed in a visible form, but they are the action of the Holy Spirit,"[1] which is invisible.

For this precise reason, in the Divine Liturgy, the Holy Gifts are covered by veils to emphasize the mystery. Furthermore, at certain points in the Divine Liturgy the curtain of the icon screen is closed, to reinforce the sacramental dimension of the liturgical action. Indeed, veils hide in order to reveal: they hide something visible, to stress the fact that what we see with our human eyes is not what is actually happing. What is actually happening is much greater, something that is not bearable by our human eyes and not expressible by our human tongue. The real action is invisible. As Saint Paul the Apostle puts it, "For now we see through a glass, darkly; but then face to face: now I know in part; but then shall I know even as also I am known" (1 Cor 13.12). We are participants in the mystery of Christ, the mystery of our salvation, which opens to us the path towards the Kingdom of God.

---

[1]Symeon of Thessalonica, *De Sacramentis* 41 (PG 155:181a).

The Church is first of all a sacramental entity, because the Church exists in order to enable us to participate in this mystery of Christ, in this great mystery of salvation. As Saint Maximus the Confessor explains:

> In Scripture, the mystery of Christ is itself called "Christ," and the great Apostle bears witness to this when he says that "the mystery hidden from the ages and the generations has now been manifested" [Col 1.24] . . . This is the great and hidden mystery. This is the blessed end for which all things were brought into existence.[2]

And this mystery of salvation in Christ is realized for us through the sacramental rites of the Church. There is no other purpose for the Church to exist.

As Saint Nicolas Cabasilas wrote, "the Church is represented in the holy mysteries." And he underlines that this is neither merely in symbols (ἐν συμβόλοις), nor by analogy, but by identity of reality (ἀλλὰ πράγματος ταυτότης). He had in mind that through the Eucharist, through our communion in the Holy Mysteries, by partaking in the sanctified bread and wine, we receive the real body and blood of Christ, and thus we become truly members of the Body of Christ which is the Church. Thus, again echoing Saint Nicolas Cabasilas, "it is not unreasonable to say that the holy mysteries represent the Church."[3]

But the sacramental dimension of the Church is signified not only by the Eucharist, but by every mystery of the Church and every sacramental rite of the Church, begnning with our baptism. Indeed, Saint Nicolas Cabasilas wrote elsewhere that our incorporation into Christ begins at our baptism, through our participation in his death and resurrection, signified by the threefold immersion in the bapstismal font, since ". . . burying our bodies in water as though in the grave, and . . . emerging thrice: this indicates that Christ, having made us partakers in his death and burial, will vouchsafe to admit us to a share in his new life."[4]

---

[2]Maximus the Confessor, *Questions to Thalassios* 60 (PG 90:620c-621c, 624bc); in English: St Maximos the Confessor, *On Difficulties in Sacred Scripture: The Responses to Thalassios*, trans. Maximos Constas, The Fathers of the Church 136 (Washington, DC: The Catholic University of America Press, 2018), 427.

[3]Nicolas Cabasilas, *Explanation of the Divine Liturgy* 13.1–3 (SC 4bis:231–233); Nicholas Cabasilas, *Commentary on the Divine Liturgy*, tr. J. M. Hussey and P. A. McNulty (Crestwood, NY: St Vladimir's Seminary Press, 1998), 91–92.

[4]Nicolas Cabasilas, *Explanation of the Divine Liturgy* 4.3 (SC 4bis:76–78; Cabasilas, *Commentary*, 33).

All the sacramental actions and rites of the Church, through ritual language, signify in a visible way mysteries that remain invisible, but that are nevertheless real and effective. The liturgical book of the Orthodox Church that contains all these sacramental rites is the *Euchologion*, also known as the *Trebnik* or the *Great Book of Needs*. The purpose of the present volume is precisely to "unveil" these mysteries by telling the history of these rites, by explaining their meaning, and by describing their actions. Thus, this fourth volume of the Orthodox Liturgy Series completes the third, where our intention was to "decode" the *Typikon*, which regulates the different services of the prayer of the Hours and of the annual liturgical cycle.

I would like to thank my colleague and friend, Professor Paul Meyendorff, for encouraging me to complete this second volume and for assisting me with its publication. I also thank Fr Benedict Churchill for his great help in editing the text and making it more accessible to the English reader. And I thank Saint Vladimir's Seminary Press for publishing it in the valuable Orthodox Liturgy Series; I hope that it will be useful to the clergy and laity of the Orthodox Church, as well as to anyone interested in the Byzantine liturgical tradition.

Archbishop Job of Telmessos

CHAPTER ONE

Christian Initiation

1. Historical Overview

Christian initiation—or the sacrament of baptism, as it is more commonly designated, or the mystery of illumination, as it is called in the patristic literature—is the series of rites through which a person is incorporated into the Church, according to the commandment of Christ to his apostles: "Go ye therefore, and teach all nations, baptizing them in the name of the Father, and of the Son, and of the Holy Ghost" (Mt 28.19). Through baptism we become members of the Church, which is the Body of Christ. The different rites of Christian initiation were never separated in the East as they came to be in the West, where, starting as early as the third century, and mostly for pastoral reasons, a separate rite of "confirmation" appeared, conferred by the bishop, often years after the baptism conferred by the parish priest. This separation led the Latin West to the concept of three different sacraments—baptism, confirmation, and the Eucharist—that were integrated into the official list of seven sacraments elaborated in the twelfth century. This list of seven sacraments was eventually adopted in the Greek East between the thirteenth and the fifteenth century, although the rites of baptism and chrismation were never disunited in the Byzantine practice, and they also remained connected to the celebration of the Eucharist, which is the mystery of the gathering or assembly (*synaxis*) and the manifestation of the Church as the Body of Christ.

Since Christian initiation is incorporation into the Church as the Body of Christ, it implies serious preparation and examination. This is why in the early Church, the bishop, as the head of the local community, was the person who conferred baptism. Those being baptized were mostly adults. This explains why the contemporary rites of Christian initiation in the Orthodox Church continue to follow the pattern of adult baptism, even though they are commonly celebrated today for infants. A person who asked to be baptized (that is, to be integrated into the Christian community) of his own will, also had to be recommended by a member of the Church. This is why a sponsor (who later became what we call today the godparent) was required. The sponsor had to witness to the moral life of the candidate. If the candidate did not fulfill the moral requirements of Christian life, his baptism was postponed.[1] If his moral life was fitting, then his name was inscribed on the list of those to be baptized.

Baptism was always preceded by a period of catechesis, during which the candidate was instructed by the bishop in the fundamental elements of the Christian faith. He was always accompanied by his sponsor. This period could sometimes last for several years, but it was a period of at least eight weeks prior to baptism; it consisted of lectures on the major passages from Holy Scripture about the mystery of salvation, and the explanation of the Symbol of Faith. A good example of such a catechesis is found in the famous *Catechical Homilies* of Saint Cyril of Jerusalem. Our liturgical texts even today make a distinction between "catechumens," that is, persons receiving instruction in preparation for their baptism, and "those who are preparing for holy illumination," that is, the catechumens entering their final stage of preparation, who are to be baptized in the following weeks. Throughout this period, priests would recite prayers of exorcism over the candidate.[2] Baptism was then followed by a one-week period of mystagogy, an explanation of the liturgical rites of Christian initiation. The *Mystagogical Homilies* of Saint Cyril of Jerusalem provide a remarkable example of these.[3]

It is important to emphasize that such an important and serious preparation was organized over time. In the early Church, baptism was celebrated in connection with Pascha, because baptism according to St Paul signifies our death and our resurrection with Christ (Rom 6.3–4). It occurred during the paschal vigil, on the eve of Pascha, which corresponds to our vesperal Liturgy of Saint Basil the Great, celebrated on Great and Holy Saturday.

---

[1]Egeria, *Itinerarium* 45.4 (SC 296:306); in English: *Egeria: Diary of a Pilgrimage*, ed. Johannes Quasten, Walter J. Burghardt, and Thomas Comerford Lawler, trans. George E. Gingras, Ancient Christian Writers 38 (New York and Mahwah, NJ: The Newman Press, 1970), 122 (hereafter Egeria, *Diary*). [Cf. Hippolytus, *Apostolic Tradition* 15–17 (Dix 16–17), in *Hippolytus: On the Apostolic Tradition*, Alistair C. Stewart, tr. and ed., Popular Patristics Series 54 (Yonkers, NY: St Vladimir's Seminary Press, 2018), 116–23.—*Ed.*]

[2]Ibid., 46 (SC 296:306–308).

[3][In Greek and English: Cyril of Jerusalem, *Lectures on the Christian Sacraments: The Procatechesis and the Five Mystagogical Catecheses Ascribed to St Cyril of Jerusalem*, trans. Maxwell Johnson, Popular Patristics Series 57 (Yonkers, NY: St Vladimir's Seminary Press, 2017).—*Ed.*]

Baptism took place in the baptistery during the long series of Old Testament readings prescribed at Vespers; these were read for the faithful, who were waiting in the nave of the Church for the entrance of the bishop with the newly baptized Christians.[4] For this reason, the period of catechesis that immediately preceded baptism corresponded to the period of Great Lent. The coincidence of this period of preparation for baptism with a period of fasting followed the recommendation of the early Church that baptism be preceded by fasting.[5] One must note that in the early Church, there were no individual baptisms. Catechumens were instructed together as a group, and then they were baptized together on the eve of Pascha. Eventually, when the number of catechumens became too large, the Church introduced other days in the liturgical year for baptism: Lazarus Saturday, Pentecost, Theophany, Nativity.[6] This explains why, at the Divine Liturgy on these feast days we still sing the Pauline verse: *As many as have been baptized in Christ, have put on Christ* (Gal 3.27). The week of post-baptismal mystagogy coincided with Bright Week, during which the newly baptized attended Divine Liturgy daily as they received their final instruction.

Things changed significantly when the Roman Empire became mostly Christian, and adult baptism consequently became rare. Indeed, the tendency was not to wait for the children of Christians to grow to adulthood before baptizing them. Thus baptism gradually took place at an earlier and earlier age, until infant baptism became widespread. This new situation led to new rites. Since children were born to Christian families who were attending church services, they needed to receive a status between their birth and the moment of their baptism. One has to remember that at one point, the norm in Byzantium was to baptize children not as infants, but more or less at the age of reason, so that they would be conscious of their initiation into the Church and would be able to follow a pre-baptismal catechesis that was shorter than the instruction for adults, but that still lasted for a month.[7] This

---

[4]Juan Mateos, *Le Typikon de la Grande Église: Ms. Sainte-Croix no. 40, Xe siècle;* Introduction, texte critique, traduction et notes par Juan Mateos, S.J., Vol. 2: *Le cycle des fêtes mobiles, OCA* 166 (Rome: Pontificium Institutum Orientalium Studiorum, 1963), 84–86.

[5]*Didache* 7 (SC 248 bis:170–172); in English: *On the Two Ways: Life or Death, Light or Darkness: Foundational Texts in the Tradition,* Alistair Stewart(-Sykes), tr. and ed., Popular Patristics Series 42 (Yonkers, NY: St Vladimir's Seminary Press, 2011), 9.

[6]*Typikon de la Grande Église,* 1:185; 2:62, 136.

[7]This explains why in later Byzantine times, the date of enrolling those who were to be baptized was the third Sunday of Great Lent (Sunday of the Cross), one month before Pascha. Cf. *Le Typikon de la Grande Église,* 2:38.

is the reason why the Byzantine Church created new rites connected to the birth of the child: the naming of the child on the eighth day after birth and the entrance of the child into the church on the fortieth day, in imitation of events in the life of Christ (Lk 2.21–38).[8] This gave an ecclesiastical status to the child who began his preparation for his future baptism at this point. For this reason, Miguel Arranz speaks of a "first catechumenate."[9] Such a practice seemed to last during almost the whole of the first millennium, since at the very end of that time, people were still discussing whether it was possible to baptize infants who were not able to renounce Satan and confess the faith for themselves.[10] Later, when infant baptism was widespread, Saint Symeon of Thessalonica discussed the question of free will and catechesis in the case of infant baptism, and he explained that the godparent ought to be a practicing Christian capable of raising the child in the Orthodox faith.[11] Thus when infant baptism became normative, pre-baptismal instruction was replaced by post-baptismal instruction that is commonly known as catechism classes or, more recently in some places, Sunday school or church school.

Thus, as we can see, Christian initiation is constituted of several rites, which were initially spread throughout the period of Great Lent and Bright Week. Today, they are gathered together in one single ceremony. The prayer to make someone a catechumen at the beginning of the service used to be said at the beginning of the period of the catechumenate, with an imposition of hands.[12] The three prayers of exorcism used to be repeated during the whole period of the catechumenate. The fourth prayer was said just before the moment of baptism,[13] with the rite of renunciation of Satan and adherence to Christ. This ancient rite was accompanied in the early Church by the recitation of the Symbol of Faith in front of the bishop, as the ultimate

---

[8]Stefano Parenti and Elena Velkovska, eds, *L'Euchologio Barberini gr. 336* (Rome: Edizioni Liturgiche, 2000) 117–118 [hereafter *Barberini* in footnotes, and in the text "Barberini *Euchologion*" or "Barberini manuscript" or "Barberini codex"]; this euchologion will often be cited in comparisons with later works.

[9]M. Arranz, "Les sacrements de l'ancien Euchologe constantinopolitain (3): II: Admission dans l'Eglise des enfants des familles chrétiennes (premier catéchuménat)," *OCP* 49 (1983): 284–302.

[10]Cf. Vassa Kontouma, "Baptême et communion des jeunes enfants: la lettre de Jean d'Antioche à Théodore d'Éphèse (998/999)," *Revue des études byzantines* 69 (2011): 85–204.

[11]Symeon of Thessalonica, *De sacramentis* 62 (PG 155:213ab).

[12]*Apostolic Constitutions* 8.39.4 (SC 336:94; ANF 7:476).

[13]*Barberini*, 122.

examination of the period of the catechumenate, and this usually took place on Great and Holy Friday at the service of Trithekti.[14]

The actual rite of baptism took place in the baptistery on Great and Holy Saturday, during the paschal vigil. It began with the blessing of the water and of the oil. The candidates stood naked, thus showing that they had put off "the old man."[15] The rite of the pre-baptismal anointing is interpreted by the *Apostolic Constitutions* as a sign of "remission of sins, and the first preparation for baptism,"[16] as one can see in the prayer of the *Euchologion.* In the early Church, the whole body was anointed with this oil by the deacon or by the deaconess.[17] The anointing with oil always preceded the threefold immersion that took place in the baptistery, in the name of each of the three persons of the Holy Trinity; this triple immersion also signifes Christ's burial for three days in the tomb and his resurrection on the third day.[18] After the immersion and the appropriate prayer, in which the celebrant gave thanks to God for giving the neophyte a new birth and the remission of sins, and asked for the seal of the gift of the Holy Spirit and the Communion of the body and blood of Christ, the neophyte was anointed with holy *Myron* (i.e., *Chrism*) in the sign of the cross on the forehead, eyes, nostrils, lips, ears, and breast, with the formula *the seal of the gift of the Holy Spirit.*[19] St Cyril of Jerusalem compares the rite of chrismation after baptism with the manifestation of the Holy Spirit after Christ's baptism in the Jordan river (Mt 3.16). For him this signifies that the neophyte who has put on Christ and has become an image of Christ (a word that literally means *the anointed one.*)[20] For this reason, the Pauline verse, *As many as have been baptized into Christ, have put on Christ* (Gal 3.27), was sung at that point. The neophytes were given a "luminous" (white) robe, showing that they

[14]*Apostolic Constitutions* 8.41.4 (SC 336:96–100; ANF 7.476); Egeria, *Itinerarium* 46.5 (SC 296:310–312; Egeria, *Diary,* 124); Cyril of Jerusalem, *Mystagogical Homilies* 1.4–5, 9 (SC 126:88, 98; *Cyril, Lectures,* PPS 57:86–89, 92–95); *Typikon de la Grande Église,* 2:78. [In the cathedral rite of the Church of Constantinople, *Trithekti* was a lenten mid-day service of antiphons, readings, and prayers; for its structure see Juan Mateos, *Le Typikon de la Grande Église* 1:xxiv—Ed.]

[15]Cyril of Jerusalem, *Mystagogical Homilies* 2.2 (SC 126:104–106; PPS 57:95–99).

[16]*Apostolic Constitutions* 8.42.2 (SC 336:100; ANF 7:476).

[17]*Barberini,* 130.

[18]Cyril of Jerusalem, *Mystagogical Homilies* 2.3–4 (SC 126:106–112; PPS 57:98–101).

[19]Cyril of Jerusalem, *Mystagogical Homilies* 3.4 (SC 126:126; PPS 57:106–109); *Barberini,* 130–131.

[20]Cyril of Jerusalem, *Mystagogical Homilies* 3.1 (SC 126:120; PPS 57:104–105).

had become children of light through the mystery of holy illumination, and had received the remission of sins.[21] Finally, just after the readings from the Old Testament of Vespers, during the recitation of Psalm 31, there was a procession with the neophytes from the baptistery to the nave of the main church, where the Divine Liturgy was celebrated, and at this Liturgy the neophytes received Holy Communion.[22]

In the early Church, the neophytes would then stay in the church for eight days, receiving their mystagogical instruction, which could be attended only by baptized Christians.[23] On the eighth day, only one prayer of ablution (the first one of our contemporary rite) was recited over the neophytes, and this concluded the rites of Christian initiation. There was no tonsure, since the origin of the current prayer of tonsure has nothing to do with the rites of Christian initiation: it is found in the ancient *Euchologion* as a prayer for the first haircut of children.[24] When infant baptism became widespread, this prayer was later added to the rites of Christian initiation, although it has no intrinsic connection with it.

2. The Rites Connected with the Birth of a Child

2.1. The Prayers on the Day of Birth

The contemporary *Euchologion* contains three prayers for the birth of a child, said by the priest at the place of the birth. They are unknown in the most ancient manuscript of the *Euchologion, Barberini gr. 336*, dated to the second half of the eighth century. This rite is known by Saint Symeon of Thessalonica at the end of the fourteenth century, who explains it essentially as a penitential prayer for the mother, to give her recovery after childbirth and for the remission of her sins, having in mind the biblical interpretation found in the prayers that "childbirth is accomplished in sin and sensual desire,"[25] and secondly for the child so that he may live and be baptized in due time.

---

[21]Pseudo-Dionysius the Areopagite, O*n the Ecclesiastical Hierarchy* 2.7, 3.8 (PG 3:396d, 404c; Pseudo-Dionysius, *The Complete Works*, tr. Colm Luibheid, The Classics of Western Spirituality [New York: Paulist Press, 1987; hereafter Luibheid], 203, 208); Symeon of Thessalonica, *Dialogue in Christ* 67 (PG 155:232d).

[22]*Barberini*, 131; *Typikon de la Grande Église*, 2:88–90.

[23]Egeria, *Itinerarium* 47.1–4 (SC 296:312–314; Egeria, *Diary*, 125–26).

[24]*Barberini*, 198.

[25]Symeon of Thessalonica, *Dialogue in Christ* 58 (PG 155:208d); cf. Lev 12.1–5; Ps 50.7; Jn 1.13.

2.2. *The Naming of a Child on the Eighth Day*

Table 1.1: The Order for the Naming of a Child on the Eighth Day

1. Usual beginning prayers
2. Troparion of the day
3. Prayer over the child
4. Troparion of the feast of the Meeting of the Lord
5. Dismissal

This rite is celebrated in the narthex.[26] The prayer for naming a child on the eighth day is already attested in the Barberini *Euchologion*.[27] The inspiration for this rite is the circumcision and naming of Christ in the Temple on the eighth day (Lk 2.21), according to the interpretation given by Saint Symeon of Thessalonica.[28] It ought to be performed in the narthex of the church. The prayer concerns the child, asking that he may in due time be united to the holy Church and partake of the holy mysteries of Christ. This corroborates what we have said before: this rite, already known in the second half of the eighth century, was composed in order to give a certain status to the children of Christian parents as these children waited for their baptism to take place when they were older.

2.3. *The Entrance of the Child into the Church on the Fortieth Day*

Table 1.2: The Order of the Entrance of a Child into the Church on the Fortieth Day

1. Beginning Prayers
2. Troparion of the day
3. Prayer over the mother and the child
4. Prayer for the mother
5. Prayer for the child
6. Prayer of inclination
7. Rite of entrance into the church [and altar]
8. Canticle of Symeon (Lk 2.29–32)
9. Dismissal

[26][Or in the home.—*Ed.*]
[27]*Barberini*, 117.
[28]Symeon of Thessalonica, *Dialogue in Christ* 60 (PG 155:209ab).

This rite is celebrated in the narthex. The prayer for the entrance of the child into the church on the fortieth day after his birth (no. 5 in the above list) is already attested in the Barberini manuscript.[29] The rite was inspired by the meeting of Christ and Symeon in the Temple on the fortieth day (Lk 2.22–38), as can be seen in the prayer for the child (no. 5) and the presence of the canticle of Symeon at the conclusion of the rite (no. 8). This is also the interpretation given by Saint Symeon of Thessalonica,[30] who says that purification is granted to the mother (because "childbearing is impure, since it is linked with the passion of desire"[31]) and this purification allows her to receive Holy Communion. He refers here to the prayer for the mother (no. 4), unknown by the Barberini *Euchologion*. He then adds that prayers are offered also for the child, so that in due time he may be united to the body of the Church and be born again of water and Spirit.

After the prayers, the rite prescribes that the priest take up the child, and to make with it the sign of the cross before the doors of the church, while saying: *The servant of God, N., is churched, in the name of the Father, and of the Son, and of the Holy Spirit. Amen.* He then carries the child into the church, saying: *I will enter into thy house: I will worship toward thy holy temple.* Coming to the center of the church, he says: *The servant of God, N., is churched, in the name of the Father, and of the Son, and of the Holy Spirit. Amen. In the midst of the congregation I will sing praises to thee.* Then, before the holy doors of the altar, he says: *The servant of God, N., is churched, in the name of the Father, and of the Son, and of the Holy Spirit. Amen.*

In contemporary practice, if the child is male, the priest then carries him into the sanctuary, making the sign of the cross with the child at the four sides of the holy table. If the child is female, she is carried only as far as the holy doors. One should note that this practice of bringing the child into the church, and eventually into the sanctuary, is unknown in the Barberini *Euchologion*, which had only one prayer for the child on the fortieth day (no. 5).

The rite of the entrance of the child into the church on the fortieth day presents several challenges today.

First, it raises the disputed question of the purity of the mother. The biblical interpretation that childbearing is impure (cf. Lev 12.1–5; Ps 50.7; Jn 1.13), and that because of this, the mother who gives birth to a child is

---

[29] *Barberini*, 118.
[30] Symeon of Thessalonica, *Dialogue in Christ* 60 (PG 155:212a).
[31] Ibid.

impure, is challenged by our contemporary society.[32] From a rather negative perspective, this biblical or patristic interpretation sees human sexuality as a consequence of the fall, and therefore of sin, and oriented to assuring the perpetuity of the human race in the face of death, which is also a consequence of sin. In a more positive perspective, the notion of purity and impurity as developed in the Old Testament shows a feeling of awe and respect before the sacredness and mystery of life. In this sense, blood, as the center of life, ought not to be touched or eaten, and therefore, any contact with blood required a period of purification.[33] Regardless of our opinion on this issue today, it is important to stress that the rite of the entrance of the child into the church on the fortieth day, as attested in the second half of the eighth century, did not know any prayer for the mother and therefore had no reference to her impurity. For this reason, if the question of the impurity of the mother raises some issues among the faithful today, we suggest, for pastoral reasons, that only the most ancient prayer be kept (no. 5 in the preceding table: *O Lord, our God, who on the fortieth day*), given that it makes no reference to that issue, and to follow it by the prayer of inclination (no. 6), while omitting the others (no. 3 and no. 4).[34]

Second, in contemporary practice, during the rite of the entrance of the child into the church, only boys are taken into the altar, and this practice is perceived by some of our contemporaries as discriminatory. It is interesting to note that until the fourteenth century, both boys and girls were brought into the altar in the same manner.[35] The reason most likely is that this rite was performed on the fortieth day after the birth of the child and therefore, there was no question of female ritual impurity at that age. Saint Symeon of Thessalonica does not mention a difference of practice according to the sex of the child. He merely notes that the child is taken into the altar only if it has been baptized.[36] This might suggest to us today that, if the question of so-called "sex discrimination" arises in connection with this rite, and if to

[32]Cf. Vassa Larin, "What is 'Ritual Im/purity' and why," *SVTQ* 52.3–4 (2008): 275–292.

[33][Cf. Jacob Milgrom, *Leviticus 1–16: A New Translation with Introduction and Commentary* (New Haven, CT: Yale University Press, 1998), 766–68.—*Ed.*]

[34][Priests must consult with their bishops in this matter. In the US, both the Orthodox Church in America and the Antiochian Archdiocese have blessed alternate orders for this service.—*Ed.*]

[35]M. Arranz, "Les sacrements de l'ancien Euchologe constantinopolitain (3): II: Admission dans l'Eglise des enfants des familles chrétiennes (premier catéchuménat)," 294.

[36]Symeon of Thessalonica, *Dialogue in Christ* 60 (PG 155:212b).

some people it is inconceivable to bring female babies into the altar, then all children could simply not be presented at the altar, but only brought in front of the holy doors of the iconostasis. The testimony of Saint Symeon shows also that by the end of the fourteenth century baptism had been advanced to a very early age, sometimes even preceding the fortieth day, thus rendering this fortieth-day rite a contradiction in terms when celebrated after baptism.

Indeed, the practice of performing this entire rite of entrance into the church and altar *after* baptism is an aberration, since, as we have already said, this rite was composed to give a status to the children of Christian parents within the Church *before* their baptism, which once took place when the child was older.[37] This is precisely what the oldest prayer of the rite [no. 5] implies when it states: *so that being accounted worthy of holy baptism, he may obtain the portion of thine Elect of thy Kingdom.* Many priests are embarrassed by this phrase and omit it from the prayer, as has been suggested by some modern editions. This clearly shows that performing this rite *after* baptism is an aberration, since the real entrance into the Church is baptism, and theologically there is absolutely no need to perform any rite of incorporation into the Church after the holy mystery of baptism. Therefore, the rite of the entrance of a child into the church should be performed only before baptism, on the fortieth day after birth. With regard to an adult catechumen, serving this rite before baptism is complete nonsense, since the rite was created specifically for children.

3. Pre-Baptismal Rites

Table 1.3: The Order of the Pre-Baptismal Rites

---

1. Prayer to make a catechumen
2. Three prayers of exorcism
3. Prayer for the catechumen before the moment of baptism

---

[37][This order has become the norm in the Russian tradition. The Slavonic *Trebnik* (*Euchologion*) includes the following rubric toward the end of the prayers for a woman on the fortieth day after birth (an addition to the earlier text, in brackets): "If the infant is baptized, then the priest performs the churching, but if not, then he does this after the baptism." Cf. *Great Book of Needs* vol. 1 (South Canaan, PA: St Tikhon's Seminary Press, 2000), 14.—*Ed.*]

4. Renunciation of Satan, adherence to Christ, and recitation of the Symbol
of Faith

5. Final prayer

The rites preceding baptism take place in the baptistery or in the narthex
of the church. The rubrics mention that the priest breathes thrice on the
face of the candidate for baptism and signs him thrice on the forehead and
breast, and then he says the prayer to make a catechumen, while laying his
hand on the head of the candidate, as used to be done in the early Church.[38]
The candidate for baptism should wear only a shirt without a belt, and he
should be barefoot and with his head uncovered. Symeon of Thessalonica
interprets the breathing, which is made thrice because of the Holy Trinity, as
recalling the first creation (Gen 2.7), and the sign of the cross as recalling the
saving sacrifice of the incarnate Word of God on the cross. The candidate is
naked under his shirt, thus signifying his state of sinfulness.[39]

This prayer is followed by three prayers of exorcism. Symeon of Thessalonica emphasizes that these prayers should all be read with great attention,
without rushing, and aloud. He mentions that there was in fact a practice
to read them several times in the week prior to baptism, in a vestige of the
ancient practice of reading them daily during the whole period of the catechumenate.[40] The three prayers of exorcism are followed by a fourth, which
was originally the prayer for the catechumen immediately before baptism;
in this the priest prays that there be driven out from the catechumen *every
evil and unclean spirit hiding and lurking in his heart, the spirit of error, the
spirit of evil, the spirit of idolatry and of all covetousness; the spirit of lying and
of all uncleanness, that operates according to the instruction of the devil.* This
prayer includes once again the priest's threefold breathing in the sign of the
cross, as he says these words, and according to Saint Symeon of Thessalonica
this breathing signifies a new creation. Some priests are embarrassed to
read these prayers, originally intended for adult catechumens, over infants,
supposing that infants are not troubled by these passions. It is important to

[38]*Apostolic Constitutions*, 8.39.4 (SC 336:94; ANF 7:476). On the pre-baptismal rites,
see M. Arranz, "Les sacrements de l'ancien Euchologe constantinopolitain (4): III-a: Préparation au baptême: 1. Second catéchuménat," *OCP* 50 (1984): 43–64; "Les sacrements de
l'ancien Euchologe constantinopolitain (5): III-b: Préparation au baptême: 2. Renonciation
à Satan et adhésion au Christ," *OCP* 50 (1984): 372–397.
[39]Symeon of Thessalonica, *Dialogue in Christ* 62 (PG 155:213c–216b).
[40]Ibid., 61 (PG 155:212d).

stress that this prayer also has a protective effect, as Saint Symeon explains that demons like to make their dwelling in the hearts of those who are not yet baptized in order to incline them later towards sin.[41]

This prayer is followed by the renunciation of Satan. According to an ancient practice, this renunciation is made facing west, since, as Saint Cyril of Jerusalem explains, "the west is the place where darkness appears," since the sun sets in the west. Because of this, Symeon reminds the newly illumined: "symbolically keeping your eyes toward the west, you renounced that dark and gloomy prince."[42] The catechumen renounces Satan three times, each time answering the priest's question: *Do you renounce Satan, and all his works, and all his angels, and all his service, and all his pride?* by saying: *I do renounce him.*[43] He is then invited by the priest to blow and spit upon him. According to Saint Symeon, this action means to reject Satan from one's heart.[44] Then, facing east—"the place of light" as Saint Cyril of Jerusalem explains it,[45] and therefore symbolizing Christ who is the Light of the world (Jn 8.12)—the catechumen unites himself to Christ. He answers the priest's question: *Do you unite yourself to Christ?* by saying: *I do unite myself to him.* Again the priest asks: *Do you unite yourself to Christ?* and the catechumen responds: *I do unite myself to him.* The priest asks: *Have you united yourself to Christ?* and the catechumen affirms: *I have united myself to Christ.* Finally, the priest asks: *And do you believe in him?* The catechumen confesses: *I believe in him as King and God,* and then he recites the Symbol of Faith. The *Euchologion* specifies that all this ought to be repeated three times. We find a witness of the threefold confession of faith in the Areopagite.[46] One has to keep in mind that the origin of the Symbol of Faith is the baptismal symbol that was taught during the period of catechumenate, which was to be recited in front of the bishop before the mystery of baptism to ensure that the candidate had a correct knowledge of the Orthodox faith. After the threefold confession of faith, the priest asks the catechumen three more times: *Have you united yourself to Christ?* Again the catechumen

---

[41]Ibid., 62 (PG 155:217c). [Cf. St Diadochos of Photiki, *On Spiritual Knowledge and Discrimination: One Hundred Texts* 76; English translation in *Philokalia* 1:279.—*Ed.*]

[42]Cyril of Jerusalem, *Mystagogical Homilies* 1.4 (SC 126:88; PPS 57:87).

[43]The translations of these exchanges are taken from the booklet, *Baptism* (New York: Department of Religious Education of the Orthodox church in America, 1972).

[44]Symeon of Thessalonica, *Dialogue in Christ* 62 (PG 155:220a).

[45]Cyril of Jerusalem, *Mystagogical Homilies* 1.9 (SC 126:98; PPS 57:93).

[46]Pseudo-Dionysius the Areopagite, *On the Ecclesiastical Hierarchy* 2.2.7 (PG 3:396b; Luibheid, 203).

responds: *I have united myself to Christ.* And then the priest adds: *Bow down before him.* And the catechumen answers: *I bow down before the Father, and the Son, and the Holy Spirit, the Trinity one in essence and undivided.* Then the priest glorifies God saying: *Blessed is God, who desires that all men should be saved and come to the knowledge of the truth, now and ever, and unto ages of ages.* And he reads the final prayer, which asks God to call the catechumen to the mystery of holy illumination and grant him the grace of baptism, in order to put off the old man (cf. Col 3.9) and renew him in eternal life.

4. The Mystery of Holy Illumination

Table 1.4: The Order of the Mystery of Holy Illumination

1. Opening blessing: *Blessed is the kingdom,* as at the Divine Liturgy
2. Litany
3. Prayer of the priest
4. Prayer of blessing the water
5. Prayer of inclination—blessing of the oil
6. Pre-baptismal anointing
7. Baptism
8. Psalm 31
9. Vesting with a white garment
10. Prayer of chrismation and chrismation
11. *As many as have been baptized into Christ,* reading of the Epistle and Gospel
12. Litany [and dismissal]
13. Prayers of ablution and ablution
14. Prayers of tonsure and tonsure
15. Litany and dismissal

The ceremony of baptism used to take place in the baptistery, a separate building or at least a separate room in the church complex.[47] Where there is

---

[47]On baptismal rites, cf. M. Arranz, "Les sacrements de l'ancien Euchologe constantinopolitain (6): IV-a: L'illumination de la nuit de Pâques: 1-a. Bénédiction de l'eau et de l'huile baptismales," *OCP* 51 (1985): 60–86; "Les sacrements de l'ancien Euchologe constantinopolitain (7): IV-b: L'illumination de la nuit de Pâques: 1-b. Bénédiction de l'eau et de l'huile baptismales (suite et fin)," *OCP* 52 (1986): 145–78; "Les sacrements de l'ancien Euchologe constantinopolitain (8): IV-c: L'illumination de la nuit de Pâques: 2. Onction

no baptistery, it would be proper to celebrate the rite in the narthex, although for practical reasons today it is often celebrated in the nave. Although baptism can be celebrated elsewhere in cases of emergency, the celebration of baptism at home has been criticized by theologians such as Alexander Schmemann, because that practice does not render properly the meaning of baptism as the entrance into the ecclesial community.[48] For this reason, Canon 59 of the Council in Trullo forbids the celebration of baptism in private chapels—it must be celebrated only in parish churches.[49] Thus baptism should never be considered a private event, but an event of the ecclesial community, and this is why Saint Symeon of Thessalonica considers that "it is indispensable that all the faithful be present, to the extent that this is possible."[50]

The ceremony begins with the exclamation of the chief celebrant: *Blessed is the Kingdom,* as at the Divine Liturgy; this is followed by the litany, in which special petitions are added for the blessing of the water and for the candidate for baptism. Normally, the litany ought to be intoned by the deacon while the priest, in a low voice, says a penitential sacerdotal prayer (similar to the one said by the priest during the Cherubic hymn of the Divine Liturgy), in which he acknowledges his unworthiness and asks God to grant him the power from on high to accomplish this great mystery. If there is no deacon, the priest says his prayer after the litany.

When the litany and the prayer of the priest have been concluded, the priest says aloud the prayer of blessing of the water, which has a structure similar to the eucharistic prayers (anaphoras). Water must be blessed at each ceremony. To use holy water blessed on the feast of Theophany, or to use water from a previous baptism, is not proper. Nevertheless, several persons can be baptized at the same time in the same baptismal font. Saint Symeon of Thessalonica prescribes that the holy water from baptism should be disposed of with reverence, after the ceremony, and in a special place, where nobody can step on it—that is, either in a special well, in a river, or in the sea.[51] During the prayer of sanctification of the water, the priest blows

pré-baptismale. 3. Immersion baptismale. 4. Onction post-baptismale. 5. Entrée dans le temple et liturgie. Appendice: Les autres jours de baptême," *OCP* 53 (1987): 59–106.

[48]Cf. Alexander Schmemann, *Of Water and Spirit* (Crestwood, NY: St Vladimir's Seminary Press, 1974), 8.

[49]Périclès-Pierre Joannou, *Discipline générale antique (IVe–IXe s.),* Vol. 1.1, *Les canons des conciles oecuméniques* (Grottaferrata [Rome]: Tipografia Italo-Orientale "S. Nilo," 1962), 195.

[50]Symeon of Thessalonica, *Dialogue in Christ* 62 (PG 155:221b).

[51]Symeon of Thessalonica, *Dialogue in Christ* 70 (PG 155:237a).

three times over the water and makes the sign of the cross three times with his right hand, while saying: *Let all hostile powers be crushed beneath the sign of the image of thy Cross.* Saint Symeon of Thessalonica says that the priest thus inscribes over the water the image of Christ and invokes the grace of the Holy Spirit, so that the baptismal font may be filled by the presence of Christ and of the Holy Spirit.[52]

After this prayer, the chief celebrant gives the peace. The prayer of inclination that follows is in fact the prayer to bless the oil that will be used for the pre-baptismal anointing. Today some priests observe a decadent practice and omit this prayer, while using oil that was blessed at a previous ceremony. This usage should be avoided. Saint Symeon of Thessalonica says in his commentary that the the holy oil left over from baptism should be burned in a lamp in the sanctuary.[53] The prayer must be read, since it is an essential part of the mystery—and furthermore it is very rich theologically. Indeed, it gives the symbolic explanation of the olive in reference to Noah (Gn 8.11), as a sign of change and salvation and as a prefiguration of the mystery of grace. It also emphasizes the meaning of the pre-baptismal anointing as an unction of incorruption, an armor of righteousness, a renewal of the soul and body, and a deliverance from all action of the devil. In Greek pracice, the ancient tradition of anointing the entire body of the candidate is still observed, so the godparents usually bring a bottle of olive oil to be used for the ceremony.[54] This practice should be encouraged. When the priest has said the prayer, he takes the bottle of oil and pours from it three times into the baptismal font in the sign of the cross, while singing *Alleluia.* Saint Symeon of Thessalonica sees in this rite a manifestation of the fact that the water has been sanctified by the presence of Christ and of the Holy Spirit, and a sign of the mercy of God.[55] After glorifying God by saying: *Blessed is God, who illumineth and sanctifieth every man that cometh into the world, now and ever and unto the ages of ages,* the priest anoints the candidate with the newly blessed oil, with the formula: *The servant of God is anointed with the oil of gladness, in the name of the Father, and of the Son, and of the Holy Spirit.* In former times, after this formula the deacon (or deaconess) would anoint the candidate's whole body.[56] Today, after

---

[52]Symeon of Thessalonica, *Dialogue in Christ* 62 (PG 155:225ab).

[53]Symeon of Thessalonica, *Dialogue in Christ* 70 (PG 155:237a).

[54]*Barberini*, 130.

[55]Symeon of Thessalonica, *Dialogue in Christ* 62 (PG 155:225b).

[56]*Barberini*, 130. [In contemporary Greek practice the godparents anoint the entire body with oil, as the deacons did in antiquity.—*Ed.*]

making the sign of the cross on the forehead while saying this, the priest anoints the candidate on the breast and shoulders, while saying: *For the healing of soul and body*—then making the sign of the cross on the ears: *For the hearing of faith;*—next, making the sign of the cross on the hands: *Thy hands have made me and fashioned me;*—then making the sign of the cross on the feet: *That he may walk in the path of thy commandments* (or in the Greek books, *That he may walk in thy footsteps*).

Then comes the solemn moment of the actual baptism, when the priest immerses the candidate three times in the baptismal font, with the words: *The servant of God, N., is baptized in the name of the Father, Amen* (first immersion), *and of the Son, Amen* (second immersion), *and of the Holy Spirit, Amen* (third immersion). This Trinitarian formula, which is fundamental for the validity of the mystery of baptism, is directly derived from the commandment of Christ to his apostles: "Go ye therefore and teach all nations, baptizing them in the name of the Father, and of the Son, and of the Holy Ghost" (Mt 28.19). Saint Symeon of Thessalonica stresses that the formula *The servant of God, N., is baptized* shows that he is baptized according to his own will, and Symeon interprets the threefold immersion as a confession of the Holy Trinity and a symbol of the three-day burial of Christ and of his resurrection on the third day.[57] In fact, the fiftieth Apostolic Canon had already specified that the threefold immersion is compulsory in order to manifest baptism as a sign of Christ's death and resurrection.[58] One should note that the proper way to baptize is through full immersion, since the etymological meaning of *to baptize* is *to immerse* in water. The *Didache* (1st c.) prescribes that water be poured three times over the head of the candidate only in exceptional cases, when there is no possibility of immersing the candidate in water.[59] It should be recommended that every parish have an adequate baptismal font, or even better, a real baptistery where adult baptisms could also take place.

The rite of baptism is followed by the chanting of Psalm 31, and while this is being chanted, the priest usually washes his hands, which are covered with oil, and the candidate is wiped dry. After the psalm, the priest gives the neophyte a white garment, while saying: *The servant of God, N., is clothed with the robe of righteousness, in the name of the Father, and of the Son, and of the Holy Spirit,* and then the troparion: *A robe of light* is sung.

[57]Symeon of Thessalonica, *Dialogue in Christ* 63–64 (PG 155:228d–229a).
[58]*Apostolic Constitutions* 8.47.50 (SC 336:290–294; ANF 7:503).
[59]*Didache* 7 (SC 248:170; PPS 41:39).

Then the priest says the prayer of chrismation: *Blessed art thou, Lord God Almighty*, and then he anoints the neophyte with the holy Chrism (also called *Myron*), by making the sign of the cross on the forehead, the eyes, the nostrils, the mouth, the ears, the breast, the hands, and the feet, and saying each time: *The seal of the gift of the Holy Spirit. Amen.*

The Pauline verse: *As many as have been baptized in Christ, have put on Christ* (Gal 3.27), is then sung, while the priest, holding the neophyte by the hand with his epitrachelion, together with the godparents walk around the baptismal font three times. According to Saint Symeon of Thessalonica, this procession around the baptismal font is a kind of dance expressing the joy of being reborn from the spiritual womb that is the baptismal font, through the power of the Spirit of God.[60] But in the early Church, at this point there was a procession of the bishop, his clergy, and the neophytes from the baptistery to the nave of the main church, where the Divine Liturgy was celebrated, starting with the Scripture readings. This is why, in the contemporary ceremony, the readings of the Epistle (Rom 6.3–11) and of the Gospel (Mt 28.16–20), which are fundamental for the theology of baptism, occur after the procession. These are in fact the daily readings of the vesperal Divine Liturgy of Great Saturday, when baptism was initially celebrated.

The readings are followed by the litany and the dismissal, since the *Euchologion* presumes that the post-baptismal rites will be celebrated on the eighth day of baptism. This is a vestige of the practice of the early Church, when the neophytes remained in church for eight days for mystagogical instruction. Today, the post-baptismal rites are usually accomplished immediately after the baptism, and therefore at this point we usually omit not only the dismissal but the litany as well, since it will be repeated at the end, after the post-baptismal rites, which consist of the prayers of ablution, the ablution, the prayers of tonsure, and the tonsure.[61]

The rite of ablution is preceded by two prayers and a prayer of inclination. Of these, only the first: *O Thou, who by holy baptism hast granted forgiveness of sins to thy servant*, is mentioned in the Barberini manuscript.[62] Thus we suggest that if an abbreviation is needed for pastoral reasons, this is the prayer to retain. The priest then soaks the end of a linen cloth in clean

---

[60]Symeon of Thessalonica, *Dialogue in Christ* 67 (PG 155:233a).

[61]On post-baptismal rites, cf. M. Arranz, "Les sacrements de l'ancien Euchologe constantinopolitain (9): IV-d: L'illumination de la nuit de Pâques: 6. Ablution et tonsure des néophytes," *OCP* 55 (1989): 33–62.

[62]*Barberini*, 131–32.

water and sprinkles the newly baptized person, with the words: *Thou art justified, thou art enlightened.* Then he dips a new sponge or a ball of cotton in water and wipes the neophyte's face, head, breast, and all the other places that have been anointed with holy oil and holy Chrism, while he says: *Thou art baptized, thou art enlightened, thou art anointed with Chrism, thou art sanctified, thou art washed: in the name of the Father, and of the Son, and of the Holy Spirit. Amen.* The purpose of this rite is to wash and wipe away the oil remaining from the anointing, before the neophyte returns home. Saint Symeon of Thessalonica explains that in the early Church, the neophytes were vested with a special robe that they wore for seven days, during which they were not allowed to wash themselves. Only on the eighth day, after the week of mystagogy, the priest washed the parts of the body that had been anointed so that the holy Chrism might not be profaned.[63]

The ablution is followed by the rite of tonsure, which consists of a prayer and a prayer of inclination. Only the prayer of inclination: *O Lord our God, who through the fulfilment of the baptismal font*, is attested by the Barberini manuscript, although it is not found there among the baptismal rites, but elsewhere among prayers for various occasions.[64] As we explained above, this was originally a prayer for the first haircut of the child, but it was later added to the post-baptismal rites. Saint Symeon of Thessalonica, on the basis of the content of the first prayer, sees in this rite a kind of offering of the first fruits of the newly baptized child to Christ.[65] In our opinion, founded on historical research, the rite of tonsure has no place in the case of an adult baptism. The priest then tonsures the hair of the newly baptized child in a form of the cross saying: *The hair of the head of the servant of God, N., is tonsured in the name of the Father, and of the Son, and of the Holy Spirit. Amen.*

The ceremony ends with the litany and the dismissal.

5. Baptismal Liturgy

The Orthodox Church is usually quite proud to have retained the unity of the three sacraments of Christian initiation (baptism-chrismation-Eucharist), but in fact, most Orthodox do not receive Holy Communion at their baptism. Most receive Communion at a Divine Liturgy celebrated later, either

[63]Symeon of Thessalonica, *Dialogue in Christ* 68 (PG 155:236a).
[64]*Barberini*, 198.
[65]Symeon of Thessalonica, *Dialogue in Christ* 67 (PG 155:232c).

on the same day or a few days after the ceremony of baptism. Unfortunately, pastoral practice reveals that in many cases the parents do not consider it important to bring the newly baptized child to receive Communion. For this reason, many Orthodox theologians of the twentieth century, such as Alexander Schmemann and Ioannis Phountoulis,[66] advocated the restoration of baptismal Liturgies, or in other words, the celebration of Christian initiation within the Divine Liturgy of a local ecclesial community, as was the practice of the early Church.

With regard to these attempts at restoration, some remarks must made concerning the ancient practice of the Church. First of all, baptism in the early Church was of course neither private nor individual. This means that it was always communal, not only because it implied the attendance of the local ecclesial community, but also because baptism was never conferred on a single individual, but on a group of catechumens. For this reason, the celebration of baptism was not so frequent as it is today. It occurred only on a very few specific days during the year, four times at the most (Pascha, Lazarus Saturday, Pentecost, Theophany).[67] It was celebrated by the bishop, as the head of the local ecclesial community, in the presence of his priests and the deacons and deaconesses, in a separate building or room—the baptistery—while the ecclesial community was listening to Old Testament readings and awaiting the solemn entrance of the bishop, with the clergy and the neophytes, into the nave of the main church.[68] One might consider these historical remarks when reintroducing the celebration of baptism in the Divine Liturgy.

The order of the celebration of a baptismal liturgy is quite simple. The pre-baptismal rites are accomplished before the beginning of the Divine Liturgy, or even on the eve. The Divine Liturgy begins with the regular opening blessing: *Blessed is the Kingdom,* and the regular order of the mystery of illumination is followed until the the Pauline verse—*As many as have been baptized in Christ, have put on Christ* (Gal 3.27). From this point, the

[66]Alexander Schmemann, *Of Water and Spirit* (Crestwood, NY: St Vladimir's Seminary Press, 1974), 169–70; Ioannis Phountoulis, *Λειτουργική, Α΄, εἰσαγωγή στη Θεία λατρεία* (Thessaloniki, 1993), 288–89. On this subject, cf. Nenad Milosevic, *To Christ and the Church: The Divine Eucharist as the All-Encompassing Mystery of the Church* (Los Angeles: Sebastian Press, 2012), 48–57.
[67]*Typikon de la Grande Église,* 1:184; 2:62, 136. At 1:158, this source also mentions the singing of the Pauline verse on the feast of the Nativity, but it says nothing about baptism on that day.
[68]*Typikon de la Grande Église,* 2:84–88.

regular order of the Divine Liturgy continues, starting from the daily readings, to which the readings for baptism are added. To omit the antiphons
and the Little Entrance is not a problem, since these elements come from the
stational celebration, and were later added to the ancient Divine Liturgies,
which always started with the readings, as we shall see in the next chapter.
Even in our contemporary practice, antiphons are omitted at Vesperal Liturgies, when the Divine Liturgy starts with the epistle and gospel readings
just after the Old Testament readings of Vespers. The post-baptismal rites
(ablution, tonsure) are done at the end of the Divine Liturgy, or even after it,
since they used to be a separate service on the eighth day after baptism.

6. Reception of Non-Orthodox Christians into the Orthodox Church

The mystery of baptism is a person's entry into the Church. From very
ancient times, the Church was concerned with the reception into her midst
of people who were baptized outside her canonical limits, whether they
were heretics, schismatics, or, in our times, members of other Christian
confessions. The canonical norm for the reception of non-Orthodox Christians into the Orthodox Church is set out in Canon 95 of the Council in
Trullo (691), which develops the earlier Canon 7 of the Second Ecumenical
Council (Constantinople, 381). According to this canon, by the end of the
seventh century there were three different cases:

a) Heretics, such as Manicheans, Marcionites, Montanists, Modalists, or
Eunomians, who rejected the three persons of the Holy Trinity—sometimes identifying the Father with the Son, or in the case of the Eunomians excluding the Son from the divine *ousia*, and therefore practicing
baptism through a single immersion—were received through *baptism*
because their heterodox baptism was considered to be invalid;

b) Heretics, such as moderate Arians, Apollinarists, and Tetradites,
who confessed the Holy Trinity in an erroneous way, were received
through *chrismation* together with the signing of an appropriate *libellus* renouncing their particular heresy;

c) Heretics, such as Nestorians and Monophysites, who confessed Christ
in an erroneous way, were received by signing only an appropriate
libellus or confession of faith, wherein their heresy was renounced,
and by receiving *Holy Communion*.

As we can see, the criterion for acknowledging the baptism of heretics when they decided to return to the Orthodox Church was their trinitarian baptism, in the name of the Father, and of the Son, and of the Holy Spirit. These guidelines were applied in the second millennium for the reception of Christians from other confessions into the Orthodox Church.[69]

In the twelfth century, the Byzantine canonist Theodore Balsamon, Patriarch of Antioch (d. 1193), states that Latins were to be received either by the submission of a *libellus*, together with the indirect support of the reapplication of Chrism, or by partaking of Holy Communion following the renunciation of Latin practices.[70] The Great Council convened in the Church of the Theotokos Pammakaristos in Constantinople in 1484 and presided over by Ecumenical Patriarch Symeon produced a rite for the reception of Latins, which prescribed that they ought to be anointed by holy Chrism and submit a *libellus*.[71] Patriarch Dositheus II of Jerusalem published the rite of the Council of Constantinople (1484) in his *Τόμος Ἀγάπης* (*Tomos agapēs*) in Iassy in 1698.[72] Patriarch Dositheos also stated in his time that Protestants ought not to be re-baptized when coming to the Orthodox Church.[73] This became the norm in the Orthodox Church, that is to say, not to re-baptize Roman Catholics or Protestants.

The contemporary partisans of rebaptizing non-Orthodox usually refer to a Pseudo-Synod of 1755, which never took place, but which is in fact a decision signed by three patriarchs (Cyril V of Constantinople, Matthew of Alexandria, and Parthenios of Jerusalem), which called for the rebaptism of Western Christian wishing to join the Orthodox Church.[74] Because

[69]Cf. P. L'Huillier, "Les divers modes de réception des catholiques-romains dans l'Orthodoxie," *Le Messager orthodoxe* 82 (1979): 15–23; J. Erickson, "Reception of Non-Orthodox into the Orthodox Church: Contemporary Practice," *SVTQ* 41 (1997): 1–17.

[70]G. A. Rhalles and M. Potles, *Σύνταγμα*, vol. 4 (Athens, 1854), 460; cf. V. Phidas, "Τὸ κύρος τοῦ βαπτίσματος τῶν αἱρετικῶν καὶ τὸ ζήτημα τοῦ ἀναβαπτισμοῦ," *Orthodoxia* 11 (2004): 434.

[71]George Dion. Dragas, "The Manner of Reception of Roman Catholic Converts into the Orthodox Church," Greek Orthodox Theological Review 44 (1999): 235–271, at 237–42; Phidas, "Τὸ κύρος τοῦ βαπτίσματος" 437–38.

[72]I. Karmiris, *Τὰ δογματικὰ καὶ συμβολικὰ μνημεία τῆς Ὀρθόδοξου Καθολικῆς Ἐκκλησίας*, vol. 2 (Athens, 1953), 987–89; Rhalles-Potles, *op. cit.*, t. V, pp. 143–47; English translation of the rite in Dragas, "The Manner of Reception of Roman Catholic Converts into the Orthodox Church," 238–41.

[73]Dositheos of Jerusalem, *Confession of Faith* 15, in *The Acts and Decrees of the Synod of Jerusalem*, tr. J. N. W. B. Robertson (London: Thomas Baker, 1899), 110–181 at 138–139; I. Karmiris, *Τὰ δογματικά*, 758.

[74]Cf. Phidas, "Τὸ κύρος τοῦ βαπτίσματος," 444–49; English translation of the declaration

the definition had three patriarchal signatures, it was considered valid and made its way through the publication of the *Pedalion* (or *Rudder*) of Saint Nicodemus the Hagiorite. Nevertheless, this definition was rejected by the Holy Synod of the Ecumenical Patriarchate—the reason why Patriarch Sylvester of Antioch refused to sign the Definition—and eventually Patriarch Cyril V was deposed by his Holy Synod for a second time in 1757. Thus the practice of rebaptizing Western Christians who desire to join the Orthodox Church has no canonical foundation.

Today the appropriate and most common rite for the reception of non-Orthodox Christians is through chrismation. To give us an idea of the differences, in the following table we compare the rite for the reception of Latins of the Council of Constantinople (1484)[75] with the rite in the contemporary edition of the *Small Euchologion* of Athens of 1974.[76]

Table 1.5: The Order for the reception of
Roman Catholics into the Orthodox Church

Order of 1484	Small Euchologion, Athens, 1974.
1. Usual beginning prayers	1. Usual beginning prayers
2. Psalm 50	2. Psalm 50
3. Questions by the bishop on the faith (councils, *filioque*, azymes)	
4. Symbol of Faith	3. Symbol of Faith
5. Anointing with holy Chrism, with the formula: *The seal of the gift of the Holy Spirit*	4. Anointing with holy Chrism, with the formula: *The seal of the gift of the Holy Spirit*
6. Prayer of absolution	5. Prayer of absolution
7. Psalm 144	
8. Litany	6. Litany
9. Dismissal	7. Dismissal
10. Signature of the *libellus*	8. Signature of the *libellus*

in Dragas, "The Manner of Reception," 243–48; Vassa Kontouma, "La Définition des trois patriarches sur l'anabaptisme (1755/56)," *Annuaire de l'École pratique des hautes études (EPHE)*, Section des sciences religieuses, 121 (2014): 255–67.

[75] I. Karmiris, *Τὰ δογματικά*, 987–89; English translation of the rite: Dragas, "The Manner of Reception," 238–41.

[76] *Μικρὸν Εὐχολόγιον* (Athens, 1974), 87–9.

CHAPTER TWO

The Divine Liturgies

1. Historical Overview

The Divine Liturgy is the celebration of the Eucharist, which according to Pseudo-Dionysius is the "sacrament of sacraments" that fulfils all the other sacramental rites.[1] For this reason, the celebration of all the mysteries of Church used to be connected with the Divine Liturgy. The Eucharist is also the manifestation of the ecclesial community as the Body of Christ. Thus Saint Paul speaks of the Church just after speaking about our Lord's institution of the Eucharist (1 Cor 11–12), and he calls Christians members of the one Body of Christ. The same idea appears in the eucharistic prayer of the *Didache*, which compares the wheat coming from different mountains to make one bread, to Christians coming together to make one Church.[2] Only the baptized could gather for the celebration of Eucharist, although catechumens were allowed to attend the Liturgy of the Word.

The earliest surviving description of the order of the eucharistic Liturgy is given to us by St Justin Martyr in his *First Apology* (*c*. 155): he mentions the exchange of a kiss of peace, the offering of bread and a chalice of wine mixed with water, a prayer of thanksgiving, praise, and giving glory to the Father though the Son and the Holy Spirit, the Communion of the bread and the chalice, given by the deacon, and a final thanksgiving.[3] In the early Church, the eucharistic prayer (Anaphora) would be improvised by the chief celebrant, though it always followed the same pattern. Finally, the text of the Anaphora was fixed in written form. Although there was a multiplicity of anaphoras in the early Church, ultimately the liturgical practice of Constantinople retained only two of them, both of an Antiochian type— one attributed to St Basil the Great, and the other to St John Chrysostom;

---

[1]Pseudo-Dionysius the Areopagite, *On the Ecclesiastical Hierarchy* 3.3.1 (PG 3:424c–425a; Luibheid, 209).

[2]*Didache*, 10.4 (SC 248:177; PPS 41:40, where the relevant text appears under no. 9).

[3]Justin Martyr, *Apology* 1.65 (SC 507:302–304; ANF 6:104–105).

this latter is is based on the ancient Anaphora of the Twelve Apostles.[4] The Barberini manuscript contains only the Anaphoras of St John and St Basil.[5] Before the period of the iconoclast controversy (726–843), the Divine Liturgy of Saint Basil the Great was the more common of the two, but after that period it ceased to be served frequently, and was restricted to ten of the most solemn liturgical days of the year (the eve of the Nativity of Christ, the feast of St Basil, the eve of Theophany, Great Thursday, Great Saturday, and the first five Sundays of Great Lent); thus the Divine Liturgy of St John Chrysostom, presumably because of the conciseness of its Anaphora, became the Liturgy served on most days.

In the early Church, the Divine Liturgy started with the Liturgy of the Word,[6] with the readings of the Old and of the New Testaments—"of the Law and the Prophets, and our Epistles, and Acts [of the Apostles], and the Gospels"—followed by the homily, as attested in the Divine Liturgy of the *Apostolic Constitutions* (c. 380).[7] Scholars generally consider that the Old Testament readings for the Divine Liturgy were not included when a new lectionary was compiled in Constantinople during the iconoclast controversy, as attested by the *Typikon of the Great Church*. Old Testament readings were preserved for feast days and were placed in Vespers.

Thus everything that comes before the biblical readings today (technically called the *enarxis*, which designates the entrance rites) was added at a later stage.[8]

The prothesis (or proskomidē or proskomedia),[9] the service of preparation of the bread and wine before the beginning of the Divine Liturgy, appeared during the time of the iconoclast controversy (726–843). The first

[4]In the twelfth century, the Byzantine canonist Theodore Balsamon, Patriarch of Antioch (d. 1193) wrote in a reply to Patriarch Mark III of Alexandria, that the Liturgies of St Mark and of St James ought not to be celebrated (Eusèbe Renaudot, *Liturgiarum Orientalium Collectio* [Paris: Coignard, 1716], 1:lxxxviii).

[5]*Barberini*, 57–82.

[6]On this part of the Divine Liturgy, cf. J. Mateos, *La célébration de la parole dans la liturgie byzantine*, OCA 191 (Rome: Pontificium Institutum Orientalium Studiorum, 1971); English translation by S. Hawkes-Teeples: *The Liturgy of the Word* (Fairfax, VA: Eastern Christian Publications, 2016).

[7]*Apostolic Constitutions* 8.5.11 (SC 336:150; ANF 7:483).

[8]Juan Mateos, "Évolution historique de la liturgie de saint Jean Chrysostome. Première partie: De la bénédiction initiale au Trisagion," OCP 15 (1965): 333–351, OCP 16 (1966): 3–18, OCP 16 (1966): 133–161 = J. Mateos, *La célébration de la parole dans la liturgie byzantine*, OCA 191:27–90.

[9]P. M. Mandalà, *La protesi della liturgia nel rito bizantino-greco* (Grottoferrata: Scuola Tipografica Italo-Orientale San Nilo, 1935).

testimony of the prothesis, served in the skevophylakion before the three antiphons,[10] interpreted in connection with the sacrifice of Christ the Lamb on the cross, is in the *Ecclesiastical History* of Patriarch Germanus of Constantinople (+733).[11] Before that period, there were no particular rites performed over the bread and the wine that would be offered at the Anaphora. The Barberini *Euchologion* contains only a prayer said in the skevophylakion over the bread placed on the diskos.[12] The order of the prothesis was ultimately fixed by the *Diataxis of the Divine Liturgy*[13] of St Philotheos Kokkinos, Patriarch of Constantinople (1353–54, 1364–76), which describes in detail the entrance prayers that ought to be said by the celebrants, the prayers that are recited while vesting, and how the priest must perform the prothesis. This liturgical document forever fixed the celebration of the prothesis by the priest, thus putting an end to an earlier practice in which the gifts of bread and wine were prepared by the deacon alone.

The antiphons that are sung at the beginning of the Divine Liturgy today in fact come from the stational celebration of the Divine Liturgy in Constantinople; there the faithful usually gathered with the bishop and the clergy in the basilica of Hagia Sophia, and walked in procession towards another church for the celebration of the Divine Liturgy,[14] while singing proper hymns. The antiphons were originally verses of a psalm chanted by a chanter at a station during the procession. The litanies and the priestly prayers accompanied each antiphon. This structure explains why even today antiphons are omitted when we serve a Divine Liturgy that begins with Vespers: the New Testament readings follow the readings of the Old Testament prescribed at Vespers. Stational liturgies seem to have disappeared during the iconoclast controversy, and consequently the three antiphons

[10][The *skevophylakion* was a room in which the sacred vessels were kept, and where the bread and wine were prepared for the Liturgy. At a certain point, these were brought in procession from the skevophylakion and taken into the sanctuary, and the contemporary Great Entrance is the continuation of that procession.—*Ed.*]

[11]Germanus of Constantinople, *Ecclesiastical History*, 20–22, in *Saint Germanus of Constantinople: On the Divine Liturgy*, Greek text with English translation, Paul Meyendorff, ed. and trans., Popular Patristics Series 8 (Crestwood, NY: St Vladimir's Seminary Press, 1984), 71 (hereafter *Divine Liturgy*).

[12]*Barberini*, 57.

[13]Panagiotis N. Trempelas, Αἱ τρεῖς λειτουργίαι (Athens: Ekdoseis tes megales patriarkhikes epistemonikes, 1935), 1–16.

[14]Cf. R. Janin, "Les processions religieuses à Byzance," *Revue des études byzantines* 24 (1966): 69–88, where the author gives all the references to the *Typikon of the Great Church*.

were added as the initial part of the Divine Liturgy. The first testimony of
the three antiphons in this place is found in the *Ecclesiastical History* of
Patriarch Germanus of Constantinople (d. 733).[15]

The rite of the Little Entrance, followed by the singing of the troparia
and of the Trisagion, corresponded to the actual entrance into the church
where the Eucharist was to be celebrated. According to a Byzantine legend,
the Trisagion is an angelic hymn that was heard by a child who was taken
up into heaven during an earthquake that took place during the reign of
Theodosius II, when Proclus was patriarch of Constantinople (434–46).[16]
It was introduced in the Byzantine Liturgy after Peter the Fuller introduced
it among the non-Chalcedonians in Antioch in the second half of the fifth
century (with a theopaschite addition).[17] At the same time, the troparion
Only-begotten Son (Ὁ Μονογενής), attributed to either Emperor Justinian
or Severus of Antioch, was introduced in the Divine Liturgy of both the
Chalcedonians and non-Chalcedonians. The first accounts of both chants in
the liturgy are from the beginning of the sixth century.[18] In the Constantinopolitan stational liturgy, it was sung at Hagia Sophia before leaving for the
procession, and sung on the way as well; it was followed by troparia, while
Glory to the Father . . . was sung when stopping at the different stations,
and then the Trisagion was sung again while entering the church where the
Divine Liturgy was to be served.[19] It is significant that in the service for the
consecration of a church, after the procession with the holy relics around
the church that is being dedicated, we still find a prayer of entrance and the
singing of the Trisagion.

The readings and the homily are followed by the Augmented Litany (also
called the Litany of Fervent Supplication) and its prayer, the litany and the

[15]Germanus of Constantinople, *Divine Liturgy* 23 (PPS 8:73).
[16]Cf. Jean-Michel Hanssens, *Institutiones liturgicæ de ritibus orientalibus*, vol. 3 (Rome:
Pontificia Università Gregoriana, 1932), no. 885.
[17]The non-Chalcedonians held a Christological view of the Trisagion, adding to it the
formula "who was crucified for us." Cf. Sebastià Janeras, "Le Trisagion: une formule brève
en liturgie comparée," R. Taft and G. Winkler, eds, *Acts of the International Congress of Comparative Liturgy: Fifty years after A. Baumstark*, OCA 265 (Rome: Pontificium Institutum
Orientalium Studiorum, 2001), 534–562; Sebastià Janeras, "Les Byzantins et le Trisagion
christologique," *Miscellanea Liturgica in onore di Sua Eminenza il Cardinale Giacomo Lercaro*, vol. 2 (Rome: Desclée, 1967), 469–99.
[18]Venance Grumel, "L'auteur et la date de la composition du tropaire Ὁ Μονογενής,"
EO 22 (1923): 398–418.
[19]Janin, "Les processions religieuses à Byzance," 72; Juan Mateos, *La célébration de la
parole dans la liturgie byzantine*, OCA 191:91–115.

prayer for the catechumens and their dismissal, and two Litanies of the Faithful and their prayers. All ancient Liturgies witness a similar structure. For example, in the Divine Liturgy of the *Apostolic Constitutions*, the readings were followed by a prayer for the catechumens and their dismissal, a prayer for the possessed and their dismissal, a prayer for those preparing for holy illumination and their dismissal, a prayer for the penitents and their dismissal, and finally a litany and a prayer for the faithful.[20] The dismissal of the catechumens marks the end of the Liturgy of the Word and the beginning of the second part of the Divine Liturgy—the Liturgy of the Eucharist, in which only baptized Christians in good standing can participate.

The first major moment of the Liturgy of the Eucharist is the Great Entrance,[21] during which the Cherubic hymn is sung and the transfer of the gifts from the prothesis to the altar takes place. Some scholars noted that in the early Church the faithful could offer their gifts only after the dismissal of the catechumens, since these ought not to know the content of the mysteries (*disciplina arcani*).[22] Others, based on archeological research, demonstrated that the origin of the Great Entrance was the transfer of the gifts to the altar table from the *diakonikon*, or later, from the *skevophylakion*—these were located either near the entrance of the church building or outside it, and the faithful placed their gifts there upon arriving for the service.[23] We should note that it is a contemporary practice among the Orthodox faithful to offer bread (prosphora) and wine for the Eucharist. Ancient canons regulate the offering of gifts by the faithful; they require that things that have served in the holy mysteries must be consumed by clergy, and that catechumens cannot partake of them.[24] In the Divine Liturgy of the *Apostolic Constitutions* (c. 380), the holy gifts were brought to the bishop by the deacons.[25]

[20]*Apostolic Constitutions* 8.6.3—8.11.6 (SC 336:152–174; ANF 7:483–486).

[21]On the Great Entrance, see Robert Taft, *The Great Entrance*, OCA 200 (Rome: Pontificium Institutum Orientalium Studiorum), 1978.

[22]Cf. A. L. Katansky, "Ocherk istorii liturgii nashei Pravoslavnoi Tserkvi," *Khristianskoe chtenie* 2 (1868): 525–576, at 547–548 [1.9]; A. Petrovsky, "Drevnii akt prinosheniya veshchestva dlya tainstva evkharistii i posledovanie proskomidii," *Khristianskoe chtenie* 84.3 (1904): 406–431; Taft, *The Great Entrance*, 14–15.

[23]G. A. Soteriou, "Ἡ Πρόθεσις καὶ τὸ Διακονικὸν ἐν τῇ Ἀρχαίᾳ Ἐκκλησίᾳ," *Θεολογία* 1/18 (1940): 76–100; D. Stričević, "Dyakonikon i protezis u ranokhristsankimi tsrkvama," *Starinar* 9 (1958): 59–66.

[24]Cf. Canons 8 of Theophilus of Alexandria and 93 of Basil the Great, in Périclès-Pierre Joannou, *Discipline générale antique (IVe–IXe s.)*, vol. 2: *Les canons des Pères Grecs* (Grottaferrata [Rome]: Tipografia Italo-Orientale "San Nilo," 1963), 269, 189–191.

[25]*Apostolic Constitutions*, 8.12.3–4 (SC 336, 178; ANF 7:486).

Already in the fifth century, Theodore of Mopsuestia interpreted the placing of the holy gifts on the altar as the deposition of the crucified Christ in the tomb (he also noted that the Great Entrance took place in silence).[26] The Cherubic hymn that is sung today during the Great Entrance is indirectly attested in the Barberini codex, which calls for the celebrant to say the priestly prayer for himself while the Cherubic hymn is being sung.[27] The contemporary practice of interrupting the singing of the Cherubic hymn in order to make commemorations, appeared only around the twelfth or thirteenth centuries,[28] although the commemoration of the diptychs before the Anaphora is attested by Pseudo-Dionysius in the fifth century.[29] St Cyril of Jerusalem (end of the 4th c.), although not mentioning any transfer of gifts, says that the celebrants wash their hands before exchanging the kiss of peace and reciting the Anaphora.[30] The hand washing has remained in our contemporary practice only at the Hierarchical Liturgy, since the priest washes his hands before the actual beginning of the Divine Liturgy, before serving the prothesis (proskomedia). The Great Entrance is followed by the Litany of Supplication and the prayer of proskomidē. This Litany of Supplication, normally intoned by the deacon after the Great Entrance, is a late addition, given that the *Protheoria* of Theodore of Andida (1055–63) does not mention it.[31] The Barberini manuscript mentions only the prayer of the proskomidē, which is to be said by the celebrant when the faithful have finished singing the "mystical" (Cherubic) hymn.[32] The Litany of Supplication was probably introduced at that place to "cover" the recitation of the prayer of the proskomidē once it became silent, after the seventh century.[33] Robert

[26]Theodore of Mopsuestia, *Homily* 15.24 (*Les homélies catéchétiques de Théodore de Mopsueste*, Raymond-M. Tonneau and Robert Devreesse, eds. [Vatican City: Biblioteca Apostolica Vaticana, 1949], 503).

[27]*Barberini*, 62.

[28]Taft, *The Great Entrance*, 228.

[29]Pseudo-Dionysius the Areopagite, *On the Ecclesiastical Hierarchy* 3.2, 3.3.9 (PG 3:425c, 437b; Luibheid, 211, 218–219).

[30]Cyril of Jerusalem, *Mystagogical Homilies* 5.2 (SC 126:146; see also *Apostolic Constitutions*, 8.11.12 (SC 336:176; ANF 7:486); Pseudo-Dionysius the Areopagite. *On the Ecclesiastical Hierarchy* 3.2 (PG 3:425c, 437d; Luibheid, 211, 219).

[31]*Protheoria* 17 and 19 (PG 140:440 and 444).

[32]*Barberini*, 62 and 75.

[33]John Moschus (+ c. 619) advocates for the silent recitation of the prayers of proskomidē and the Anaphora to avoid abusive cases that he recalls; see John Moschus, *The Spiritual Meadow*, 25 and 196 (SC 12:65 and 266); English in John Moschos, *The Spiritual Meadow*, Introduction, translation, and notes by John Wortley, Cistercian Studies 139 (Collegeville, MN: The Liturgical Press, 2008), 17 and 77–78.

Taft's opinion is that this litany was first introduced into the Divine Liturgy before the Lord's Prayer under the influence of the Liturgy of the Presanctified Gifts, in which the litany appears after the entrance, as at every service of Vespers, and that then it was added to the Divine Liturgies after the Great Entrance on that model.[34]

The exclamation of the prayer of proskomidē is followed by the greeting of the chief celebrant: *Peace be to all*, and the exchange of the kiss of peace among the celebrants. The presence of the kiss of peace is ancient, and in the early Church it involved the whole assembly, although by groups, as described by the *Apostolic Constitutions:* "And let the deacon say to all, Salute ye one another with the holy kiss. And let the clergy salute the bishop, the men of the laity salute the men, the women the women."[35] The exchange of the kiss of peace is followed by the exclamation of the deacon: *The doors, the doors!* This is a remnant of the early Church practice, according to which "subdeacons stand near the doors of the men while deaconesses stand near the doors of the women, so that neither anyone would exit, nor the doors be open, even to let someone enter, during the time of the Anaphora."[36] This exclamation is followed by the recitation of the Symbol of Faith. It was introduced into the Divine Liturgy in 511, after its introduction among the non-Chalcedonians by Peter the Fuller in Antioch in 476, after the Council of Chalcedon (451).[37] Some scholars, following the commentary of Saint Maximus the Confessor, see in the expression "the catholic hymnology" (καθολικὴ ὑμνολογία) in the *Ecclesiastical Hierarchy* of Pseudo-Dionysius (5th c.) the first mention of the Symbol of Faith in the Divine Liturgy.[38]

The recitation of the Symbol of Faith is followed by the prayer of the Anaphora, which is the heart of the Divine Liturgy. According to the Antiochian tradition, it is introduced by the Pauline verse: *The grace of our Lord Jesus Christ, the love of God the Father, and the communion of*

[34]R. Taft, *The Great Entrance*, OCA 200 (Rome: Pontificio Istituto Orientale: 1978), 335.

[35]*Apostolic Constitutions* 8.11.9 (SC 336:174; ANF 7:486).

[36]*Apostolic Constitutions* 8.11.11 (SC 336, 176; translated by the author; cf. ANF 7:486).

[37]Theodore the Reader, *Historia Ecclesiastica*, 2.32 and 48 (PG 86a:201, 209). By reciting the creed at every eucharistic gathering, the non-Chalcedonians wanted to stress that they were remaining faithful to the first Ecumenical Council. Later, the Chalcedonians introduced it as well, during the rule of the non-Chalcedonian emperor Anastasius, to secure the political support of the emperor by showing their faithfulness to the Council of Nicea.

[38]Pseudo-Dionysius the Areopagite, *On the Ecclesiastical Hierarchy* 3.2 (PG 3:425c; Luibheid, 211).

the Holy Spirit be with you all (2 Cor 13.13). The classic structure of the Anaphoras of the Antiochian type contains praise of God, an anamnesis of the creation, the *Sanctus*, an anamnesis of the economy of salvation and of the Mystical Supper, an epiclesis, and a prayer of intercession. Our contemporary Anaphoras of Saint John Chrysostom and of Saint Basil the Great follow that ancient pattern. The *Sanctus* is a very ancient element of the celebration of the Eucharist. Saint Maximus the Confessor (7th c.) interprets the singing of the *Sanctus* (which he calls the Trisagion) as the encounter of the faithful with the angels in faith and their elevation to the same honor while entering into the divine mystery, a participation made possible through baptism and sanctification.[39] The text of the *Sanctus* passed from Jewish use to Christian use at a very early time; it is already cited in the Apocalypse of John (4.8) and in the Letter of Clement of Rome to the Corinthians.[40] The *Sanctus* in its Antiochian form has two parts: the *Sanctus* proper, consisting of the acclamation from Isaiah 6.3; and the *Benedictus*, a christological acclamation taken from Matthew 21.9, an echo of Psalm 117.26.[41] The epiclesis is a prayer that asks for the transformation of the sacred gifts through the coming of the Holy Spirit. It is a very ancient part of the Anaphora.[42] Saint Cyril of Jerusalem wrote that through this prayer, "we beseech the God who loves mankind to send the Holy Spirit on the gifts that are presented, to make the bread the body of Christ and the wine the blood of Christ, since everything that is touched by the Holy Spirit becomes sanctified and transformed."[43]

The Anaphora is concluded by the diptychs. From the end of the fourth century, the term *diptychs* designated tablets on which the names of living and departed Christians were inscribed in order to be commemorated in the Church's prayers. According to the ancient Constantinopolitan usage, when the chief celebrant was reading the concluding part of the Anaphora (the prayer of intercession), a deacon would read the names inscribed on

---

[39]Maximus the Confessor, *Mystagogy* 24 (PG 91:704c and 709b; *Saint Maximus the Confessor: On the Ecclesiastical Mystagogy*, Greek text with English translation by Jonathan J. Armstrong, in collaboration with Shawn Fowler and Tim Wellings, Popular Patristics Series 59 [Yonkers, NY: St Vladimir's Seminary Press, 2019], 87 and 92).

[40]Clement of Rome, *Letter to the Corinthians* 34.6 (SC 167:154–156; ANF 9:239).

[41]Cf. E. Mazza, *The Celebration of the Eucharist: The Origin of the Rite and the Development of its Interpretation* (Collegeville, MN: Liturgical Press, 1999), 285.

[42]Some prayers may be considered epicleses even they do not explicitly ask for the coming of the Holy Spirit; see Mazza, *The Celebration of the Eucharist*, 144.

[43]Cyril of Jerusalem, *Mystagogical Homilies* 5.7 (SC 126:154; PPS 57:124–125).

the diptychs in a low voice.[44] A vestige of this remains where our contemporary liturgical books call for the deacon to say, at the end of the prayer of intercession: *and everyone that each of us has in mind, and each and everyone.*

The Anaphora is followed by the pre-Communion rites.[45] The chief celebrant turns to the assembly to bless the people with the words: *And may the mercies of our great God and Savior Jesus Christ be with all of you.* The deacon then intones the Litany of Supplication. This sequence is attested in the second half of the eighth century by the Barberini *Euchologion.*[46] As we noted above, this litany is a later addition to the Liturgy, most likely under the influence of the Liturgy of the Presanctified Gifts, where the Litany of Supplication appears after the entrance, before the Lord's Prayer.[47] During the Litany of Supplication, the chief celebrant says the pre-Communion prayer, in which he asks God to make the assembly worthy of receiving Communion. A similar prayer was known in the Alexandrian tradition, in the *Euchologion of Serapion* (mid-4th c.).[48] The Litany of Supplication and the pre-Communion prayer are followed by the Lord's Prayer (Our Father), introduced by the exclamation of the celebrant: *And make us worthy, O Master, that with boldness and without condemnation we may dare to call on thee, the heavenly God, as Father, and to say. . . .* St Cyril of Jerusalem (*c.* 380) is the first to mention the Our Father as a pre-Communion prayer because of its allusion to "super-substantial" (ἐπιούσιος, *epiousios*) bread.[49]

After the Lord's Prayer, the chief celebrant gives the peace to the assembly: *Peace be unto all*, and then says the prayer of inclination, already attested in this place in the second half of the eighth century by the Barberini manuscript.[50] In the Byzantine tradition, the prayer of inclination is normally a dismissal prayer.[51] R. Taft noted that, unlike the prayer of inclination before Communion in the Divine Liturgy of Saint Basil the Great, the prayer of

[44]Cf. R. Taft, *The Diptychs*, OCA 238 (Rome: Pontificio Istituto Orientale, 1991), 7–10.

[45]On pre-Communion rites, see Robert Taft, *The Precommunion Rites,* OCA 261 (Rome: Pontificio Istituto Orientale, 2000).

[46]*Barberini, 68 and 80.*

[47]Taft, *Precommunion Rites,* 86–87.

[48]M. Johnson, *The Prayers of Sarapion of Thmuis: A Literary, Liturgical and Theological Analysis*, OCA 249 (Rome: Pontificio Istituto Orientale, 1995), 50–51.

[49]Cyril of Jerusalem, *Mystagogical Homilies* 5:11–18 (SC 126:160–168; PPS 57:126–133).

[50]Barberini, 69 and 81.

[51]Taft, *Precommunion Rites,* 155–157.

inclination in the Divine Liturgy of Saint John Chrysostom does not make any reference to Communion. He concluded that this prayer was moved from the end of the Liturgy to this place, as a dismissal of the non-communicants who departed before Communion.[52]

After the exclamation of the prayer of inclination, the chief celebrant elevates the Lamb, saying: *The Holy Things are for the holy,* and the assembly responds: *One is holy, one is Lord: Jesus Christ, to the glory of God the Father.* This was once the invitation to Communion, attested around 380 by the *Apostolic Constitutions* and by St Cyril of Jerusalem.[53] After this elevation, the holy bread is broken into four portions. This rite of fraction (μελισμός) is very ancient. In the New Testament, the Eucharist is referred to as "the breaking of the bread" (cf. Lk 24.35, Acts 2.42, Acts 20.7, Acts 27.35). One portion of the Lamb is put into the chalice. Theodore of Mopsuestia (*c.* 388–92) comments on the mixture of the bread and the wine by saying that "although they are two [i.e., bread and wine], they are nevertheless one in power, and are the memorial of the death and the passion of the body of our Lord, when his blood was shed on the cross for us all."[54] Then, hot water (*zeon*) is added to the chalice. The Barberini manuscript does not mention this action, which was added in the twelfth century[55] to emphasize that in the Eucharist we partake of the body and blood of the living, risen Christ, by the activity of the Holy Spirit.[56]

The *Apostolic Constitutions* give a precise order for holy Communion: "The bishop, then the presbyters, and deacons, and sub-deacons, and the readers, and the singers, and the ascetics; and then of the women, the deaconesses, and the virgins, and the widows; then the children; and then all the people in order, with reverence and godly fear, without tumult."[57] This order is still observed in the Orthodox Church today, where the bishop receives Communion first, before distributing Communion to the clergy—

[52]Taft, *Precommunion Rites,* 195–196.

[53]*Apostolic Constitutions* 8.13.11 (SC 336:208; ANF 7:490); Cyril of Jerusalem, *Mystagogical Homilies* 5.19 (SC 126:168; *Lectures on the Christian Sacraments,* PPS 57:132–133).

[54]Theodore of Mopsuestia, *Homily* 16.15; A. Mingana, "Commentary of Theodore of Mopsuestia on the Lord's Prayer and on the Sacrament of Baptism and the Eucharist," *Woodbrooke Studies* 6 (1933): 105.

[55]Taft, *The Precommunion Rites,* 473.

[56]Cf. Nicolas Cabasilas, *Explanation of the Divine Liturgy* 37.1–3 (SC 4-bis: 226–228; Cabasilas, *Commentary,* 90–91); St. Symeon of Thessalonica, *The Liturgical Commentaries,* ed. and tr. Steven Hawkes-Teeples, Studies and Texts 168 (Toronto: Pontifical Institute of Mediaeval Studies, 2011), 150.

[57]*Apostolic Constitutions* 8.13.14 (SC 336:208–10, ANF 8:490).

to priests and deacons—and then to the faithful, among whom children usually receive Communion first.[58] The *Apostolic Constitutions* and St Cyril of Jerusalem mention Psalm 33 as a Communion hymn, because of the verse: *Taste and see that the Lord is good* (Ps 33.9).[59] The Byzantine tradition later developed a whole repertoire of Communion chants (*koinonika*) for different days and feasts of the year.[60]

The ancient formula of Communion, as attested by the *Apostolic Constitutions*, was: *The body of Christ,* said by bishop while he was distributing the body, and: *The blood of Christ,* said by the deacon while giving the chalice.[61] Saint Cyril of Jerusalem specifies that the faithful receive the body of Christ on their right hand placed over their left hand.[62] This was the practice for the laity until the eighth century,[63] and this is still the way clergy receive the body of Christ. The practice of giving the laity the body mixed with the blood of Christ with a spoon seems to have been implemented only in the ninth century. Canon 10 of the Prima-Secunda Council of Constantinople (861) is the first document to mention the spoon (λαβίδα, *labida*) among the different liturgical vessels.[64]

In the ancient Church, Communion was followed by a prayer of thanksgiving.[65] This is still the contemporary practice: Communion is followed by a litany said by the deacon and a prayer of thanksgiving concluding with an exclamation by the chief celebrant. But following it, the priest says one more prayer: the Ambo Prayer (ἐπιστάμβωνος, *epistambonos*), already attested in the Barberini *Euchologion*.[66] Contemporary liturgical books add after the Ambo Prayer: *Blessed be the name of the Lord* and Psalm 33, with the

[58]On Communion rites and the end of the Divine Liturgy, cf. R. Taft, *The Communion, Thanksgiving and Concluding Rites*, OCA 281 (Rome: Pontificio Istituto Orientale, 2008).

[59]*Apostolic Constitutions*, 8.13.16 (SC 336, 210, ANF 7:491); Cyril of Jerusalem, *Mystagogical Homilies* 5.20 (SC 126:168–70; PPS 57:132–135).

[60]Cf. Taft, *Precommunion Rites*, 263–267.

[61]*Apostolic Constitutions* 8.13.15 (SC 336.210; ANF 7:490–91).

[62]Cyril of Jerusalem, *Mystagogical Homilies* 5.21 (SC 126:170; PPS 57:134–35).

[63]Canon 101 of the Council in Trullo (691–92) prescribes that the laity receive the body of Christ in their hands, and not in some vessel; cf. P. Joannou, *Discipline générale antique*, 1.1:237–39.

[64]Périclès-Pierre Joannou, *Discipline générale antique (IVe–IXe s.)*, vol. 1.2, *Les canons des Synodes Particulieres* (Grottaferrata [Rome]: Tipografia Italo-Orientale "San Nilo," 1962), 466–67.

[65]*Apostolic Constitutions* 8.14.1 (SC 336:210; ANF 7:491); Cyril of Jerusalem, *Mystagogical Homilies* 5:22 (SC 126:172; PPS 57:134–35).

[66]*Barberini*, 70.

distribution of the antidoron (according to the rubric of the Slavic books), and a dismissal. This final part first appeared in the eleventh century, most likely under the influence of the dismissal of the major services of the Hours, as attested by *Paris Coislin 213* (1027) at the end of the anointing of the sick in conjunction with the Divine Liturgy.[67]

2. The Preparation

The Divine Liturgy is preceded by a service that is not often seen by the faithful: the preparation rites that were codified in the fourteenth century by the *Diataxis of the Divine Liturgy*[68] of St Philotheos Kokkinos, Patriarch of Constantinople. It includes the entrance prayers, the vesting, and the prothesis.

2.1. Entrance Prayers

The entrance prayers (or the *kairos* as the Greeks call them) are said by the chief celebrant and his concelebrants in front of the iconostasis. The prayers are said by the deacon, except the prayer of the chief celebrant, in which he asks God for strength to offer the bloodless sacrifice, since all liturgical actions are God's action, for our Lord Jesus Christ is mystically the chief celebrant of all liturgical sacramental services. The order is as follows:

Table 2.1: The Order of the Entrance Prayers

1. Usual beginning prayers
2. Troparia *Have mercy on us, O Lord*
3. Veneration of the icon of Christ with the troparion: *We venerate thy most pure image*
4. Veneration of the icon of the Theotokos with the troparion: *Make us worthy of mercy*

[In the Greek practice, the celebrants venerate also the other icons on the iconostasis, while saying the relevant troparia]

---

[67]M. Arranz, *L'Eucologio costantinopolitano agli inizi del secolo XI: Hagiasmatarion & Archieratikon (Rituale & Pontificale) con l'aggiunta del Leiturgikon (Messale)* (Rome: Pontificia Università Gregoriana, 1996), 381–82.
[68]P. Trempelas, *Αἱ τρεῖς λειτουργίαι* (Athens, 1935), 1–16.

---

5. Prayer of the chief celebrant: *O Lord, stretch forth thy hand*
[In the contemporary Greek practice, this is followed by the dismissal]
6. Entrance into the sanctuary, while saying Ps 5.8–13: *I will enter thy house*

2.2. Vesting

The entrance prayers are followed by the vesting. For the celebration of the Divine Liturgy, the celebrants put on all their liturgical vestments. The fact that the prayers of vesting are given immediately before the prothesis means that the priest who performs the prothesis ought to be fully vested. (I note here that performing the prothesis without the phelonion is not proper, but rather a decadent practice that may be observed in some parishes, particularly among the Greeks.) A special prayer is prescribed when putting on each vestment, since each one of these has a special meaning.[69]

The vestments of the deacon are the sticharion, the orarion, and the cuffs (*epimanikia*). In the theology of priesthood developed by Pseudo-Dionysius and Saint Symeon of Thessalonica, the deacon, as a servant, is compared to the angelic orders. For this reason, Symeon says that the sticharion is the vestment that symbolizes the angelic order and the orarion manifests the angelic wings.[70] For St Nicolas Cabasilas, the deacon's sticharion has wide sleeves to show that he is at service.[71] For Saint Symeon, the epimanikia, which are worn by all the celebrants without exception, represent the divine energy that is acting through the celebrant, since our Lord Jesus Christ is the main celebrant.[72]

The priest puts on a sticharion with tight sleeves, the epitrachelion, the belt (zonē), the cuffs (epimanikia) and the phelonion. For Saint Symeon of Thessalonica, the epitrachelion manifests the grace of priesthood, which is given from above, and it shows that the priest must submit himself to Christ who is the main celebrant.[73] The belt signifies that Christ is serving for our

---

[69]On the history of the liturgical vestments, cf. W. Woodfin, *The Embodied Icon: Liturgical Vestments and Sacramental Power in Byzantium* (Oxford: Oxford University Press, 2012).

[70]Symeon of Thessalonica, *The Liturgical Commentaries*, 98–100; PG 155:709–12.

[71]Nicolas Cabasilas, *Explanation of the sacred vestments* 1 (SC 4-bis: 364).

[72]Symeon of Thessalonica, *The Liturgical Commentaries*, 104–106; PG 155:713.

[73]Symeon of Thessalonica, *The Liturgical Commentaries*, 98–102 (PG 155:709 and 713); see also Nicolas Cabasilas, *Explanation of the sacred vestments* 2 (SC 4-bis:364).

salvation.[74] The phelonion shows that through his incarnation, crucifixion, and resurrection, God the Word has united heaven and earth.[75] Some priests may wear also an epigonation and a cross, but these are actually bishop's attributes that are awarded by the bishop to some priests because of their particular work and responsibilities.[76]

The bishop puts on a sticharion with tight sleeves, the epitrachelion, the belt (zonē) and the cuffs (epimanikia) as the priest does. He puts on the epigonation, which signifies the victory over sin through the resurrection of Christ.[77] Instead of the phelonion, he puts on the sakkos; this was originally a vestment of the emperor, which eventually replaced the phelonion for bishops. Over the sakkos the puts on the omophorion, which signifies the incarnation of God the Word and the lost sheep that the Savior came to save and put on his shoulders.[78] The bishop also wears the cross, the encolpion, and the miter.

At the conclusion of the vesting, the celebrants wash their hands while saying the psalm verses: *I will wash my hands in innocence* (Ps 25.6–12). As we have seen before, in the early Church, the washing of the hands (*lavabo*) took place before the Anaphora,[79] as is still the case for the bishop serving the Hierarchical Liturgy. With the appearance of the prothesis in the eighth century, the hand washing was moved just before it.

2.3. *The Prothesis*

In our contemporary practice, the prothesis [*proskomidē, proskomedia*] is performed over one large prosphora in the Greek practice, and over five smaller prosphoras in the Russian practice. Sometimes, on the Holy Mountain, two prosphoras are used. This is the echo of fluctuations throughout history, where we may find accounts of one, two, five, seven, or even nine prosphoras used in the prothesis. According to the *Diataxis of the Divine Liturgy* of Saint Philotheos Kokkinos, five prosphoras ought to be used: the

[74]Symeon of Thessalonica, *The Liturgical Commentaries,* 104 (PG 155:713).
[75]Symeon of Thessalonica, *The Liturgical Commentaries,* 106 (PG 155:716).
[76]Symeon of Thessalonica, *Dialogue in Christ* 83 (PG 155:261d-264a).
[77]Symeon of Thessalonica, *The Liturgical Commentaries,* 104 (PG 155:713c).
[78]Symeon of Thessalonica, *The Liturgical Commentaries,* 108–100 (PG 155:709 and 716).
[79]Cyril of Jerusalem, *Mystagogical Homilies* 5.2 (SC 126:146; PPS 57:120–123); *Apostolic Constitutions,* 8.11.12 (SC 336:176; ANF 7:486); Pseudo-Dionysius the Areopagite, *On the Ecclesiastical Hierarchy* 3.2, 3.3.10 (PG 3:425c, 437d; Luibheid, 211, 219).

first for the Lamb, the second for the Theotokos' particle, the third for the nine particles for different ranks of saints, the fourth for particles for the living, and the fifth for the particles for the dead.[80]

Taking the first prosphora, from which the Lamb will be cut (that is, the piece of bread that will be sanctified as the body of Christ), the priest says three times: *In remembrance of our Lord and God and Savior Jesus Christ,* each time making the sign of the cross with the spear. He then pierces the prosphora with the spear to the right of the seal (that is, on the side of the seal with "IC" and "NI"), and he cuts along the right side while saying: *As a sheep he was led to the slaughter* (Is 53.7). Then cutting the left side, he says: *And as a blameless lamb before its shearers is dumb, so he opens not his mouth.* Cutting the upper side, he says: *In his humiliation his judgment was taken away.* Cutting the lower side, he says: *Who shall declare his generation?* The deacon then points to the holy bread with his orarion, saying: *Take up, master,* and the priest, piercing the prosphora on the bottom right side and cutting, then lifts out the Lamb, saying: *For his life is taken up from the earth.* The priest inverts the Lamb, placing the seal upon the diskos, while the deacon says: *Sacrifice, master,* and then the priest cuts the Lamb cross-wise, taking care not to cut through the seal, saying: *Sacrificed is the Lamb of God, who takes away the sin of the world, for the life of the world and its salvation* (cf. Jn 1.29). The priest inverts the Lamb again so that the seal is on top, while the deacon says: *Pierce, master.* The priest then pierces the right side of the Lamb under the letters "IC" saying: *One of the soldiers pierced his side with a spear, and immediately there came forth blood and water. He who saw it has borne witness, and his witness is true* (Jn 19.34–35). At this moment, the deacon takes the wine and water and says to the priest: *Bless, master, the holy union,* and as the deacon pours the wine and water into the chalice, the priest blesses the diaconal action with the sign of the cross while saying: *Blessed is the union of thy holy things, always, now and ever and unto ages of ages. Amen.*

St Germanus of Constantinople, to whom *The Ecclesiastical History* [or *On the Divine* Liturgy] is usually attributed, says, "the proskomedē, which takes place on the altar located in the skevophylakion, signifies the place of Calvary, where Jesus was crucified."[81] St Nicolas Cabasilas and St Symeon of Thessalonica emphasized the first transformation that takes place at the

---

[80]P. Trempelas, *Αἱ τρεῖς λειτουργίαι,* 2–4; Symeon of Thessalonica, *De sacra liturgia,* 84:93–94 (PG 155:264a, 280c-284d).

[81]Germanus of Constantinople, *Divine Liturgy* 36 (PPS 8:85).

prothesis: the bread and wine are taken out of profane space and enter sacred space by becoming the antitypes (τὰ ἀντίτυπα, *ta antitypa*) of the body and blood of Christ, as the Anaphora of Saint Basil calls them,[82] awaiting their ultimate transformation into the body and blood of Christ through the epiclesis.[83] In the prothesis, water is mixed with wine. This reflects the common practice for wine drinking in antiquity. Nevertheless, the mystagogical interpretations of the Divine Liturgy link this with the narrative of the crucifixion in the gospels, when blood and water flowed from the pierced side of Christ (cf. Jn 19.34). Saint Germanus of Constantinople says that "the wine and water are the blood and the water which came out from his side."[84] Canon 32 of the Council in Trullo criticizes the Armenians for not adding water to the eucharistic wine.[85] This argument against the Armenians was later reproduced in the commentary of Saint Symeon of Thessalonica.[86]

The priest then takes the second prosphora and removes a triangular particle saying: *In honor and memory of our most blessed Lady Theotokos and Ever-virgin Mary. Through her prayers, O Lord, accept this sacrifice upon thine altar above the heavens.* And he places it on the right side of the Lamb, saying: *The Queen stood on thy right side, arrayed in golden robes, all glorious* (Ps 44.9).

The priest takes the third prosphora, from which he cuts nine small triangular particles for the nine orders (ranks) of saints. The practice of taking one square particle with the nine orders of saints, as one can see in many parishes, especially among the Greeks, is not proper but rather decadent, since the only square piece on the diskos ought to be the Lamb. There is a variant among the Greek and Slavonic books concerning the commemorations for the first two particles, which reflect variants in the manuscript tradition. Here is the list:

---

[82]Trempelas, *Αἱ τρεῖς λειτουργίαι*, 183.

[83]Cf. Nicolas Cabasilas, *Explanation of the Divine Liturgy* 6.1–6 and 11.1 (SC 4-bis: 80–82 and 98; Cabasilas, *Commentary*, 119–120); Symeon of Thessalonica, *De sacra liturgia* 96 (PG 155:288b).

[84]Germanus of Constantinople, *Divine Liturgy*, 22 (PPS 8:71).

[85]Joannou, *Discipline générale antique*, 1.1:162–66. Cf. Robert Taft, "Water into Wine. The Twice-mixed Chalice in the Byzantine Eucharist," *Le Muséon* 100 (1987): 323–42.

[86]Symeon of Thessalonica, *The Liturgical Commentaries*, 204–214 (PG 155:276–80).

Table 2.2: The Order of the Proskomedia

Greek books	Slavic books
1. The holy Archangels Michael and Gabriel and all the angelic powers	1. Saint John the Baptist
2. Saint John the Baptist and the holy and glorious prophets	2. The holy and glorious prophets
3. The holy, glorious and all-laudable apostles	3. The holy, glorious and all-laudable apostles
4. Our fathers among the saints and hierarchs	4. Our fathers among the saints and hierarchs
5. The holy apostle and Archdeacon Stephen the Protomartyr and the holy martyrs	5. The holy apostle and Archdeacon Stephen the Protomartyr and the holy martyrs
6. The venerable and God-bearing monastic fathers and mothers	6. The venerable and God-bearing monastic fathers and mothers
7. The holy Wonderworkers and Unmercenary Physicians	7. The holy Wonderworkers and Unmercenary Physicians
8. The holy and righteous Ancestors of God, Joachim and Anna, and the saint of the day	8. The holy and righteous Ancestors of God, Joachim and Anna, the Patron Saint of the church, and the saint of the day
9. Saint John Chrysostom or Basil the Great, depending on whose liturgy is being served	9. Saint John Chrysostom or Basil the Great, depending on whose liturgy is being served

The priest then takes a particle from the fourth prosphora and, placing it at the foot of the Lamb, he commemorates the local bishop. He then remembers any other living faithful, removing small particles from the fourth prosphora (or from other prosphoras that have been offered by the faithful) for each and placing them next to the first, while each name is being mentioned.

Finally, the priest takes a particle from the fifth prosphora and, placing it below the row of particles just mentioned, he remembers the departed patriarchs, bishops, priests, deacons, and monastics; then the departed Orthodox rulers, and the founders of the local church; and while he remembers any other departed faithful, he removes small particles from this fifth prosphora, or from other prosphoras that have been offered by the faithful, while each name is mentioned.

When he finishes remembering the departed, the priest says the prayer: *Remember all of our Orthodox fathers and brethren who have departed in the hope of resurrection to eternal life in thy communion, O Lord who lovest mankind.* The priest then concludes by taking a small particle for himself, saying: *Remember, O Lord, mine unworthiness also, and forgive me all my sins, both voluntary and involuntary.* The deacon presents the censer to the priest, saying: *Bless, master, the incense.* The priest blesses the censer saying: *We offer thee incense, O Christ our God* ... Then he censes the asterisk and covers the diskos with it, while saying: *And the star came and stood over the place where the young Child was* (Mt 2.9). Here we see a symbolic link between the prothesis and the nativity of Christ. Saint Symeon of Thessalonica sees in the prothesis "a figure of the cave and manger."[87] This explains why very often the icon of the Nativity is depicted over the prothesis table. But this is a rather late interpretation of the prothesis, introduced into the mystagogies when the interpretation of the order of the Divine Liturgy as the chronology of the life of Christ was firmly established. Next, the priest covers the diskos with a veil, censing it first while saying: *The Lord reigns; he is robed in majesty* ... (Ps 92). Then the priest censes the second veil and places it over the chalice, saying: *Thy virtue has covered the heavens, O Christ, and the earth is full of thy praise.* Then, censing the aër (large veil), the priest says: *Cover us with the shelter of thy wings* ... and he places this veil over both the chalice and the diskos. He then takes the censer and censes the holy gifts, saying three times: *Blessed is our God, who is thus well pleased: glory to thee,* and the deacon answers: *always, now and ever, and unto ages of ages.* The priest then says the prayer of the prothesis: *O God, our God, who didst send the heavenly Bread* ... , and he concludes the prothesis with the dismissal. After the dismissal, the deacon censes the table of the prothesis and the altar table, while praying the troparion of Great Saturday: *In the tomb with the body* ... and then, reciting Psalm 50, he continues censing the whole church in the prescribed order.

After the censing, the chief celebrant and the deacon make the sign of the cross and bow three times, and say the opening dialogue, introduced in the fourteenth century by the *Diataxis* of St Philotheos Kokkinos.[88] The chief celebrant recites the prayer to the Holy Spirit (*O Heavenly King*), followed by the verses: *Glory to God in the highest* (twice), and: *O Lord, thou shalt open*

---

[87]Symeon of Thessalonica, *The Liturgical Commentaries*, 232 (PG 155:285d).
[88]P. Trempelas, *Αἱ τρεῖς λειτουργίαι*, 5.

my lips, crossing himself and making a bow after each. Then the deacon says, *It is the time for the Lord to act. Bless, master.* The chief celebrant blesses him, saying: *Blessed is our God.* . . . The deacon replies: *Amen. Pray for me, master.* The chief celebrant says: *May the Lord direct thy steps.* The deacon replies: *Remember me, holy master.* The chief celebrant replies: *May the Lord God remember thee in his kingdom.* . . . The deacon answers: *Amen*, exits the sanctuary, comes in front of the holy doors of the iconostasis, says quietly: *O Lord, thou shalt open my lips* . . . and then he says aloud: *Bless, master.*

3. The Liturgy of the Word

The Divine Liturgy begins with the exclamation of the first priest: *Blessed is the Kingdom,* as he makes the sign of the cross with the gospel book over the holy table; this is followed by the Great Litany (also known as the Litany of Peace) by the deacon. The first stage of the Divine Liturgy is the enarxis, which is a vestige of the ancient procession that took place in Constantinople from Hagia Sophia to the church where the Divine Liturgy was to be served. This procession had three stops, or stations, at each of which a litany was intoned by the deacon and a prayer by the priest, and then an antiphon was sung. The Little Entrance, which today is preceded by the Prayer of the Entrance said by the priest, is the vestige of the actual entrance into the church in which the Divine Liturgy was to be celebrated in that stational arrangement. The contemporary order of the Liturgy of the Word is as follows:

Table 2.3: The Order of the Liturgy of the Word

---

1. Enarxis (Service of the three antiphons)
   a) Great Litany, prayer and First Antiphon
   b) Little Litany, prayer and Second Antiphon. Glory . . . Both now . . . *O Only-begotten Son*
   c) Little Litany, prayer and Third Antiphon
2. Prayer of the Entrance and Little Entrance
3. Troparia and Kontakia
4. Prayer of the Trisagion and the Trisagion
5. Peace. Readings (Epistle and Gospel), with prayer of the Gospel

---

6. Homily

7. Augmented Litany (sometimes called the Litany of Fervent Supplication) with a prayer

8. Litany and prayer for the catechumens, dismissal of the catechumens

The contemporary liturgical practice employs festal antiphons on Great Feasts; these are found in the *Menaion*. Daily antiphons, composed of selected verses from Psalms 91, 92, and 94, are sung at daily Liturgies, as well as on ordinary Sundays according to the contemporary Greek practice; these can be found in the *Apostol* book. They are mentioned in the *Ecclesiastical History* attributed to Saint Germanus of Constantinople.[89] For particularly festive Sundays and for major feasts, the so-called *Typika* are sung. These are in fact the first part of the service of the Typika, which is found in the *Horologion* and consists of Psalms 102, 145, and the Beatitudes. The incorporation of these elements into the Divine Liturgy was prescribed in the twelfth century by the *Typikon* of the Evergetis Monastery, because the service of the Typika was suppressed on these festive days.[90] Thus, in the twelfth century, the first part of the Typika replaced the service of the three antiphons. The Second Antiphon is always followed by the troparion *O only-begotten Son* (Ὁ Μονογενής, *ho Monogenēs*), attributed either to Emperor Justinian or Severus of Antioch; this was introduced into the Liturgy at the beginning of the sixth century.

Toward the end of the Third Antiphon, the Entrance takes place (this is sometimes called the Little Entrance in contrast with the Great Entrance later in the Liturgy). The priest gives the gospel book to the deacon, and, preceded by one or two candle-bearers, they exit through the northern deacon's door. Once they arrive in front of the holy doors of the iconostasis (as they would have arrived in front of the main doors of the church in the ancient stational liturgy), the priest says the prayer of the entrance and blesses saying: *Blessed is the entrance of thy saints* . . . . Since this entrance was historically the actual entrance of the assembly into the church, even today the holy doors of the iconastasis are usually kept closed until the Little Entrance, and a celebrating bishop enters the sanctuary only after the Little Entrance. In his *Mystagogy*, St Maximus the Confessor (580–662) interpreted this entrance of the people with the bishop into the church as the

[89]Germanus of Constantinople, *Divine Liturgy* 23–24, PPS 8:72–75.
[90]Dmitrievsky, *Opisanie*, 1:603.

passage from ignorance to knowledge of God, from evil to virtue.[91] A century later, when the stational liturgy was likely abandoned and the service of the three antiphons became the initial part of the Divine Liturgy, the Little Entrance was re-interpreted as "the coming of the Son of God and his entrance into the world," as Saint Germanus of Constantinople puts it.[92] The deacon says: *Wisdom! Stand upright!* and the assembly sings the entrance hymn (*eisodikon*): *Come, let us worship and fall down before Christ. O Son of God*—on Sundays: *who art risen from the dead*; on other days: *who art wondrous in thy saints—save us who sing to thee, Alleluia!* or, on a great feast, the proper *eisodikon* (entrance verse) prescribed by the *Typikon*.

The Little Entrance is followed by the singing of the troparia and the kontakia. Usually the troparia of the temple, of the day of the week, of the feast or of the saint celebrated on that day, of the deceased (if there is a commemoration of the departed), followed by kontakia of the temple, of the day of the week, of the feast or of the saint celebrated on that day, of the deceased (if there is a commemoration), and a concluding kontakion (usually in honor of the Theotokos). In the contemporary Greek practice, only troparia and the concluding kontakion are sung. A hierarchical ordering is observed: a troparion in honor of Christ takes precedence over a troparion in honor of the Theotokos, which takes precedence over a troparion of a saint. This explains why on a major feast, like the Nativity of Christ, the troparia of the temple and of the weekday are suppressed, and only the troparion and the kontakion of the feast are sung. The *Typikon* prescribes a special order of troparia and kontakia during the periods of forefeasts or afterfeasts. The following table gives the usual order of the singing of the troparia and the kontakia:

Table 2.4: The Order of Troparia and Kontakia at the Divine Liturgy

In a church of the Savior	In a church of the Theotokos	In a church of a saint
Troparion of the church*	Troparion of the church*	Troparion of the weekday
Troparion of the weekday	Troparion of the weekday	Troparion of the church

[91]Maximus the Confessor, *Mystagogy* 9 (PG 91:688d–689a; Maximus, *Ecclesiastical Mystagogy*, PPS 59:73–74).

[92]Germanus of Constantinople, Divine Liturgy 24, PPS 8:72–75.

Troparion of the saint of the day (1 or 2)	Troparion of the saint of the day (1 or 2)	Troparion of the saint of the day (1 or 2)
Kontakion of the weekday	Kontakion of the weekday	Kontakion of the weekday
		Kontakion of the church
Kontakion of the saint of the day (1 or 2)	Kontakion of the saint of the day (1 or 2)	Kontakion of the saint of the day (1 or 2)
Glory: Kontakion of the departed (*With the saints give rest*)	Glory: Kontakion of the departed (*With the saints give rest*)	Glory: Kontakion of the departed (*With the saints give rest*)
Both now: Kontakion of the church*	Both now: Kontakion of the church	Both now: *Steadfast protectress of Christians*
*Replaced on Wednesday and Friday by the troparion of the Cross.	*On Wednesday and Friday, the troparion of the Cross precedes the troparion of the church.	

The singing of the troparia and of the kontakia is followed by the prayer of the Trisagion and the singing of the Trisagion. On several great feasts of the Lord—the Nativity of Christ, Theophany, Lazarus Saturday, Pascha, and Pentecost—the Trisagion is replaced by the Pauline verse: *As many as have been baptized in Christ, have put on Christ* (Gal 3.27), in memory of the baptism that took place on these days in the early Church. On the feast of the Exaltation of the Cross (September 14), on the third Sunday of Great Lent (Sunday of the Cross), and on the feast of the Procession of the Cross (August 1), the Trisagion is replaced by the troparion *Before thy cross*.

The Trisagion is followed by the readings of the day. There is usually one epistle reading and one gospel reading prescribed for a Divine Liturgy, although when several commemorations coincide, the *Typikon* may prescribe two or even three readings from the epistles and gospels. The contemporary Greek practice, following the new *Typikon of the Great Church*, avoids this practice and prescribes only one epistle reading and one gospel reading for any Divine Liturgy. The readings are preceded by the greeting of the chief celebrant: *Peace be unto all*. This exclamation once marked the beginning of the Divine Liturgy.[93] It is a pity (if not a mistake) that it was

[93]P. Trempelas, *Αἱ τρεῖς λειτουργίαι*, 48–49. Cf. J. Mateos, "Évolution historique de la liturgie de saint Jean Chrysostome. Deuxième partie: Les lectures," *POC* 18 (1968): 305–25 = J. Mateos, *La célébration de la parole dans la liturgie byzantine*, OCA 191:127–147.

suppressed in contemporary Greek liturgical books. The peace is followed by the prokeimenon (found in the *Apostol*), which is chanted by the reader (and repeated by the chanters). The reading of the epistle is followed by the singing of *Alleluia*, with the appropriate psalm verses (found in the *Apostol*). It was during this rather long chant sequence that the deacon performed the censing before the reading of the gospel. Unfortunately, contemporary usage has reduced the singing of the Alleluia with the appointed verses; for practical reasons this reduction has led to doing the censing during the reading of the epistle, and this is not proper. The singing of the Alleluia and the censing are a preparation and an acclamation prior to the reading of the gospel. According to the practice of the early Church, the biblical readings ought to be followed by a homily, since preaching is an integral part of the Liturgy of the Word.[94] The homily is followed by the Augmented Litany and its prayer and the Litany for the Catechumens and its prayer, and after this the catechumens are dismissed. During the Augmented Litany, the antimension is unfolded over the holy table in preparation for the transfer of the Holy Gifts. The upper part of it is usually unfolded during the Litany for the Catechumens, when the deacon says: *That he may reveal to them the gospel of righteousness.*

4. The Liturgy of the Eucharist

After the dismissal of the catechumens, the Liturgy of the Eucharist begins. From this point, each Divine Liturgy (both of Saint John Chrysostom and of Saint Basil the Great) has its own proper prayers. The order of the Liturgy of the Eucharist is the following:

Table 2.5: The Order of the Liturgy of the Eucharist

1. Two Little Litanies with their prayers for the Faithful
2. Cherubic Hymn and sacerdotal prayer
3. Great Entrance
4. Litany of Supplication and Prayer of the Proskomidē
5. Peace, Kiss of Peace, and Symbol of Faith

---

[94]Cf. Tertullian, *Apologeticum* 39.1–4; *Apostolic Constitutions* 8.5.11–12 (SC 336:150; ANF 7:483).

6. Anaphora

7. Diptychs

8. Litany of Supplication and pre-Communion prayer

9. Lord's Prayer (Our Father)

10. Peace and Prayer of Inclination

11. *The Holy Things are for the holy,* fraction, commixture, zeon

12. Communion (in order, with clergy receiving before the laity)

13. Litany and Prayer of Thanksgiving.

14. Ambo Prayer

15. Prayer before consuming the holy Gifts

16. *Blessed be the name of the Lord* (Ps 33), and dismissal

The dismissal of the catechumens is followed by two Little Litanies with their prayers for the faithful. Then the Cherubic Hymn is sung. During this the chief celebrant recites the sacerdotal prayer: *No one who is bound with the desires and pleasures of the flesh,* in a low voice; in this he prays that he may be made worthy, by the power of the Holy Spirit given through the mystery of the priesthood, to celebrate the mystery of the Eucharist. This prayer is extremely important for the theology of the Eucharist and of the priesthood, since it presents our Lord Jesus Christ both as the unique sacrifice offered once for all and as the only priest (cf. Heb 10.12): *he that offers and is offered, that accepts and is distributed* (ὁ προσφέρων καὶ προσφερόμενος καὶ προσδεχόμενος καὶ διαδιδόμενος). After this prayer, the chief celebrant says the first half of the Cherubikon three times, and each time the deacon completes it. The chief celebrant then censes the altar table, the iconostasis, and the assembly from the solea, bows with the deacon three times in front of the holy table, kisses it, bows to the assembly, and goes to the prothesis table. (Note that in the Russian practice, the deacon performs the censing, in a slightly different order: the altar table, the prothesis, the high place and the rest of the sanctuary, the icon screen, and the people.)

After censing the holy gifts on the prothesis table, the priest puts the aër over the shoulders of the deacon and gives him the diskos, and he takes the chalice himself. Preceded by one or two candle bearers, they carry the holy gifts and exit through the northern deacon's door. In contemporary practice, the Cherubic hymn is interrupted, so that the deacon and the priest may make commemorations; the most widespread and basic formula is: *May the Lord God remember all of us in his Kingdom always, now and forever and to the ages of ages*. The chanters respond: *Amen*, and sing the rest of the Cherubikon, as the priest and the deacon enter the sanctuary through the holy doors. The chief celebrant places the chalice and the diskos on the unfolded antimension on the holy table, takes the veils away, and covers both diskos and chalice with the aër, which he takes from the shoulders of the deacon. The transfer of the gifts from the prothesis table (seen as Golgotha) to the holy table (seen as the Tomb) and their covering with the aër has been allegorically interpreted as a transfer of Christ from Golgotha and his burial.[95] For this reason, the depiction of Christ in the Tomb was often depicted on the aër, and this custom later gave birth to the first epitaphia. The placing of the gifts on the holy table as a depiction of the burial of Christ is accentuated by the closing of the holy doors and of the curtain of the iconostasis. The curtain remains closed until the Symbol of Faith (Russian practice), or even until the end of the Anaphora (Athonite practice).

After the gifts are covered, the chief celebrant censes them while saying: *Do good, O Lord, to Sion* . . . and then a dialogue ensues between the chief celebrant and the deacon; this was introduced by St Philotheos Kokkinos in the fourteenth century.[96] The chief celebrant says to the deacon: *Pray for me, brother and concelebrant*. The deacon replies: *The Holy Spirit shall come upon thee* . . . . The chief celebrant then says: *The Holy Spirit himself shall minister together with us all the days of our life*. The deacon then asks: *Remember me, holy master*. The chief celebrant ends this dialogue by saying: *May the Lord God remember thee in his kingdom* . . . . Saint Symeon of Thessalonica emphasizes that "the bishop requests a prayer from all acknowledging his human weakness and in fear and trembling before the task."[97]

The Great Entrance is followed by the Litany of Supplication intoned by the deacon, while the chief celebrant says the Prayer of the Proskomidē. This prayer is often understood as a prayer for the Gifts being presented and offered, but in fact it asks God that the celebrants who have come to the holy altar may be made worthy that the Holy Gifts may be accepted and the Holy Spirit may come upon them to sanctify them. The *Protheoria* explains it in this way: "After the deposition of the Holy Gifts, the bishop, saying the

---

[95] Germanus of Constantinople, *Divine Liturgy* 41, PPS 8:88–89.
[96] P. Trempelas, *Αἱ τρεῖς λειτουργίαι*, 10.
[97] Symeon of Thessalonica, *The Liturgical Commentaries,* 131 (PG 155:729d).

prayer for himself and for the people, asks that the sacrifice, offered to God the Father, of his immolated only-begotten Son, may be pleasing."[98] After the exclamation, the chief celebrant blesses the assembly saying: *Peace be unto all.* The assembly responds: *And to thy spirit.* The deacon intones the invitation for the kiss of peace, saying: *Let us love one another, that with one mind we may confess*—and the assembly responds: *Father, Son, and Holy Spirit: the Trinity, one in essence and undivided.* The chief celebrant venerates the covered Holy Gifts, saying privately: *I will love thee, O Lord, my strength. The Lord is my firm foundation, my refuge, and my deliverer* (thrice). If there is a concelebration, all the concelebrants do the same and then exchange the kiss of peace (the priests with the chief celebrant and among themselves, the deacons among themselves). The deacon exclaims: *The doors! The doors! In wisdom, let us attend,* and the assembly says the Symbol of Faith. In the contemporary Russian practice, the Symbol of Faith is usually sung, most often by a choir, although there is no reason for the Symbol of Faith to be sung, since it is neither a hymn nor a chant. In the contemporary Greek practice, it is recited either by a non-celebrating bishop or clergyman, or by an honored guest. But the Barberini *Euchologion* prescribes that it be said by the people.[99] During the Symbol of Faith, the priest waves the aër over the holy gifts. This seems to be a later development, from the fifteenth century. St Symeon of Thessalonica in his commentary says that "they hold the sacred veil over the gifts until the sacred creed is completed because it is necessary that everything concerning Jesus be professed in purity and that he then be seen unveiled."[100] Nevertheless, the contemporary practice is to wave it, not until the end of the Symbol of Faith, but only until the phrase: *and on the third day he rose again, according to the Scriptures.* For this reason, the waving of the aër is often interpreted today as signifying the earthquake at the death of Christ (cf. Mt 27.51).

The recitation of the Symbol of Faith is followed by the prayer of the Anaphora, introduced by the Pauline verse said by the chief celebrant while he turns towards the assembly to bless the people: *The grace of our Lord Jesus Christ, the love of God the Father, and the communion of the Holy Spirit be with you all* (2 Cor 13.13). The assembly replies: *And with thy spirit.* The chief celebrant then says, still facing the people (or, in the Russian practice, facing the altar): *Let us lift up our hearts,* to which the assembly replies: *We*

---

[98] *Protheoria* 19 (PG 140:444).
[99] *Barberini,* 63 and 75.
[100] Symeon of Thessalonica, *The Liturgical Commentaries,* 132 (PG 155:732c).

lift them up unto the Lord. Facing the altar, the chief celebrant says: *Let us give thanks to the Lord,* to which the assembly used to reply: *It is meet and right,* as attested by the *Apostolic Constitutions.*[101] The remaining words of the answer sung today (in the Russian tradition)—*to worship the Father, and the Son, and the Holy Spirit; the Trinity, one in essence, and undivided*—is a later interpolation, introduced to cover the prayer of the Anaphora, which came to be said in a low voice.[102]

Then the chief celebrant says the first part of the Anaphora, which introduces the *Sanctus.* This leads to the exclamation: *Singing the triumphal hymn, shouting, proclaiming, and saying. . . .* The assembly responds with the Sanctus: *Holy, holy, holy, Lord of Sabaoth. Heaven and earth are full of thy glory: Hosanna in the highest. Blessed is he that comes in the name of the Lord. Hosanna in the highest* (Is 6.3; Ps 117.26; Mt 21.9). The chief celebrant continues reading the prayer of the Anaphora, which recalls the institution of the Eucharist, and includes the words of Christ: *Take, eat: This is my Body which is broken for you, for the remission of sins . . . Drink of it, all of you: This is my Blood of the New Covenant, which is shed for you and for many, for the remission of sins* (cf. Mt 26.26–28). The chief celebrant then continues the prayer of the Anaphora, mentioning: *all those things which have come to pass for us: the Cross, the Tomb, the Resurrection on the third day, the Ascension into heaven, the Sitting at the right hand, and the second and glorious Coming* (Anaphora of Saint John Chrysostom), and then he exclaims: *Offering unto thee thine own of thine own, on behalf of all and for all. . . .* Saint Nicolas Cabasilas stresses that, "He who celebrates the sacrifice daily is but the minister of the grace. He brings to it nothing of his own, he would not dare to do or say anything according to his own judgement and reason. He offers only that which he has already received . . . back to God, in the manner which is laid down. Since, then, the gifts are always offered to God in a manner which is pleasing to him, they must surely always be accepted."[103] The assembly then completes this prayer by saying: *We praise thee, we bless thee, we give thanks unto thee, O Lord; and we pray unto thee, O our God.*

---

[101]*Apostolic Constitutions* 8.12.4–5 (SC 336:178–80; ANF 7:486).

[102]About the Anaphora's being said aloud or in a low voice, see: P. Trempelas, "L'audition de l'anaphore par le peuple," in *1054–1954. L'Église et les Églises,* vol. 2 (Chevetogne, 1954), 207–20.

[103]Nicolas Cabasilas, *Explanation of the Divine Liturgy* 46:10 (SC 4-bis, 262; Nicolas Cabasilas, *Commentary,* 104).

The chief celebrant continues the prayer of the Anaphora with the prayer of the *Epiclesis*. It is unfortunate that this prayer has been interrupted and divided into parts by the interpolation of various elements foreign to its origin, which make us lose track of the prayer. The first interpolation is the prayer of the Third Hour. After reading the introduction to the Epiclesis, the chief celebrant with the deacon makes three prostrations, saying each time: *O God, cleanse me a sinner*. And then, raising both hands, he says three times the troparion of the Third Hour: *O Lord, who didst send down thy most Holy Spirit*. . . . After the first recitation, the deacon, raising his orarion, says the psalm verses: *Create in me a clean heart* . . . and after the second, he says: *Cast me not away from thy presence* . . . (Ps 50.10, 11). This interpolation was introduced at some point during the fifteenth century as the celebrants' spiritual preparation for the Epiclesis.[104] Fortunately, it has been omitted from the contemporary Greek liturgical books.

The second interpolation is a dialogue between the deacon and the chief celebrant introduced in the fourteenth century by Saint Philotheos Kokkinos.[105] The deacon, pointing to the Lamb with his orarion says: *Bless, master, the holy bread*. And the chief celebrant blesses it saying: *And make this bread the precious Body of thy Christ*, to which the deacon responds *Amen*; then the deacon points to the chalice with his orarion, saying, *Bless, master, the holy cup*. And the chief celebrant blesses it, saying: *And that which is in this cup, the precious Blood of thy Christ*, to which the deacon responds: *Amen*; finally the deacon points to both the Lamb and the chalice with his orarion, and says: *Bless both, master*. The chief celebrant then blesses both the Lamb and the chalice, saying: *Making the change by thy Holy Spirit*, to which the deacon responds: *Amen. Amen. Amen*. And after making a prostration, the deacon says: *Remember me, a sinner, holy master*, to which the chief celebrant replies: *May the Lord God remember thee*. . . . Given that this later interpolation is a dialogue between the chief celebrant and the deacon, the widespread practice observed today, in which the assembly responds with the deacon's *Amen*, is erroneous, since this is not a response to the prayer, which is not yet completed, but to the different directions of the deacon. To understand better how these interpolations destroy the unity of the prayer,

[104]N. Odintsov, *Poryadok obshchestvennogo i chastnogo bogosluzheniya v drevnei Rossii do XVI v.* (Saint Petersburg, 1881), 63, 67; A. Dmitrievsky, "Bogosluzhenie v Russkoi Tserkvi za pervye pyat vekov," *Pravoslavnii sobesednik* 12 (1882): 378–379.
[105]P. Trempelas, *Αἱ τρεῖς λειτουργίαι*, 11–12.

we present here below the prayer of the epiclesis of the Anaphora of Saint John Chrysostom with and without the interpolations:

Table 2.6: The Prayers of the Epiclesis of the Liturgy of St John Chrysostom, with and without Interpolations

The prayer of epiclesis without the interpolations	The prayer of epiclesis with the interpolations
The priest: Again we offer unto thee this rational and bloodless worship, and ask thee and pray thee and supplicate thee: Send down thy Holy Spirit upon us and upon these Gifts here offered; and make this bread the precious Body of thy Christ, and that which is in this cup the precious Blood of thy Christ; making the change by thy Holy Spirit; that they may be to those who partake for vigilance of soul, for the remission of sins, for the communion of thy Holy Spirit, for the fulfillment of the kingdom of heaven, for boldness towards thee, and not for judgment or condemnation.

Again we offer unto thee this rational worship for those who have fallen asleep in the faith: ancestors, fathers, patriarchs, prophets, apostles, preachers, evangelists, martyrs, confessors, ascetics, and every righteous spirit made perfect in faith. | *The* priest: Again we offer unto thee this rational and bloodless worship, and ask thee and pray thee and supplicate thee: Send down thy Holy Spirit upon us and upon these Gifts here offered;

The priest and the deacon make three reverences, saying at each: O God, cleanse me a sinner.

The priest (in a low voice): O Lord, who didst send down thy most Holy Spirit upon thine apostles at the third hour: Take him not from us, O Good One, but renew him in us who pray unto thee.

The deacon (in a low voice): Create in me a clean heart, O God, and renew a right spirit within me.

The priest (in a low voice): O Lord, who didst send down thy most Holy Spirit . . .

The deacon (in a low voice): Cast me not away from thy presence, and take not thy Holy Spirit from me.

The priest (in a low voice): O Lord, who didst send down thy most Holy Spirit . . .

The deacon, pointing to the Lamb with his orarion, says: Bless, Master, the holy bread.

And the priest makes the sign of the cross over the Lamb and says: And make this bread the precious Body of thy Christ; |

The deacon, pointing to the chalice with his orarion, says: Amen. Bless, Master, the holy cup.

The priest, while making the sign of the cross over the chalice, says: And that which is in this cup the precious Blood of thy Christ;

The deacon, pointing to the holy Gifts with his orarion, says: Amen. Bless both, Master.

The priest, making the sign of the cross over both the Lamb and the chalice, says: Making the change by thy Holy Spirit;

The deacon: Amen. Amen. Amen.

The deacon: Remember me, a sinner, holy master.

The priest: May the Lord God remember thee in his kingdom, always, now and ever, and unto ages of ages. Amen.

The priest says in a low voice: That they may be to those who partake for vigilance of soul, for the remission of sins, for the communion of thy Holy Spirit, for the fulfillment of the kingdom of heaven, for boldness towards thee, and not for judgment or condemnation.

Again we offer unto thee this rational worship for those who have fallen asleep in the faith: ancestors, fathers, patriarchs, prophets, apostles, preachers, evangelists, martyrs, confessors, ascetics, and every righteous spirit made perfect in faith.[106]

---

[106]The text of these prayers is from the *Hieratikon*, 133–137, which places the prayer *Again we offer* after the prayer of the Third Hour, and also provides slightly different directions.

There is a third erroneous interpolation, this one in the Epiclesis prayer of the Anaphora of St Basil, under the influence of the Anaphora of St John Chrysostom—the words: *Changing them by thy Holy Spirit,* of the Anaphora of Chrysostom were interpolated after the words: *for the life of the world,* of the Anaphora of Basil, under the influence of the dialogue interpolated into the Anaphora of Chrysostom, as we can see in the table below. This interpolation has nothing to do in the text of the Prayer of Epiclesis of St Basil the Great, and fortunately it is not included in the contemporary Greek editions (or in the new edition of the Orthodox Church in America's *Hieratikon*).

Table 2.7: The Prayer of the Epiclesis of the Liturgy of St Basil, with and without interpolations

The prayer of the Epiclesis without the interpolations	The prayer of the Epiclesis with the interpolations
Therefore, all-holy Master, we also—thy sinful and unworthy servants, who have been made worthy to minister at thy holy altar, not because of our own righteousness (for we have done nothing good upon the earth) but because of thy mercy and compassion, which thou hast richly poured out on us—now dare to approach thy holy altar, and, presenting the antitypes of the holy Body and Blood of thy Christ, we pray thee and call upon thee, O Holy of Holies, that by the favor of thy goodness thy Holy spirit may come upon us and upon these Gifts now offered, to bless them, and to hallow and to show this bread to be truly the precious Body of our Lord and God and Savior Jesus Christ, and this cup to be truly the precious Blood of our Lord and God and Savior Jesus Christ, shed for the life of the world.	*The priest (in a low voice):* Therefore, all-holy Master, we also—thy sinful and unworthy servants, who have been made worthy to minister at thy holy altar, not because of our own righteousness (for we have done nothing good upon the earth) but because of thy mercy and compassion, which thou hast richly poured out on us—now dare to approach thy holy altar, and, presenting the antitypes of the holy Body and Blood of thy Christ, we pray thee and call upon thee, O Holy of Holies, that by the favor of thy goodness thy Holy spirit may come upon us and upon these Gifts now offered, to bless them, and to hallow and to show—
And unite to one another all of us who partake of the one bread	*The priest and the deacon make three reverences, saying at each:* O God, cleanse me a sinner.
	The priest (in a low voice): O Lord, who didst send down thy most Holy Spirit upon thine apostles at the third hour: Take him not from us, O

and cup unto communion of the one Holy Spirit, and grant that none of us may partake of the holy Body and Blood of thy Christ for judgment or condemnation. Instead, may we find mercy and grace will the the saints who through the ages have been well-pleasing unto thee: ancestors, fathers, patriarchs, prophets, apostles, preachers, evangelists, martyrs, confessors, teachers, and every righteous spirit made perfect in faith.

Good One, but renew him in us who pray unto thee.

The deacon (in a low voice): Create in me a clean heart, O God, and renew a right spirit within me.

The priest (in a low voice): O Lord, who didst send down thy most Holy Spirit . . .

The deacon (in a low voice): Cast me not away from thy presence, and take not thy Holy Spirit from me.

The priest (in a low voice): O Lord, who didst send down thy most Holy Spirit . . .

The deacon, pointing to the Lamb with his orarion, says: Bless, Master, the holy bread.

And the priest makes the sign of the cross over the Lamb and says: —this bread to be truly the precious Body of our Lord and God and Savior Jesus Christ;

The deacon, pointing to the chalice with his orarion, says: Amen. Bless, Master, the holy cup.

The priest, making the sign of the cross over the chalice, says: And this cup to be truly the precious Blood of our Lord and God and Savior Jesus Christ;

The deacon: Amen.

The priest says: Shed for the life of the world.

The deacon, pointing to the holy Gifts with his orarion, says: Amen. Bless both, Master.

The priest, making the sign of the cross over both the Lamb and the chalice, says: Making the change by thy Holy Spirit;

The deacon: Amen. Amen. Amen.

The deacon: Remember me, a sinner, holy master.

The priest: May the Lord God remember thee in his kingdom, always, now and ever, and unto ages of ages. Amen.

The priest says in a low voice: And unite to one another all of us who partake of the one bread and cup unto communion of the one Holy Spirit, and grant that none of us may partake of the holy Body and Blood of thy Christ for judgment or condemnation. Instead, may we find mercy and grace with the the the saints who through the ages have been well-pleasing unto thee: ancestors, fathers, patriarchs, prophets, apostles, preachers, evangelists, martyrs, confessors, teachers, and every righteous spirit made perfect in faith.[107]

After the prayer of the Epiclesis, the chief celebrant exclaims: *Especially for our most holy, most pure, most blessed and glorious Lady Theotokos and Ever-virgin Mary.* The assembly then sings a hymn in honor of the Theotokos—usually, *It is truly meet,* but sometimes a different hymn, as appointed by the *Typikon.* During this chant, the chief celebrant concludes the Anaphora with the prayer of intercession and the diptychs. During the prayer of intercession, after commemorating the saints and the departed, the chief celebrant commemorates the bishops, the priests, the deacons, the monks, the civil authorities, and finally the ruling bishop saying: *Among the first, remember O Lord, our Archbishop . . . .* In the services of the Orthodox Church, the ruling bishop is also commemorated at the Great Litany, at the Augmented Litany, and at the end of the Anaphora. In the Russian practice, he is also commemorated at the Great Entrance. Commemorations at the

---

[107]Text of these prayers is largely from the *Hieratikon,* 185–188, which places the prayer *Therefore, all-holy Master* after the prayer of the Third Hour, provides slightly different directions, and no longer includes the words from the Liturgy of St John Chrysostom, *making the change by thy Holy Spirit.*

Great Entrance appeared only after the fourteenth century, when the celebrants began to commemorate the emperor and the patriarch when they were actually present.[108] In the Russian practice, starting from the time of Patriarch Nikon (mid-17th c.), the patriarch is also commemorated, before the ruling bishop, but this late practice is unjustified, since the priest is required to commemorate only the bishop in whose name he is serving the mysteries.[109] The commemoration of the bishop at the end of the Anaphora is attested by the Barberini manuscript.[110] This is the most ancient place the bishop is commemorated, and it is mentioned as early as the fourth century by the *Apostolic Constitutions*.[111]

After the exclamation of the prayer (*And grant that with one mouth*), the chief celebrant turns to the assembly to bless the people with the words: *And may the mercies of our great God and Savior Jesus Christ be with all of you*, and the the deacon's Litany of Supplication follows. During the petitions of this litany before the Lord's Prayer, the chief celebrant says the pre-Communion prayer. The litany and the pre-Communion prayer are followed by the Lord's Prayer itself (*Our Father*), introduced by the exclamation of the celebrant: *And make us worthy, O Master, that with boldness and without condemnation we may dare to call on thee, the heavenly God, as Father, and to say* . . . The Lord's Prayer ought to be said by the assembly, in the same way as the Symbol of Faith.

After the Lord's Prayer, the chief celebrant blesses the assembly saying: *Peace be unto all*, and then he says the prayer of inclination. After its exclamation, the deacon says: *Let us attend*, and the chief celebrant elevates the Lamb saying: *The Holy Things are for the holy*. The assembly responds: *One is holy, one is Lord: Jesus Christ, to the glory of God the Father*. According to Saint Symeon of Thessalonica, the elevation of the Lamb "typifies the crucifixion of the Savior for us."[112] The deacon says in a low voice: *Break, master, the holy bread*. The chief celebrant breaks the Lamb into four portions (IC, XC, NI, KA) while saying in a low voice: *Broken and distributed is the Lamb*

---

[108]Taft, *The Great Entrance*, 230–231. Cf. Pseudo-Kodinos, *Traité des offices*, ed. Jean Verpeaux (Paris: Centre National de la Recherche Scientifique, 1996), 266.

[109]Cf. Apostolic Canon 39. Joannou, *Discipline générale antique*, 1.2:27. [In the contemporary Russian tradition, the patriarch is always commemorated along with the ruling bishop: in the Great and Augmented Litanies, at the Great Entrance, and after the consecration of the Gifts: *Among the first. . . .—Ed.*]

[110]*Barberini*, 79.

[111]*Apostolic Constitutions* 8.12.40 (SC 336:201; ANF 7:490).

[112]Symeon of Thessalonica, *The Liturgical Commentaries*, 254 (PG 155:297d).

of God: broken, yet not divided; ever eaten, yet never consumed, but sanctifying those who partake thereof. The deacon says: *Fill, master, the holy cup,* and the chief celebrant puts one portion of the Lamb (IC) into the chalice, saying: *The fullness of the Holy Spirit.* The deacon says, while presenting the zeon (warm water): *Bless, master, the warm water.* The chief celebrant blesses it saying: *Blessed is the warmth of thy holy things always, now and ever and unto ages of ages.* Then the deacon pours the proper amount of the zeon into the chalice (that is, enough so that the chalice becomes warm), while saying: *The warmth of faith, full of the Holy Spirit. Amen.* The rite of the zeon emphasizes that we receive in Holy Communion the body and blood of the living, resurrected Christ.[113] This is also expressed by the opening of the holy doors of the iconostasis for the Communion of the faithful, thereby signifying the open tomb.

At Communion, the clergy receive first. In our contemporary practice, prayers before Communion are often said at this point by the clergy (and even by the faithful). These are even printed in the liturgical books at this place. But it has to be emphasized that it is not proper to add these prayers to the Divine Liturgy, for they are taken from the Service of Preparation for Holy Communion of the *Horologion*; the Divine Liturgy, on the other hand, has its own prayers of preparation (the pre-Communion prayer and the prayer of inclination in the Divine Liturgy of Saint Basil). The prayers before Communion of the Service of Preparation ought to be said at home on the eve in preparation for the Divine Liturgy, and not during the Divine Liturgy itself. While the clergy are receiving Communion, the assembly should sing the proper Communion chant (*koinonikon*), according to the *Typikon*.

The priest partakes from the holy bread (from the portion XC), and then gives a piece to the deacon (according to the Russian practice, he first gives a portion to the deacon and then takes a portion for himself, so that all the clergy may commune at the same time together). Then the priest drinks from the chalice (once in the prevailing Greek practice, thrice according to the Russian practice), and then he communes the deacon from the chalice. Then the priest puts the other portions (NI and KA) into the chalice for the Communion of faithful. According to the ancient Byzantine practice, all the particles on the diskos were put into the chalice. At the turn of the fourteenth to the fifteenth century, Saint Symeon of Thessalonica discussed this practice, underlining that these particles were not transformed into

---

[113]Cf. Nicolas Cabasilas, *Explanation of the Divine Liturgy* 37:1–3 (SC 4-bis: 226–228); Symeon of Thessalonica, *The Liturgical Commentaries*, 150.

the body of Christ, and for this reason, the priest ought to commune the faithful from the portions of the holy bread only and not from the particles, although they all became one in the chalice.[114] In the eighteenth century, St Nicodemus the Hagiorite prescribed in his *Pedalion* (or *Rudder*) that Communion should be given to the faithful from the holy Lamb first, and then the rest of the particles should be put into the chalice.[115] That was already the practice introduced by Peter Moghila in his *Sluzhebnik* in the seventeenth century.[116] Then the the laity receive Communion, after the invitation by the deacon: *In the fear of God, with faith and love, draw near.* The assembly responds by singing: *Blessed is he that comes in the name of the Lord.* . . . While the faithful are receiving Communion, the assembly sings the Communion hymn: *Receive the body of Christ* . . . .

After Communion, the priest blesses the people, saying: *O God, save thy people, and bless thine inheritance.* The assembly responds by singing the troparion: *We have seen the true Light.* The priest usually puts the rest of the particles into the chalice at this point, while saying in a low voice: *Wash away, O Lord, the sins of all those remembered here, by thy precious Blood; through the prayers of all thy saints.* Then he censes the holy gifts three times, saying: *Be thou exalted, O God, above the heavens, and thy glory over all the earth.* He gives the diskos to the deacon, who takes it to the prothesis table. Then, making the sign of the cross over the antimension with the chalice, The priest says in a low voice: *Blessed is our God,* and then turns towards the assembly, blesses the people with the chalice, and says: *Always, now and ever and unto ages of ages.* The assembly then sings the troparion: *Let our mouths be filled with thy praise* . . . .[117]

The Litany of Thanksgiving after Communion is intoned by the deacon, and the prayer of thanksgiving follows;[118] it concludes with an exclamation by the chief celebrant. Following this exclamation, the priest says the Ambo Prayer (ἐπιστάμβωνος, *epistambōnos*), facing the sanctuary in our contemporary practice. This prayer actually used to be said on the ambo that was in the middle of the church, facing the west (that is, the exit of the church),

---

[114]Symeon of Thessalonica, *The Liturgical Commentaries*, 224 (*De sacra liturgia* 94, PG 155:284d–285a).

[115]See *Πηδάλιον* (Thessaloniki, 1998), 243.

[116]Peter Moghila, *Sluzhebnik* (Kiev, 1639), 65–66, 374–75.

[117]Note that there are some local variations in the order of these actions.

[118][The contemporary Slavonic service book places this prayer after the Communion of the clergy and before the Communion of the faithful.—*Ed.*]

as a final blessing at the end of the liturgy.[119] The chief celebrant then says the prayer for consuming the holy gifts (*O Christ our God, who art thyself the fulfillment of the law and the prophets*). The Ambo Prayer is followed by *Blessed be the name of the Lord* and, according to the rubric of the Slavic books, by Psalm 33, during which the antidoron ought to be distributed (although it is usually distributed after the dismissal that follows immediately afterwards). After blessing the assembly by saying: *The blessing of the Lord be upon you through his grace and love for mankind, always, now and ever and unto ages of ages*, the chief celebrant intones the dismissal.

5. Hierarchical Liturgy

The Divine Liturgy presided over by a bishop follows basically the same order as a Divine Liturgy presided over by a priest, but there are some details that we shall now describe. First, the bishop is normally greeted in the narthex, where he puts on the mantia. In the Russian practice, this takes place before (or sometimes after) the reading of the Third and Sixth Hours. The priest who has served the prothesis holds a tray with the cross on it. The bishop venerates the cross and presents it to the concelebrating priests to venerate. In the Greek practice, since Matins (Orthros) is served immediately before the Divine Liturgy, the bishop is greeted in the narthex during Matins, after the sixth ode, before the reading of the Synaxarion. After the Synaxarion reading, the bishop blesses the assembly in the middle of the nave and goes to his throne, where he blesses the concelebrants. He stays there until the Praises, when he descends from his throne to read the entrance prayers.

The entrance prayers, read immediately after the greeting in the Russian practice, are said in front of the iconostasis in the usual way. After the prayer of the chief celebrant, the bishop blesses the assembly once again and either goes to the middle of the church to be vested solemnly (Russian practice) or to the altar (Greek practice). During the vesting, the deacon says the appointed prayers. If the bishop is vested solemnly in the middle of the church, the vesting is concluded by the bishop's blessing with the dikirion and the trikirion, as the choir chants the acclamation (*Ton despotin*).

For the beginning of the Divine Liturgy, the bishop stands on the cathedra in the middle of the church (Russian practice) or on his throne on the

---

[119] A. Jacob, "Où était récitée la prière de l'ambon?" *Byzantion* 51 (1981): 306–15.

side (Greek practice), until the Little Entrance. The concelebrating priests stand side by side with him, in order of seniority. The first priest enters the altar just before the beginning of the Divine Liturgy, to say the opening blessing (*Blessed is the kingdom*). He also says the exclamation of the litany. The other concelebrants enter in order, after each exclamation of the Little Litanies. The bishop recites the prayer of the prothesis and the prayers of the antiphons. At the Little Entrance, the concelebrants come out of the sanctuary and stand side by side with the bishop, in the middle of the nave. After *Wisdom! Stand upright!* the bishop blesses the assembly with the dikirion and the trikirion while intoning the entrance verse (*eisodikon*), and then he enters the sanctuary, where he censes the holy table and the sanctuary, then he exits to cense the iconostasis, and finally, from the solea, the assembly, then he enters the sanctuary again.

One of the most solemn moments of the Hierarchical Liturgy is the blessing of the assembly with the dikirion and the trikirion at the Trisagion. After the exclamation of the bishop *For holy art thou*, the Trisagion is sung in a special way, in which the first three iterations are doubled:

Table 2.8: The Order of the Trisagion at a Bishop's Liturgy

Greek practice	Russian practice
1a) by the right choir	1a) by the choir
1b) by the left choir	1b) by the clergy
2a) by the clergy	2a) by the choir
2b) by the right choir	2b) by a trio: Bishop blesses from solea
3a) by the clergy	3a) by the choir
Glory . . . both now . . . Holy Immortal—by the choir	3b) by the clergy: Bishop blesses from synthronon
3b) *Holy God*—in three parts, by the clergy:	*Glory . . . both now . . . Holy Immortal*
Bishop blesses from solea	Concluding *Holy God*
Dynamis: Concluding *Holy God*	

In Greek practice, when the clergy sing the Trisagion for the first time (2a), the bishop takes the dikirion and makes the sign of the cross over the gospel book on the altar table. Then, when the clergy sing the Trisagion for the second time (3a), he makes the sign of the cross with the trikirion over the gospel book. St Symeon of Thessalonica says that this signifies that it is through the incarnation of the Son of God, who is true God and true man (the dikirion represents the two natures of Christ), that the Holy Trinity was manifested (the trikirion represents the three persons of the Trinity).[120] Then the bishop blesses the assembly three times with the dikirion and the trikirion, after each iteration of Holy God, while saying each time: *O Lord, O Lord, look down from heaven, and see, and visit this vineyard which thy right hand hath planted, and establish it* (Ps 79.15–16). In the Russian practice, this is said only once, while the bishop blesses the assembly with the dikirion and the cross, before the trio sings the Holy God. Once the bishop has blessed the assembly, he goes to the synthronon. In the Russian practice, the bishop then blesses the assembly from the synthronon with the trikirion. In the Greek practice, after the Trisagion, the clergy and the choir sing *O Lord, save the pious*, followed by the *phēmē* (acclamation) of the patriarch and of the ruling bishop. At the end of his *phēmē*, the bishop blesses the assembly. In the Russian practice, acclamations are sung only at a patriarchal liturgy. At the prokeimenon of the epistle, the bishop takes off the great omophorion. Since the omophorion symbolizes the incarnation of Christ,[121] Saint Symeon of Thessalonika explains that "during the reading of the gospel, the bishop removes the omophorion, . . . since [the Lord] is perceived to be speaking through the gospel and is present, at that time [the bishop] does not wear the icon of his incarnation."[122] The omophorion is taken off to show that the symbol becomes a reality through the reading of the gospel. For this reason, in the Russian practice, the omophorion, held in the hands of a deacon or a subdeacon, is carried out before the gospel book, when the deacon comes out of the sanctuary to read the gospel from the bishop's cathedra or throne. After the reading of the gospel, the bishop blesses the assembly from the solea with the cross in the Greek practice, or with the dikirion and trikirion in the Russian practice, and the chanters sing the acclamation: *Eis polla eti despota.*

At the Cherubic hymn, after he has said the sacerdotal prayer, the bishop washes his hands in preparation for the Anaphora, in continuity with the practice of the early Church,[123] and then he takes off his miter and puts on

[120]Symeon of Thessalonica, *The Liturgical Commentaries*, 116 (PG 155:721bc).

[121]Symeon of Thessalonica, *The Liturgical Commentaries*, 108 (PG 155:716c).

[122]Symeon of Thessalonica, *The Liturgical Commentaries*, 121 (PG 155:724c).

[123]Cf. Cyril of Jerusalem, *Mystagogical Homilies* 5.2 (SC 126:146; PPS 57:121, 123);

the small omophorion. According to the Greek practice, he censes the holy table, the sanctuary, the iconostasis, and the assembly from the solea. He then goes to the prothesis table, where he completes the prothesis (according to the Greek practice, the priest who did the prothesis would have stopped after the commemoration of the nine ranks of saints and the commemoration of the ruling bishop). He commemorates the living, including the concelebrants who come up to him and kiss his right shoulder. He then commemorates the dead. Then, he normally covers the holy gifts with the veils, saying the proper prayers. Some see in this practice a vestige of the prothesis that was once served at the Great Entrance.[124] He then takes off his small omophorion, which is held in the procession of the Great Entrance by either one of the priests (Greek practice) or one of the subdeacons (Russian practice). He places the aër on the deacon's shoulder, and then gives him the diskos, and he gives the chalice to the senior priest. The other concelebrating priests hold the spoon, the spear, or hand crosses. The bishop awaits the procession at the holy doors. He puts on the small omophorion when the procession arrives at the holy doors in the Greek practice, while in the Russian practice he puts on the miter after the Great Entrance, but does not put on the small omophorion until the Anaphora, before the words *Take, eat*. In the Greek practice, the bishop keeps his small omophorion on from this moment until the dismissal. The deacon presents the diskos to the bishop who censes it, takes it, and makes commemoration of the living. Then the priest presents the chalice to the bishop who censes it, takes it, and makes commemoration of the departed. After the commemorations, the chanters complete the Cherubic hymn, and then the bishop blesses the assembly from the solea with the trikirion (and the dikirion in Russian practice). The deacon then intones the Litany of Supplication.

For the kiss of peace, the bishop (after removing his miter) venerates the holy gifts, saying: *I will love thee, O Lord*, and then stands on the south side of the holy table. The priests come to venerate the holy gifts according to their seniority, and then kiss the shoulders of the bishop (left and right) and his right hand,[125] while the bishop says to them: *Christ is in our midst*, to which they respond: *He is and shall be*. For the Symbol of Faith, the bishop

---

Apostolic Constitutions 8.11.12 (SC 336:176; ANF 7:486); Pseudo-Dionysius the Areopagite, *On the Ecclesiastical Hierarchy* 3.2, 3.3.10 (PG 3:425c, 437d; Luibheid, 211, 219).

[124]Taft, *The Great Entrance*, 265–70.

[125]The practice for priests in the OCA, in ROCOR, and in the MP is to kiss the bishop's right hand, then his right shoulder, then his right hand again.

bows his head over the holy table, in front of the holy gifts, as the concelebrating priests wave the aër over the holy gifts and his head, until the words *and on the third day he rose*. This rite is linked with the symbolic interpretation of the Divine Liturgy: since the aër symbolizes Christ in the tomb, and waving it symbolizes the earthquake after his death (cf. Mt 27.51), and the bishop is an image of Christ in the celebration of the holy mysteries, the bishop bows his head in front of the holy gifts under the aër, representing Christ in the tomb, and then the bishop stands upright at the phrase *and on the third day he rose again, according to the Scriptures*, signifying the resurrection of Christ.

At the beginning of the Anaphora, the bishop turns towards the assembly to bless the people with the cross according to the Greek practice (or with the dikirion and trikirion in the Russian practice), saying: *The grace of our Lord Jesus Christ . . . Let us lift up our hearts . . . Let us give thanks to the Lord . . .* (for each of these, in the Russian practice, he blesses the assembly, middle, south and north). After the Anaphora, in the Russian practice, the bishop takes off his omophorion and puts on the miter.

After the bishop has commemorated his *protos* (patriarch or archbishop) at *Among the first*, the concelebrating priests (or the senior priest in the Russian practice) repeat the prayer *Among the first*, commemorating the presiding bishop. According the Russian practice, just before this the deacon commemorates the names on the diptychs (known in the Slavic liturgical books as the великая похвала—*velikaya pokhvala*—or commonly called выкличка—*vyklichka*), naming the bishop who is offering the holy gifts, the patriarch, and all the remaining orders of the Church. In the Greek practice, the deacon commemorates the names on the the diptychs after *Among the first . . .* only at patriarchal and synodal liturgies. After the exclamation *And grant that with one mouth*, the bishop turns to the assembly to bless the people with the trikirion (and the dikirion in the Russian practice), saying: *And may the mercies of our great God and Savior Jesus Christ be with all of you*, and the deacon then intones the Litany of Supplication. In the Russian practice, after the Lord's Prayer and *Peace be unto all*, the bishop puts on the small omophorion and takes off the miter.

The bishop partakes of the holy Mysteries first. Then he gives the holy Bread to the concelebrating priests and then to the deacons, according to the order of seniority, and then he gives them the holy Chalice.

The Ambo Prayer is said by one of the concelebrating priests (usually the most senior in the Greek practice or the most junior in the Russian practice). Then the dismissal is intoned by the bishop, now wearing his miter, from the solea (or from the throne in the Greek practice); after this he blesses the assembly with the trikirion (and the dikirion in the Russian practice), as the chanters chant the acclamation (*Ton despotēn*, in the Greek practice, or *Eis polla*, in the Russia practice).

6. The Liturgy of the Presanctified Gifts

The Liturgy of Presanctified Gifts is not a "full" liturgy properly speaking, since there is no Anaphora. Its attribution in some liturgical books to Saint Gregory Dialogus, Pope of Rome, is erroneous.[126] It is in fact a Communion rite for the reception of Gifts that were sanctified in a previous Divine Liturgy, and it is added to the service of Vespers during Great Lent.[127] It follows this order:

Table 2.9: The Order of the Liturgy of the Presanctified Gifts

---

6.1. Vespers Service

---

1. Opening blessing (*Blessed is the Kingdom*) and Psalm 103

2. Great Litany

3. Kathisma (in three parts, each followed by a Little Litany, prayer, and exclamation)

4. *Lord, I call* (with 10 stichera)

5. Little Entrance (usually with the censer but with the gospel book on feast days) and *O Gladsome Light*

6. First prokeimenon and biblical reading (from Genesis or Exodus)

---

[126]Cf. N. Uspensky, "The Liturgy of Presanctified Gifts. History and Practice," in *Evening Worship in the Orthodox Church* (Crestwood, NY: St Vladimir's Seminary Press, 1985), 156–62; J. Getcha, "La liturgie hagiopolite et l'origine de la Liturgie des Présanctifiés," in Daniel Findikyan, Daniel Galadza, and André Lossky, eds, *Sion, mère des Églises: Mélanges liturgiques offerts au Père Charles Athanase Renoux*, Semaines d'études liturgiques Saint-Serge Subsidia 1 (Münster: Aschendorff, 2016), 163–78.

[127]Cf. our first volume, *The Typikon Decoded*, Orthodox Liturgy Series 3 (Yonkers, NY: St Vladimir's Seminary Press, 2012), 169–73. On the history of the Presanctified Liturgy, see Miguel Arranz, "La liturgie des Présanctifiés de l'ancien Euchologue byzantin," *OCP* 47 (1981): 332–88; N. D. Uspensky, "Liturgiya prezhdeosvyashchennykh darov: Istoriko-liturgicheskii ocherk," *Bogosluzhebnie Trudy* 15 (1976): 146–84.

7. *The Light of Christ*

8. Second prokeimenon and biblical reading (from Proverbs or Job)

6.2. Communion Rite

9. *Let my prayer arise* (and Prayer of Saint Ephrem)

10. (Reading of Epistle and Gospel on feast days)

11. Augmented Litany with prayer

12. Litany and prayer for the catechumens, dismissal of the catechumens

13. (Litany and prayer for those who are preparing for illumination, dismissal of those who are preparing for illumination)

14. Two Little Litanies with their prayers for the faithful

15. Hymn *Now the powers of heaven*

16. Great Entrance (and Prayer of Saint Ephrem)

17. Litany of Supplication and prayer, and pre-Communion prayer

18. Lord's Prayer (*Our Father*)

19. Peace and Prayer of Inclination

20. *The presanctified Holy Things are for the holy*, fraction, commixture, zeon

21. Communion

22. Litany and prayer of thanksgiving

23. Ambo Prayer

24. Prayer for consuming the Holy Gifts

25. Blessed be the name of the Lord, (Psalm 33), and dismissal

After the opening blessing (*Blessed is the Kingdom*), Psalm 103 is read. During this psalm, the priest reads the vesperal prayers, beginning with the fourth, as the first three are read during the three stases of the kathisma (the reading of kathisma 18 is split into three parts). The deacon then intones the Great Litany. At the end of each stasis, the deacon intones the Little Litany, while the priest reads one of the first three vesperal prayers and the appropriate exclamation. During the first stasis, the priest unfolds the antimension on the altar table, and he places the diskos on the antimension. He then takes the presanctified Lamb from the artophorion on the altar table and places it on the diskos. During the second stasis, he censes the altar table from all four sides, while the deacon, carrying a candle, precedes him. During the third stasis, the priest carries the diskos from the altar to the prothesis table; he is preceded again by the deacon, who carries a candle and continuously censes the holy gifts. After the priest and deacon arrive at the prothesis table, the deacon pours wine into the chalice, to which he also adds some water. The priest covers the holy gifts, saying only: *Through the prayers of our holy fathers*. . . .

At *Lord, I call*, the chanters sing six stichera from the Triodion and four from the Menaion, and then the Theotokion. During the Theotokion, the priest goes out for the Little Entrance, accompanied by the deacon, who holds the censer. Instead of the evening prokeimenon, a prokeimenon from the Triodion is sung, followed by the first reading (from Genesis during the forty days, or from Exodus in Holy Week). After the reading comes a second prokeimenon from the Triodion. Then the deacon says *Command*, and the priest: *Wisdom. Let us attend. The Light of Christ illumines all!* Holding a candle and censer in his right hand, the priest blesses the assembly, with everyone prostrate on the ground. The second reading (from Proverbs during the forty days, or from Job during Holy Week) follows. After that the reader, standing in the middle of the church, chants selected verses from Psalm 140 in the form of a great prokeimenon: *Let my prayer arise*. While this is being sung, the priest censes the altar table and then the prothesis. After the last refrain, in the Russian practice, the priest recites the Prayer of Saint Ephrem with three full prostrations, as at the end of Sunday Vespers in Lent, while in the Greek practice the priest does not recite the Prayer of St Ephrem, but does make three prostrations.

If it is a feast with the polyeleos, the epistle and gospel readings are done at this point. If not, then the Augmented Litany and the Litany for the Catechumens follow immediately. Beginning on Wednesday of the fourth week of Great Lent, an additional litany—*As many as are preparing for illumination*—is added after these two. Two Litanies for the Faithful then follow.

The Great Entrance takes place during the singing of the hymn: *Now the powers of heaven*. After the deacon has censed the sanctuary, the priest goes to the prothesis table, takes the diskos in his right hand and, holding it over the chalice held in his left hand (if there are concelebrants, the first priest holds the diskos), and moves towards the altar, passing through the north deacon's door and entering the sanctuary through the holy doors, saying nothing. The deacon continuously censes the holy gifts, and the assembly is prostrate on the floor. In Russian practice, the priest again recites the Prayer of Saint Ephrem, with three prostrations. Then the deacon intones the Litany of Supplication, during which the priest reads the pre-Communion prayer in a low voice, and after that comes the Lord's Prayer. The priest gives the peace and then says the Prayer of Inclination. The deacon then says, *Let us attend*, and the priest: *The presanctified Holy Things are for the holy*, while he elevates the presanctified Lamb under the aër. The aër and the asterisk are then removed, and the priest breaks the presanctified Lamb into four portions (IC, XC, NI, KA), while saying in a low voice: *Broken and distributed is the Lamb of God: broken, yet not divided; ever eaten, yet never consumed, but sanctifying those who partake thereof.* The deacon says: *Fill, master, the holy cup*, and the priest puts one portion of the Lamb (IC) into the chalice, saying: *Through the prayers of our holy fathers . . . .* Then the deacon pours the zeon (warm water) into the chalice until the chalice becomes warm, saying: *Through the prayers of our holy fathers . . . .* And then the Communion follows, with the clergy partaking first.

In Greek practice, the Communion of the clergy follows the typical practice. This is the ancient Byzantine practice. Russian practice, however, follows rubrics that were introduced into the *Hieratikon* in the seventeenth century, according to which the celebrant who is to consume the holy Gifts at the end of the Liturgy (usually the deacon) ought to receive Communion only from the holy Gifts on the diskos. Thus, only those who are not to consume the Gifts after the the faithful have communed drink from the chalice.[128] While the clergy partake of Communion, the koinonikon is sung: *O taste and see that the Lord is good.* The faithful receive Communion as usual, and the deacon's Litany of Thanksgiving follows, with its exclamation by the priest, the Ambo prayer intoned by the priest (*O Almighty Master*), then Psalm 33 (during which the priest distributes the antidoron saved from the preceding Sunday), and the dismissal.

---

[128][Although the OCA generally follows Russian liturgical practices, in this instance today it follows the more ancient practice, preserved in Greek (and pre-Nikonian Russian) practice.—*Ed.*]

CHAPTER THREE

Ordinations

1. Historical Overview

The source of all ministry and authority in the Church is Jesus Christ himself who communicated his ministry and authority to the apostles. In their turn, the apostles transmitted this ministry and authority to bishops and deacons of local Churches by the grace of the Holy Spirit, through the laying on of hands, as can be seen in the book of Acts (cf. Acts 13.1–5) and in the first epistle of Clement to the Corinthians.[1] St Paul, in his first epistle to the Corinthians, states that "God hath set some in the church, first apostles, secondarily prophets, thirdly teachers" (1 Cor 12.28). The *Didache* mentions these prophets in connection with the celebration of the Eucharist: "Let the prophets give thanks [εὐχαριστεῖν, *eucharistein*] as much they want" and affirms that if these prophets want to settle in a local Church, they "are worthy of their food . . . since they are your high priests [ἀρχιερεῖς, *archiereis*]."[2] The New Testament prophets, as the successors of the apostles, became the bishops to whom the presbyters ought to be tuned "as the strings are to the harp," as Saint Ignatius of Antioch puts it at the beginning of the second century.[3]

As one can see from the Christian writings of the first two centuries, the Church was served and administered by a threefold hierarchy (bishops, priests, deacons) who received their authority from Christ, through the grace of the Holy Spirit, through the laying on of hands. This is the foundation of sacerdotal ordination. From the *Ecclesiastical Hierarchy* of Pseudo-Dionysios (5th c.) to Saint Symeon of Thessalonica (14th–15th c.), an analogy is made between this threefold hierarchy of the Church and

---

[1]Clement of Rome, *First Epistle to the Corinthians* 42.1–5 (SC 167:168–170; ANF 9:241–242).

[2]*Didache* 11.4 and 13.1–3 (SC 248:184 and 190; PPS 41:41 and 42).

[3]Ignatius of Antioch, *Epistle to the Ephesians* 4.1 (SC 10:60; *Ignatius of Antioch: The Letters*, Alistair Stewart, tr., Popular Patristics Series 49 [Yonkers, NY: St Vladimir's Seminary Press, 2013], 30–31).

the Holy Trinity. The bishop—an icon of *the Father of lights*, from whom *every good and perfect gift* proceeds (Jas 1.17)—possesses the fullness of the priesthood since he performs all the sacraments, including ordinations, the consecration of churches, and the confection of Chrism. The priest receives his ministry from the bishop who ordains him and appoints him to a parish to perform the sacraments. The deacon is the assistant of the two higher degrees and without them cannot perform anything.[4] Without the sacrament of priesthood, there would be no other sacraments in the Church, and for this reason, priesthood is essential for the life of the Church. Saint Symeon affirms that "true Christianity exists by means of bishops, and through them, by the mysteries of Christ. . . . Without [the bishop] there can be no altar, no ordination, no holy myron, no baptism, and therefore, no Christian."[5]

The *Euchologion* uses two Greek terms to refer to ordinations: *cheirotonia* (χειροτονία) and *cheirothesia* (χειροθεσία). The root of both these terms is the word "hand" (χείρ, *cheir*). The term *cheirotonia* comes from the verb χειροτονεῖν (*cheirotonein*) which literally means "χεῖρας τεινεῖν" (*cheiras teinein*): to stretch out the hands. This term was already used in antiquity when talking about stretching out one's hand for the purpose of casting a vote in the assembly for elections for social responsibilities. In the Christian context, it was used for appointment to an office in the Church. It is already used in the book of Acts, where we read that "when [Paul and Barnabas] had ordained (χειροτονήσαντες, *cheirotonēsantes*) elders (πρεσβυτέρους, *presbyterous*) in every church, and had prayed with fasting, they commended them to the Lord" (Acts 14.23). It is also found in the *Didache* for the election of bishops and deacons.[6] Initially, the term *cheirothesia* was synonymous with *cheirotonia*, but Canon 14 of the Seventh Ecumenical Council (787) introduced a distinction between them. Since that time, the term *cheirothesia* is used for minor orders such as the ordination of readers,[7] and the term *cheirotonia* is reserved for ordinations to major orders. Saint Symeon of Thessalonica emphasizes that ordinations (*cheirothesiai*) to the minor orders (reader and subdeacon) are performed outside the sanctuary, as the

---

[4]Pseudo-Dionysius the Areopagite, *Ecclesiastical Hierarchy* 5.1.2, 5.1.6–7 (PG 3:501d, 505a-509a; Luibheid, 234–235, 236–239); Symeon of Thessalonica, *De sacro templo* (PG 155:724d, 728d; *The Liturgical Commentaries*, 132–33 and 136–37).

[5]Symeon of Thessalonica, *De sacro ritu sancti olei* 77 (PG 155:252ab).

[6]*Didache* 15.1 (SC 248:192; PPS 41:43).

[7]Joannou, *Discipline générale antique*, 1.1:269–71.

ordinations (*cheirotoniai*) to the major orders (deacon, priest, bishop) are performed inside the sanctuary, in front of the holy table.[8] The ordinations to the minor orders do not take place during the Divine Liturgy, but either before it, or at some other time.

The canonical tradition and Byzantine legislation regulated the age of candidates for ordinations. The minimal age for the ordination of a reader was fixed at eighteen (Novella 123 of Justinian), of a subdeacon at twenty (Canon 15 of the Council in Trullo, 691–92),[9] of a deacon at twenty-five (Canon 16 of Carthage and Canon 14 of the Council in Trullo),[10] and of a priest at thirty years (Canon 11 of the Council of Neocaesarea and Canon 14 of the Council in Trullo).[11] Although the minimal age for the ordination of a bishop was fifty years in the *Apostolic Constitutions* (*c.* 380),[12] in the sixth century it was set at no less than thirty, the minimal age for the ordination to priesthood (Novella 137 of Justinian). Priesthood constitutes an impediment to marriage, in the sense that after ordination to the subdiaconate a cleric is forbidden to marry (see Canons 3, 6, and 13 of the Council in Trullo), but married men can be ordained to every clerical rank, with the exception of the episcopate (after Canon 12 of the Council in Trullo).[13]

The cheirothesia of a reader begins with a tonsure. The origin of this rite was the tonsure performed when a man was entering the clerical state.[14] Canon 21 of the Council in Trullo (691–92) mentions that the clerical tonsure distinguished the clergy from the laity, who grew their hair long.[15] This clerical tonsure used to be in a form of a crown, but in current practice, the future reader is tonsured in the form of the cross. Canon 14 of Seventh Ecumenical Council mentions the clerical tonsure (ἡ κουρὰ τοῦ κλήρου, *hē koura tou klērou*) as a separate rite that preceded the ordination of a reader.[16] The tonsure used to be accompanied by "a prayer to make a layman a clergyman."[17]

[8]Symeon of Thessalonica, *De sacris ordinationibus* 156 (PG 155:361d–364a).
[9]Joannou, *Discipline générale antique*, 1.1:144.
[10]Joannou, *Discipline générale antique*, 1.1:143–144; 1.2:231.
[11]Joannou, *Discipline générale antique*, 1.1:143–144; 1.2:80.
[12]*Apostolic Constitutions* 2.1 (SC 320:144; ANF 7:396).
[13]Joannou, *Discipline générale antique*, 1.1:125–32.
[14]A. Neselovsky, *Chiny khirotesii i khirotonii* (Kamianets-Podol'sk, 1906), 3–19.
[15]Joannou, *Discipline générale antique*, 1.1:152–53.
[16]Joannou, *Discipline générale antique*, 1.1:269–71.
[17]Goar, 235.

The most ancient attestation of the ordination of a reader[18] is found in the *Apostolic Constitutions* (*c.* 380), through the imposition of the bishop's hand.[19] Canon 33 of the Council in Trullo (691–92) forbids the ordination of a reader who has not become a clergyman by receiving the clerical tonsure.[20] The Barberini manuscript contains the prayer for the ordination of a reader that is still used today, along with the laying on of the bishop's hand.[21] It prescribes that after the prayer, the bishop give the book of the epistles to the newly ordained reader to read. This manuscript does not mention the clerical tonsure in the ordination of the reader, because most likely at the time it was written, clerical tonsure was still a separate rite. The manuscript *Coislin 213* (11th c.) and the so-called *Euchologion of Bessarion* (Grottaferrata Γ.β.1, 13th c.) contain the tonsure rite in the form of the cross, with the words *In the name of the Father . . .* before the prayer of ordination.[22] These two manuscripts prescribe that the candidate be vested in a phelonion. There is no attestation of such a practice before the eleventh century. In his commentary, Saint Symeon of Thessalonica uses the expression "the blessed phelonion or shirt [καμίσιον]," which he interprets as "the beginning of sacred vestments."[23] The small phelonion used to be an inner vestment, worn by all the minor clergy on their cassock, and without which they could not perform any liturgical function.[24]

The most ancient attestation of the ordination of a subdeacon[25] is also found in the *Apostolic Constitutions*, through the imposition of hands by the bishop.[26] The Barberini *Euchologion* contains the prayer for the ordination of a subdeacon that is still in use today, along with the imposition of the bishop's hand.[27] After the prayer, the newly ordained subdeacon said thrice: *All the faithful* (Ὅσοι πιστοί, *hosoi pistoi*). According to A. Neselovsky, this exclamation corresponds to the current exclamation of the deacon that occurs after the Litany of the Catechumens in the Divine Liturgy, and he suggests that the ordination of the subdeacon initially took place at that precise moment in the

[18]Cf. Neselovsky, 7–64.
[19]*Apostolic Constitutions* 8.22 (SC 336:224; ANF 7:493).
[20]Joannou, *Discipline générale antique*, 1.1:166–67.
[21]*Barberini*, 175.
[22]Arranz, *Euchologio*, 163; Dmitrievsky, *Opisanie*, 2:997.
[23]Symeon of Thessalonica, *De sacris ordinationibus* 159 (PG 155:365b).
[24]Symeon of Thessalonica, *De sacris ordinationibus* 186 (PG 155:396b).
[25]Cf. Neselovsky, 73–102.
[26]*Apostolic Constitutions* 8.21 (SC 336:222; ANF 7:492–493).
[27]*Barberini*, 174.

Liturgy. In his opinion, this practice was observed until the seventh century. Later, when the ordination no longer took place during the Divine Liturgy, this exclamation was linked with the washing of the bishop's hands that follows the ordination. Again according to Neselovsky, the washing of the hands of the clergy before the Anaphora initially took place immediately after the ordination of the subdeacon, and therefore it was performed by him.[28] In the eleventh century, the reader who was to be ordained subdeacon was brought to the bishop wearing the little phelonion, which the bishop took off before the prayer of ordination, and then vested the candidate in a sticharion girded with the orarion. After the prayer of ordination, the newly ordained subdeacon brought the bowl for the washing of bishop's hands. From the fourteenth century on, the *Euchologia* prescribe that the newly ordained subdeacon stand before the holy doors of the iconostasis, with the bowl for the hand washing, while praying silently until the Great Entrance.[29]

As one can see, the moment of ordination for each degree of the priesthood is significant, since it reveals the meaning of the particular ministry of each. The ordination of a bishop[30] takes place in the first part of the Divine Liturgy, after the Trisagion, before the biblical readings; this was already the practice at the end of the fourth century, as witnessed by the *Apostolic Constitutions*,[31] which specify that the newly ordained bishop preside at the Divine Liturgy and preach after the readings. The Barberini manuscript also indicates that the ordination of the bishop takes place after the Trisagion.[32] This location of the bishop's ordination emphasizes that the episcopal ministry consists in teaching the true faith and in presiding at the eucharistic gathering. The ordination of a priest,[33] also found in the *Apostolic Constitutions*,[34] takes place before the Anaphora, right after the Great Entrance, as attested also by the Barberini *Euchologion*;[35] this locus shows that the ministry of the priest is to celebrate the divine mysteries. The ordination of a deacon,[36] already found in the *Apostolic Constitutions*,[37] takes place after

---

[28]Cf. Neselovsky, 76–77.

[29]Dmitrievsky, 2:297–298, 376, 692, 785.

[30]Neselovsky, 212–71.

[31]*Apostolic Constitutions* 8.5.9 and 11 (SC 336:148 and 150; ANF 7:482–83).

[32]*Barberini*, 165.

[33]Neselovsky, 168–212.

[34]*Apostolic Constitutions* 8.16 (SC 336:216–18; ANF 7:491–92).

[35]*Barberini*, 167.

[36]Neselovsky, 105–168.

[37]*Apostolic Constitutions* 8.17 (SC 336:218–220; ANF 7:492).

the Anaphora, before the Litany of Supplication (*Having commemorated all the saints*), as prescribed, again, in the Barberini manuscript,[38] to emphasize that the role of the deacon is only to assist the bishop or the priest in the celebration of the mysteries, but not to perform them.

For each major ordination, the candidate is brought by two of his colleagues before the holy doors of the iconostasis. There he bows towards the sanctuary, as someone of the same clerical rank says: *Command* (Κέλευσον, Повели: *keleuson, poveli* [singular]). Then he bows towards the assembly, as the exclamation is repeated by a peer: *Command* (Κελεύσατε, Повелите: *keleusate, povelite* [plural]). Finally, he is brought to the bishop through the holy doors by the senior person of the rank of the clergy to which he is to be ordained, who says: *Command, holy master* (Κέλευσον δέσποτα ἅγιε, Повели преосвященнейший владыко: *keleuson, dhespota agie; poveli, preosvjashchennejshij vladyko*) as he bows towards the bishop. Neselovsky sees the origin of the expression *Command* (Κέλευσον, *keleuson*) in the imperial ceremonial, where it asked the superior to give permission.[39] The first "Command" is addressed to the candidate himself, since no ordination can take place without the candidate's own consent, given freely and without any pressure.[40] The second is addressed to the assembly, since originally an ordination implied an election.[41] Indeed, Canon 7 of Theophilus of Alexandria prohibits secret ordinations, and stresses that ordination should take place in full churches, in the presence of all the people.[42] For this reason, priesthood is the only sacrament that never became a private celebration and therefore was never dissociated from the Divine Liturgy. One can see that this "Command" corresponds to the real election of the candidate by the whole Church, which takes place before the ordination.[43] The third "Command" is addressed to the bishop, since the authority to ordain (and to judge) the clergy is the prerogative of the bishop.[44]

In contemporary practice, the candidate is then brought around the holy table thrice by two senior clergymen of the rank to which he is to be ordained, as the clergy and the chanters sing the troparia: *O holy martyrs;*

---

[38] *Barberini,* 170.

[39] Neselovsky, 154–57.

[40] Cf. Canon 10 of Basil the Great, Joannou, *Discipline générale antique,* 2:110.

[41] *Apostolic Tradition* 9 (SC 11:39; *On the Apostolic Tradition,* PPS 54:102).

[42] Joannou, Discipline générale antique, 2:267–68.

[43] N. Afanasieff, *Ekkleziologiya: Vstuplenie v klir* (Paris, 1968), 37–38.

[44] Apostolic Canon 2, Joannou, *Discipline générale antique,* 1.2:8.

Glory to thee, O Christ God; and *Rejoice, O Isaiah*. This is a relatively late development in the rite of ordination, since Saint Symeon of Thessalonica (late 14th–early 15th c.) describes only the first troparion (which is sung twice) as universal, while stressing that the second is sung only in Thessalonica, but not in Constantinople.[45] Therefore, we can conclude that this part of the rite did not exist prior to the fourteenth century. We can also note that although the troparia are sung even in the contemporary Greek practice for the ordination of a bishop, this rite is not found in the *Archieratikon* of Moscow, which keeps the practice that was in effect before the fourteenth century, when these troparia had not yet been added to the ordination rites.[46]

The candidate then kneels to the right of the bishop, in front of the holy table. Kneeling at the ordination is attested in the fifth century by the *Ecclesiastical Hierarchy* of Pseudo-Dionysius, who sees in it a sign of submission of the candidate's life to God. He emphasizes that at the ordination of a deacon, the candidate kneels on only one knee, because he is only a servant, and that at the ordination of a priest or of a bishop, the candidate kneels on both knees because they are called to perform the holy mysteries.[47] The Barberini *Euchologion* also prescribes kneeling at ordinations.[48]

The bishop then proclaims: *The grace divine . . .* (Η Θεία χάρις, *hē theia charis*). This is the "sacred proclamation" already mentioned in the fifth century in the *Ecclesiastical Hierarchy* of Pseudo-Dionysios.[49] Originally it was not a prayer of ordination but a proclamation of the text of a document (charter) certifying that the ordination could take place, and it was presented and read by the chartophylax[50] before the candidate knelt and received the laying on of the hands of the bishop.[51] It is already found in the second half of the eighth century in the Barberini manuscript.[52] In this text, we find the word προχειρίζεται (*procheirizetai*), usually translated as *promotes*, since the candidate is being promoted to a higher level of ministry. Nevertheless,

[45]Symeon of Thessalonica, *De sacris ordinationibus* 205 (PG 155:413c).
[46]Neselovsky, 260.
[47]Pseudo-Dionysius the Areopagite, *On the Ecclesiastical Hierarchy* 5.3, 5.8 (PG 3:509d, 516ab; Lubheid, 240, 242–43).
[48]*Barberini*, 167 and 170.
[49]Pseudo-Dionysius the Areopagite. *On the Ecclesiastical Hierarchy* 5.3.5 (PG 3:512b; Lubheid, 241).
[50]The chartophylax, literally the "keeper of documents," was an ecclesiastical officer in charge of official documents and records in the patriarchal chancellery.
[51]Neselovsky, 121–122, 129–134.

we should notice in this word the same root, χείρ (*cheir*), meaning *hand*, as in the words χειροτονία (*cheirotonia*) and χειροθεσία (*cheirothesia*). Thus it refers once again to an election, usually done by raising one's hand. This text emphasizes that the divine grace chooses, elects, and promotes a person to a certain degree of priesthood.[53] It also stresses that *the divine grace . . . always heals that which is infirm and completes that which is lacking.*

This sacred exclamation used to be followed by the rite of the imposition of hands, which is very ancient, found already in the New Testament (Acts 13.1–5; 1 Tim 4.14; and 2 Tim 1.6). One should note that in the last passage cited, Saint Paul is speaking of the laying on of his hands, which testifies that the one ordaining placed both his hands on the head of the candidate. According to Saint Symeon of Thessalonica, the rite of the imposition of hands symbolically represents the grace dispensed by Christ, which comes and overshadows the one who is being ordained.[54] For the ordination of a bishop, besides the imposition of the hands of the consecrating bishop and his concelebrants, the gospel book, text side down, is placed over the head of the bishop-elect, as already attested at the end of the fourth century by the *Apostolic Constitutions.*[55] This rite shows that the bishop-elect receives the imposition of hands from Christ himself and is thus introduced into the priesthood of Christ the High Priest, as the concelebrating bishops witness the apostolic succession manifested in time and space.

The imposition of hands is always accompanied by two prayers of ordination and a litany, normally said during the second prayer by the senior clergyman of the degree to which the candidate is being ordained, in which he prays particularly for the one who is ordaining *and the works of his hands*, and for the one who is being ordained. These are already attested by the Barberini codex.[56]

The prayers of ordination are followed by the vesting. At the vesting, each time a new vestment is given, the bishop says: *Axios!* (Worthy!), and this is repeated by the clergy and the chanters (and/or the people). Given that this happens after the ordination, it has nothing to do with an election, although it is often erroneously presented as such. Rather, it is an acclamation

[52]Barberini, 165, 167 and 170.
[53]A. Pentkovsky, "Chinosledovaniya khirotonii v viznatiiskikh Evkhologiyakh VIII–XII vv." *Vizantiskii Vremenik* 61 [86] (2002): 127–30.
[54]Symeon of Thessalonica, *De sacris ordinationibus* 169 (PG 155:376bc).
[55]*Apostolic Constitutions* 8.4.6 (SC 336:142; ANF 7:482).
[56]Barberini, 165–67, 167–69 and 170–71.

testifying that the person who has just been ordained has been made worthy of the degree of the ministry to which he has been called. Saint Symeon of Thessalonica says that we say "Axios, because he has been made worthy in front of God, is perceived as such by the angels and men, and that he must conduct himself in such a way, according to the diginity of his ministry."[57] We find this acclamation already in the fifth century in the canonico-liturgical document entitled *The Testament of our Lord Jesus Christ*.[58]

The deacon receives the orarion and the ripidion (liturgical fan).[59] Canons 22 and 23 of the Council of Laodicea (end of 4th c.) witness that the orarion used to be the prerogative of the deacon and ought not to be worn by readers or even subdeacons.[60] The ripidion is attested at the end of the fourth century in the *Apostolic Constitutions*.[61] It was used by the deacon to wave over the Holy Gifts in order to chase flies away from the chalice. Saint Symeon of Thessalonica compares the service of a deacon to the service of the angels and the orarion to the wings of the angels.[62] According to the Barberini codex, after partaking of the holy Gifts, the newly ordained deacon received the chalice from the bishop to distribute the holy Blood to the faithful.[63]

The priest is vested with the epitrachelion and the phelonion. According to the Barberini manuscript, the orarion used to be joined together in order to be united in front of the candidate, in order to form the epitrachelion.[64] At that time, the newly ordained priest, immediately after his ordination, used to receive "in his hands a portion of the bread from the diskos," at the very beginning of the Anaphora, at: *It is meet and right,* and he gave it back at: *The Holy Things are for the holy.*[65] This was the practice until the eleventh century. This bread was of course not consecrated. It was given to the priest so that immediately after his ordination he could serve the Anaphora on his own bread. This is analogous to giving the epistle book to the newly

---

[57]Symeon of Thessalonica, *De sacris ordinationibus* 210 (PG 155:424b).

[58]*The Testament of the Lord: Worship and Discipline in the Early Church*, An English Version, with an Introduction and Notes by Alistair C. Stewart, Popular Patristics Series 58 (Yonkers, NY: St Vladimir's Seminary Press, 2018), 91.

[59]*Barberini*, 171.

[60]Joannou, *Discipline générale antique*, 1.2:139–40.

[61]*Apostolic Constitutions* 8.12.3 (SC 336:178; ANF 7:486).

[62]Symeon of Thessalonica, *De sacris ordinationibus* 173 (PG 155:381bc).

[63]*Barberini*, 171.

[64]*Barberini*, 169.

[65]Ibid.

ordained reader to read, or giving the ripidion to the newly ordained deacon. This practice was abandoned in the eleventh century, because of the
principle that only one liturgy (and therefore one bread) could be offered on
one altar on any one day. Thus the practice, the meaning, and the moment
of giving the bread to the newly ordained priest changed. From that period,
he received only a portion (XC) of the sanctified bread after the completion of the Anaphora, as a pledge of the mysteries he will be performing in
the future. To emphasize this, in the fourteenth century the words *Receive
this pledge* (Λάβε τὴν παρακαταθήκην ταύτην, Приими залог сей; *Labe
tēn parakatathēkēn tautēn, Priimi zalog sei*) were added. According to Saint
Symeon of Thessalonica, this portion of the rite symbolizes that the newly
ordained priest is made a custodian of the divine mysteries.[66]

In ancient times, as attested at the end of the eighth century by the Barberini codex, the newly ordained bishop received only the omophorion,
which was placed over his phelonion.[67] According to the contemporary
practice, the newly ordained bishop takes off the phelonion at that moment
and puts on the sakkos, the omophorion, the encolpion, and the miter. The
sakkos was originally an imperial garment, which was later granted to the
Ecumenical Patriarch, and from him, it was extended to all the bishops
without exception.[68] Still, Symeon of Thessalonica (late 14th–early 15th c.)
states that some among the bishops have the privilege of wearing a polys-
tavrion or a sakkos instead of the phelonion.[69] Originally, the cross and the
encolpion were not worn during liturgical celebrations. Saint Symeon of
Thessalonica describes the encolpion when he describes the bishop's mantia, and says that the bishop wears the encolpion as a sign of his confession
of faith.[70] He says that the patriarch receives the encolpion of the Church
from the emperor.[71] It became the norm for all bishops to wear a cross and
an encolpion at liturgical celebrations only after the seventeenth century.[72]
The same can be said of the miter, since the ancient tradition was to serve

[66]Symeon of Thessalonica, *De sacris ordinationibus* 182 (PG 155:389d–392a).
[67]*Barberini*, 167.
[68]Cf. Vassa Larin, *The Byzantine Hierarchical Divine Liturgy in Arsenij Suxanov's Proskinitarij: Text, Translation and Analysis of the Entrance Rites*, OCA 286 (Rome: Pontificio
Istituto Orientale, 2010), 233; Woodfin, *The Embodied Icon*, 133–77.
[69]Symeon of Thessalonica, *De sacra liturgia* 79 and 81 (PG 155:256b and 260c; *The
Liturgical Commentaries*, 214–217).
[70]Symeon of Thessalonica, *De sacra liturgia* 80 (PG 155:257a; *The Liturgical Commentaries*, 214–215).
[71]Symeon of Thessalonica, *De sacris ordinationibus* 229 (PG 155:441c).
[72]Larin, *Hierarchical Divine Liturgy*, 228–30,

the liturgy without any head covering. Saint Symeon of Thessalonica states that only the Patriarch of Alexandria wears the miter during the liturgy.[73] The miter was introduced in the liturgy after the fall of Constantinople and was first worn by the Ecumenical Patriarch only, and after the seventeenth century by all the bishops.[74] Some say that this was originally the imperial crown, which was then worn by the Ecumenical Patriarch in his capacity as ethnarch, in the absence of an emperor. Others allege that it was introduced into the liturgy by Cyril Loukaris when he became Ecumenical Patriarch (1620–38) after he had been Patriarch of Alexandria (1601–20), where the use of the miter was already attested.

After the vesting, the newly ordained person exchanges the kiss of peace with the bishop who ordained him (and with other clergy of the rank to which he has been ordained).[75] This kiss is already mentioned in the fifth century in the *Ecclesiastical Hierarchy* of Pseudo-Dionysius, who states that the newly ordained "has acceded to the priestly dignity and therefore is worthy of love from his equals and from all who belong to the sacred orders," including the bishop who ordained him.[76]

Saint Symeon of Thessalonica mentions that the newly ordained deacon and priest serve the Divine Liturgy for seven consecutive days "in honor of the gifts of the Holy Spirit, in order to learn his work."[77]

2. The Ordination of a Reader

Table 3.1: The Order of the Ordination of a Reader
(1. Prayer with imposition of the bishop's hand: *O Lord who enlightenest all creation with the light of thy wonders*)
2. Opening blessing and usual beginning prayers
3. Troparia: *O Holy Apostles . . . Grace shining forth from thy mouth like a beacon . . . Thy proclamation has gone out into all the earth . . . The shepherd's reed of thy theology . . . Glory . . . Both now . . . Through the prayers of all the saints . . .*

[73]Symeon of Thessalonica, *Expositio de divino templo* 45 (PG 155:716d–717b; *The Liturgical Commentaries*, 112–13); *Responsa ad Gabrielem Pentapolitanum* 20 (PG 155:872cd)..

[74]Cf. Woodfin, *The Embodied Icon*, 31–33; Larin, *Hierarchical Divine Liturgy*, 100, 233.

[75]*Barberini*, 167, 169, 171.

[76]Pseudo-Dionysius the Areopagite, *On the Ecclesiastical Hierarchy* 5.3.6 (PG 3:513b; Luibheid, 242).

[77]Symeon of Thessalonica, *De sacris ordinationibus* 176 (PG 155:384d).

4. Tonsure, with the words: *In the name of the Father. Amen. And of the Son. Amen. And of the Holy Spirit. Amen.*

5. Blessing of the small phelonion

6. Prayer with imposition of the bishop's hand: *O Lord God Almighty*

7. Reading of the Epistle

8. Blessing of the sticharion

9. Exhortation: *Child, the first degree of priesthood*

10. Proclamation: *Blessed be the Lord. Behold, the servant of God becomes a reader of the most holy church*

The ordination (*cheirothesia*) of a reader takes place outside the sanctuary, in the nave. In the Russian practice, it is preceded by the prayer of ordination of a candle-bearer. The bishop blesses the head of the candidate thrice and says the prayer of ordination with the imposition of his hand: *O Lord who enlightenest all creation*, which is found in an appendix in the *Euchologion* of Goar,[78] but which is no longer in use in the Greek practice.

After the opening blessing (*Blessed is our God*) and the usual beginning prayers, troparia are sung. Then the bishop performs the tonsure, in the sign of the cross, while saying: *In the name of the Father. Amen. And of the Son. Amen. And of the Holy Spirit. Amen.* The bishop blesses the small phelonion, which is put on the candidate. The bishop blesses the head of the candidate thrice again and says the prayer of ordination with the imposition of his hand: *O Lord God Almighty* (already present in the Barberini codex).[79] After the prayer, the bishop opens the book of the epistles over the head of the candidate and gives him a passage to read. The newly ordained reader announces the reading, saying: *The reading is from the Epistle of the Holy Apostle Paul to the . . .* and he reads the pericope that was given to him. Then the small phelonion is taken away and the bishop blesses the sticharion, and vests the newly ordained reader with it. Then the bishop reads the exhortation: *Child, the first degree of priesthood . . .* ; this is followed by the proclamation: *Blessed be the Lord. Behold, the servant of God becomes a reader of the most holy church. . . .* In the proclamation, the bishop mentions the church for which the reader has been ordained, since, according to Canon 6 of the Fourth Ecumenical Council, there cannot be ordinations at large, but always in connection with a specific church (parish or monastery).[80]

[78]Goar, 237.
[79]*Barberini*, 175.
[80]Joannou, *Discipline générale antique*, 1.1:74.

3. The Ordination of a Subdeacon

The ordination (*cheirothesia*) of a subdeacon takes place outside the sanctuary, in the nave. The candidate, vested with the sticharion, is brought to the bishop. The bishop blesses the orarion, and the candidate is girded with it. The bishop blesses the head of the candidate thrice and says the prayer of ordination with the imposition of his hand: *O Lord our God, who through one and the same Holy Spirit* (already found in the Barberini *Euchologion*).[81] After the prayer, the newly ordained subdeacon is given the bowl and towel for the washing of the bishop's hands, and he proceeds to perform the washing. Then he stands with the bowl and the towel in front of the iconostasis, praying silently until the Great Entrance. At the Cherubic Hymn, he is led by two other subdeacons before the holy doors to wash the hands of the bishop. At the Great Entrance, he walks behind all the clergy, and after the entrance, he stands with the subdeacons in the sanctuary at the appointed place.

4. The Ordination of a Deacon

The ordination of a deacon takes place in the sanctuary after the exclamation *And may the mercies of our great God and Savior. . . .* The candidate is brought before the holy doors of the iconostasis by two subdeacons. There he bows towards the sanctuary, as one of the subdeacons says: *Command.* Then he bows towards the assembly, as one of the subdeacons says: *Command.* Finally, he is brought to the bishop through the holy doors by the archdeacon who says: *Command, holy master*, as the candidate bows towards the bishop. Two deacons lead him around the holy table thrice, as the clergy and the chanters sing the troparia: *O Holy Martyrs*; *Glory to thee, O Christ God*; and *Rejoice, O Isaiah.* As they go around the holy table, the candidate kisses it on the four corners, and after completing each circuit around the holy table, he kisses the hand and the omophorion (or the epigonation) of the bishop, who is sitting on a chair. Then the candidate kneels on one knee to the right of the bishop, who blesses the head of the candidate thrice and proclaims: *The grace divine . . .* and then says the two prayers of ordination with the imposition of his hand: *O Lord our God, who by thy foreknowledge sendest the gift of thy Holy Spirit . . .* and: *O God, our Savior, who by thine incorruptible voice . . .* (already found in the Barberini codex).[82] The clergy

---

[81]*Barberini*, 174.
[82]*Barberini*, 170–71.

in the sanctuary, and then the chanters, respond by singing: *Kyrie, eleison,* thrice. During the second prayer, the first deacon says the litany in a low voice; in this he prays in particular for the bishop who is ordaining and for the deacon who is being ordained. Then the newly ordained deacon is vested with the orarion and the cuffs and receives the ripidion. With each item the bishop proclaims: *Axios!* and the clergy and the chanter repeat this acclamation. The newly ordained deacon kisses the bishop and then fans the holy gifts over the holy table until the *Our Father.*

5. The Ordination of a Priest

The ordination of a priest takes place in the sanctuary after the Great Entrance. During the entrance, the candidate holds the aër over his head, to emphasize that he is being called to be a custodian of the divine mysteries. He is then brought before the holy doors of the iconostasis by two deacons. There, he bows towards the sanctuary, as one of the deacons says: *Command.* Then he bows towards the assembly, as one of the deacons says: *Command.* Finally, he is brought to the bishop through the holy doors by the senior priest, who says: *Command, holy master,* as the candidate bows towards the bishop. Two priests lead him around the holy table thrice, as the clergy and the chanters sing the troparia: *O Holy Martyrs*; *Glory to thee, O Christ God*; and *Rejoice, O Isaiah.* As they go around the holy table, the candidate kisses it on the four corners, and after each circuit around the holy table, he kisses the hand and the omophorion (or the epigonation) of the bishop, who is sitting on a chair. Then the candidate kneels on both knees to the right of the bishop, who blesses the head of the candidate thrice and proclaims: *The grace divine . . .* and then says the two prayers of ordination with the imposition of his hand: *O God, who hast no beginning and no ending . . .* and *O God, great in power and inscrutable in wisdom . . .* (already present in the Barberini manuscript).[83] The clergy in the sanctuary, and then the chanters, respond by singing *Kyrie, eleison* thrice. During the second prayer, the first priest says the litany in a low voice; in this he prays in particular for the bishop who is ordaining and for the priest who is being ordained. Then the newly ordained priest is vested with the epitrachelion, the belt, and the phelonion. In Russian practice he receives the silver pectoral cross and *Hieratikon* as well. With each item the bishop proclaims: *Axios!* and the clergy and the chanter repeat this acclamation. The newly ordained

[83]*Barberini,* 167–69.

priest kisses the bishop and all his concelebrants, and then stands with the priests (usually, at the right of the first priest). At the end of the Anaphora, he receives in his hands (usually on a second diskos) the "XC" portion of the Lamb as the bishop says to him: *Receive this pledge and preserve it whole and unharmed until thy last breath, for thou shalt be held to an accounting for it in the second and fearful coming of our great Lord and God and Savior Jesus Christ.* He holds the portion of the holy Bread over the holy table while saying prayers for himself until the Lord's Prayer, when he gives it back to the bishop who puts it back on the main diskos.

6. The Ordination of a Bishop

The ordination of a bishop includes five stages, each of which has a liturgical character: 1) the election, 2) the message (μήνυμα, наречение; *mēnyma, narechenie*), 3) the confession of faith, 4) the ordination itself (χειροτονία; *cheirotonia*), and 5) the enthronement.[84] The *Archieratikon* contains only the texts for the third and fourth stages, although Saint Symeon of Thessalonica gives a detailed commentary on all five stages in his *Dialogue in Christ*.[85]

The election of the bishop, according to tradition and as it is still observed at the Ecumenical Patriarchate, takes place in a church in front of the icon of Christ and is preceded by a short service that includes the troparion and the kontakion of Pentecost. The service is presided over by the first hierarch, who censes and says the litany and the dismissal of Pentecost.[86] This makes clear that the election of the bishop is centered on Christ, since the one who is elected is called to exercise the episcopal ministry in the place and in the image of Christ (εἰς τόπον καὶ τύπον Χριστοῦ; *eis topon kai typon Christou*). His election should be made under the inspiration of the Holy Spirit, in a way similar to that of the apostles, who on the day of Pentecost were sent to announce the gospel to the ends of the world.

The election is followed by the "order of proclamation" (τάξις τοῦ μηνύματος, чин наречение; *taxis tou mēnymatos, chin narechenie*), a ceremony in which the decision of the Holy Synod is communicated to the

---

[84]Cf. our article: J. Getcha, "La liturgie de l'ordination épiscopale dans l'Église orthodoxe," *Le concile Vatican II et l'Église orthodoxe,* Analecta Chambesiana 5 (Chambésy, 2015), 160–74 [also in Greek: "Ἡ Ἀκολουθία τῆς ἐπισκοπῆς χειροτονίας στὴν Ὀρθόδοξη Ἐκκλησία," *Θεολογία* 3 (2014): 7–23].

[85]Symeon of Thessalonica, *De sacris ordinationibus* 187–223 (PG 155:396d–437b).

[86]Symeon of Thessalonica, *De sacris ordinationibus* 141 (PG 155:400d–404a); A. Neselovsky, 229–230.

man who has been elected and to his local Church. The service is held in a
church and presided over by the bishop-elect, who censes the icons of the
iconostasis. After the troparion and the kontakion of Pentecost are chanted,
he says the litany and the dismissal of the Pentecost. Then, upon hearing
the announcement of his election read by the deputy secretary of the Holy
Synod, the bishop-elect responds by giving thanks, accepting his election,
and asking for God's help. Then the bishop-elect exchanges the kiss of peace
with the members of the Holy Synod, and afterwards he signs the act of his
election in the synodical codex.[87]

The confession of faith takes place on the day of ordination, before the
Divine Liturgy. The first hierarch and the other bishops participating in the
ordination sit in the middle of the church. The bishop-elect, wearing his
priestly vestments, is presented to them by two clergymen; he stands on a
large carpet depicting an eagle (which symbolizes the episcopal ministry),
a city (which represents the local church), and three rivers (which symbol-
ize the teaching of truth).[88] In his hands the bishop-elect holds the book of
the holy gospels, in which is placed a confession of faith signed by his own
hand. For this reason, the bishop-elect says: *I, N., elected by the mercy of
God bishop of N., have written this by my hand.* He then reads three confessions of faith: the Nicene-Constantinopolitan Symbol of Faith, a confession
of faith on the mystery of the Holy Trinity, and a confession of faith on the
mystery of Christ. He then promises to be faithful to the teachings of the
holy Fathers and of the seven Ecumenical Councils, and the holy canons,
and to be a minister of the unity of the Church. The rite of the confession of
faith follows the decision of the council of Carthage (419), which prescribed
that the decisions of the councils will be taught to the bishop-elect by the
ones ordaining him, so that he would not be ignorant of them (Canon 18
[25]).[89] This prescription was reiterated by Novella 137 of Justinian in the

---

[87]Cf. *Chinovnik*, vol. 2 (Moscow, 1983), 5–9.

[88]Syméon of Thessalonica, *De sacris ordinationibus* 199–203 (PG 155:408c–412d);
Neselovsky, 231–33, 254–57; *Archieratikon* (Athens, 1994), 87–92; *Chinovnik*, 2:9–19. On
the confessions of faith, Cf. O. Raquez, "Les confessions de foi de la chirotonie épiscopale
des Églises grecques," *Traditio et progressio: Studi liturgici in onore del Prof. A. Nocent*, Studia Anselmiana 95 (Rome: Pontificio Ateneo S. Anselmo, 1988), 469–85; O. Delouis, "La
profession de foi pour l'ordination des évêques (avec un formulaire inédit du patriarche
Photius" in S. Metivier and P. Pages, eds., *Le saint, le moine et le paysan. Mélanges d'histoire
byzantine offerts à M. Kaplan*, Byzantina Sorbonensia 29 (Paris: Publications de la Sorbonne, 2016), 119–38.

[89]P. Joannou, *Discipline générale antique*, 1.2:232.

sixth century. Two deacons then present the bishop-elect to the first hierarch and the concelebrating bishops. The first hierarch blesses him saying: *The grace of the Holy Spirit, through my mediocrity, elevates thee, most-beloved of God . . . to be the Bishop-elect of the God-saved city, N.* Then the bishop-elect exchanges the kiss of peace with each bishop and goes back to stand on the eagle rug. Then two priests present the bishop-elect to the first hierarch and the concelebrating bishops. The first hierarch blesses him saying: *May the grace of the Most Holy and Life-giving Spirit be with thee always, now and ever, and unto the ages of ages.* Then the bishop-elect exchanges the kiss of peace with each bishop once more and immediately goes into the sanctuary, where he awaits the moment of his ordination in silent prayer.

According to the practice of the Ecumenical Patriarchate, the troparion and the kontakion of Pentecost are chanted after the Little Entrance, showing that the ordination of the bishop is compared to the descent of the Holy Spirit on the apostles on the day of the Pentecost.[90] The ordination takes place in the first part of the Divine Liturgy, after the Trisagion, before the biblical readings. This was already the case at the end of the fourth century, as witnessed by the *Apostolic Constitutions*,[91] which specify that the newly ordained bishop preside over the Divine Liturgy and preach after the readings. This arrangement is also attested in the Barberini *Euchologion*.[92] This order emphasizes that the episcopal ministry concerns both the teaching of the true faith and the presidency of the eucharistic gathering.

After the Trisagion, two priests bring the bishop-elect from the middle of the church to the holy doors of the iconostasis. There, he bows towards the sanctuary, as one of the priests says, *Command*. Then he bows towards the assembly, as one of the priests says, *Command*. Finally, he is brought to the presiding bishop through the holy doors by the senior concelebrating bishop who says, *Command, holy master*, as he bows towards the presiding bishop. He is received at the holy doors of the iconostasis by two bishops who take turns leading him three times around the holy table as three troparia are chanted: *O Holy martyrs*; *Glory to thee, O Christ God*; and *Rejoice, O Isaiah*. These troparia are not found in the *Archieratikon* of Moscow, which keeps an older practice from before the time when these troparia were added to the ordination rites.[93]

[90]Neselovsky, 254 n. 103. This practice is observed also in the Church of Jerusalem.
[91]*Apostolic Constitutions* 8.5.9 and 11 (SC 336:148 and 150; ANF 7:482–483).
[92]Barberini, 165.
[93]Neselovsky, 260.

The first hierarch then stands in front of the holy table as the bishop-elect kneels to his right in front of the holy table, resting his head over his crossed hands on the holy table. The first hierarch places the end of his omophorion over the head of the bishop-elect, and the opened gospel book is placed over the omophorion and held by the first hierarch and his concelebrants. The *Apostolic Constitutions* (from the end of the 4th c.) attest to the practice of placing the gospel book over the head of the bishop-elect.[94] Saint Symeon of Thessalonica says that the gospel is Christ, who is the head of the Church. Acting in the place and in the figure of Christ (εἰς τόπον καὶ τύπον Χριστοῦ; *eis topon kai typon Christou*), the new bishop thus becomes the head of his local Church.[95]

The first hierarch then says out loud, *By the vote and approbation of the most holy metropolitans, archbishops, and bishops, the grace divine* . . . . We find here the same formula that is used for the other major ordinations. This was not originally a prayer of ordination but the text of a document certifying the ordination. In the late eighth century (as testified by the Barberini codex), the text that begins with the words *The grace divine* was read as at other ordinations, and the gospel book was put over the head of the bishop-elect only after this text was read.[96] After the thirteenth century, the phrase *By the vote and approbation of the most holy metropolitans, archbishops, and bishops* was added to the original sacred proclamation (*The grace divine*), in reference to the synodical election.[97] The clergy in the sanctuary, and then the chanters, respond by singing *Kyrie, eleison* thrice.

Then the first hierarch reads the two prayers of ordination (usually in a low voice). The first prayer: *O Master, Lord our God*, already attested in the Barberini manuscript,[98] refers to the three degrees of the ministry of the *episcopate* (*apostles, prophets, teachers*), already mentioned by Saint Paul: "God hath set some in the church, first apostles, secondarily prophets, thirdly teachers" (1 Cor 12.28). Episcopacy is therefore a divine institution, as highlighted by Saint Paul and the prayer of ordination. The ancient prayer found in the *Apostolic Constitutions* emphasized as well that "The institutions [are given] to the Church through the incarnation of thy Christ, with the testimony of the Comforter, by thine apostles and us, thy teachers, the

[94]*Apostolic Constitutions* 8.4.6 (SC 336:142; ANF 7:482).
[95]Symeon of Thessalonica, *De sacris ordinationibus* 206 (PG 155:416ab).
[96]*Barberini*, 165–167.
[97]For an example see the 14th century manuscript *Dionysiou 99* (Dmitrievsky, *Opisanie*, 2:271).
[98]*Barberini*, 165–67.

bishops established by thy grace."⁹⁹ The prayer stresses that the bishop-elect is *made worthy to come under the yoke of the Gospel*, that is to say, the mission to announce the good news of salvation and to ensure orthodoxy of faith in his see. The prayer emphasizes that Christ ordains the candidate *through the infusion, the power, and the grace of [the] Holy Spirit . . . as [he] strengthened [his] holy apostles and the prophets.* The prophets mentioned here are the New Testament prophets, the successors of the apostles and the predecessors of the bishops. In his commentary, Saint Symeon of Thessalonica also notes that Christ ordains through the bishop by dispensing the grace of the Holy Spirit.¹⁰⁰

After this first prayer, one of the concelebrating bishops says the litany, during which a special petition for the one ordaining and the one being ordained is added. During the litany, the first hierarch reads the second prayer of ordination, already attested in the Barberini manuscript (*O Lord our God*);¹⁰¹ this is more likely older than the first one.¹⁰² This second prayer points out that the bishop acts in the Church in the place and in the figure of Christ (εἰς τόπον καὶ τύπον Χριστοῦ; *eis topon kai typon Christou*). This prayer echoes the teaching of Saint Ignatius of Antioch who, in the early second century, wrote of the bishop as acting in the place and figure of Christ, and by stating that the bishop has access to his throne, it also echoes the words of St Symeon of Thessalonica, who in fact follows St Ignatius in his statement that the bishop is seated first as in the place of God, in his own expression "on the throne of God himself."¹⁰³ The prayer asks that he may be *an imitator of the True Pastor* (cf. Jn 10.11–16; Lk 15.4–7) and *a steward of the episcopal grace.* Finally, the prayer reminds the bishop of his teaching ministry, which is *the preaching of the Gospel.* For this reason, as we have said before, the ordination of the bishop takes place before the biblical readings and the homily at the Divine Liturgy.

After this prayer, the vesting takes place. In the current practice of the Ecumenical Patriarchate, the miter is given at the end of the Divine Liturgy, when the pastoral staff is presented to the newly ordained bishop.

---

⁹⁹*Apostolic Constitutions* 8.5.3 (SC 336:146; this is the author's translation; cf. the somewhat different rendering in ANF 7:482).

¹⁰⁰Symeon of Thessalonica, *De sacris ordinationibus* 246 (PG 155:465a).

¹⁰¹*Barberini*, 165–67.

¹⁰²Pentkovsky, op. cit., 123–27.

¹⁰³Ignatius of Antioch, *To the Magnesians* 6.1 (SC 10bis:82–84; PPS 49:46–47), and Symeon of Thessalonica, *De sacris ordinationibus* 207 (PG 155:420a).

After the vesting, the newly ordained bishop exchanges the kiss of peace with the first hierarch and all the concelebrating bishops, and then the Divine Liturgy continues normally. According to the current practice, the newly ordained bishop stands immediately after the first hierarch, although according to the ancient practice described in the *Apostolic Constitutions* (late 4th c.), he used to preside at the Divine Liturgy immediately after his ordination. In the current practice, if there happen to be other ordinations at the Divine Liturgy they are usually performed by the newly ordained bishop.

The enthronement of the newly ordained bishop used to occur immediately, when he would ascend his throne in the synthronon at the beginning of the Divine Liturgy at which he was to preside, as one can see in the *Apostolic Constitutions*. But in the Byzantine epoch it became a widespread practice to ordain bishops in the patriarchal church.[104] For this reason, a special rite of enthronement appeared, distinct from the liturgy of ordination. In this rite the newly ordained bishop is solemnly seated on his throne as he takes possession of his local Church. By the beginning of the fifteenth century, Saint Symeon of Thessalonica notes that "the enthronement was formerly celebrated solemnly in the same way that the enthronement of a patriarch occurs today."[105] This rite used to take place at the beginning of the Divine Liturgy, at the Trisagion, at the moment when the bishop ascends his throne in the synthronon. He was then seated thrice, as the assembly acclaimed him with the cry: *Axios!* This ancient Byzantine practice is still observed for the enthronement of the patriarchs of Moscow.[106] In the contemporary practice of the Ecumenical Patriarchate, the enthronement of bishops takes place during a doxology, with the newly ordained bishop presiding on his throne in the church; during this ceremony the decision of the Holy Synod to elect him to this see is read.

7. Awards and Ranks (*Offikia*)

Besides the prayers of ordination, we find in the *Euchologia* and *Archieratika* other prayers to elevate a clergyman to a certain rank of distinction because of his seniority or because of his particular duty. These prayers are not ordinations (χειροτονία; *cheirotonia*) properly speaking, since they are

---

[104]Cf. Neselovsky, 244–47.
[105]Symeon of Thessalonica, *De sacris ordinationibus* 216 (PG 155:428d).
[106]Ibid.

not elevating the candidate to another degree of priesthood; they confer only a distinction within his degree of priesthood. Nevertheless, each of these prayers is said with an imposition of the hand and therefore is considered a *cheirothesia* (χειροθεσία).

We find the *cheirothesia* of an archdeacon already mentioned in the euchologion manuscript *Alexandria 104* (14th c.),[107] the *cheirothesia* of a protopresbyter in the euchologion manuscript *Sinai gr. 1006* (15th c.),[108] and the *cheirothesia* of an igumen in the Barberini codex (late 8th c.).[109] The Greek *Archieratikon* gives additional prayers for the *cheirothesia* of an economos, found already in *Alexandria 104*,[110] and likewise the *cheirothesia* of an archimandrite (although the Slavonic *Archieratikon* prescribes the same prayer as for an igumen). In the Russian practice, these elevations take place during the Little Entrance at the Divine Liturgy. According to the Greek practice, they usually take place at the end of a service. The prayers are read over the clergyman by the bishop, who makes the sign of the cross over the head of the candidate thrice and places his hand on him.

Saint Symeon of Thessalonica mentions that the pectoral cross and the epigonation, which are the prerogatives of the bishop, were already awarded by the bishop to some senior priests and to archimandrites.[111] This practice prevails to the present day. These distinctions are also awarded by the bishop to the clergy at the Little Entrance of the Divine Liturgy.

The Orthodox Church in Russia developed many awards during the eighteenth and nineteenth centuries, often at the initiative of the Tsar or the Tsarina. Three initial awards—the epigonation, the jeweled cross, and the rank of protopresbyter—were doubled to produce three additional, lesser awards: the nabedrennik (a new type of rectangular epigonation, which is not worn by the bishop), the gold cross, and the rank of archpriest (протоиерей; *protoierei*).[112] The miter, until then the prerogative of the bishop, was also awarded to a few senior priests, and also the red or purple

---

[107]Dmitrievsky, 2:347.
[108]Dmitrievsky, 2:618.
[109]*Barberini*, 175–176.
[110]Dmitrievsky, 2:52.
[111]Symeon of Thessalonica, *Dialogue in Christ* 83 (PG 155:261d).
[112][In English, it is not common to transliterate протоиерей. Instead, the word "archpriest" was borrowed from Anglican use. This can be confusing to Russian and Greek speakers: архиерей in Russian, like the Greek ἀρχιερεύς, refers to a "hierarch," i.e., a bishop (in Scripture, this word refers to the "high priest" in the Temple in Jerusalem).—*Ed.*]

skufia (скуфия, *skufia*) and kamilavka (камилавка), although the use of the skufia during liturgical services fell out of use.[113] The title of *igumen*, which was until then exclusively used for the abbot of a monastery, became a distinction for monastic clergy equivalent to the rank of archpriest. The Moscow Patriarchate discontinued this award in 2011. For deacons, the award of a "double" orarion, distinct from the "simple" orarion worn by all deacons, was introduced, as well as the kamilavka (камилавка). Here is the complete list of the awards for priests, in chronological order, according to the practice of the Church of Russia:

Table 3.2: Clergy Awards in the Russian Tradition

Married clergy	Monastic clergy
1. Nabedrennik	1. Nabedrennik
2. (Skufia [скуфия])	
3. Kamilavka (камилавка)	
4. Gold cross	2. Gold cross
5. Archpriest (протоиерей)	3. (Igumen)
6. Epigonation	4. Epigonation
7. Jeweled cross	5. Jeweled cross
8. Miter	
9. Protopresbyter	6. Archimandrite (with miter)

---

[113][The Russian Orthodox Church Outside of Russia is the only church that still retains this practice.—*Ed.*]

CHAPTER FOUR

The Mysteries of Healing

Introduction

In patristic literature, the Church is often presented as a spiritual hospital. St Ignatius of Antioch (beginning of the 2nd c.) writes to the Ephesians that "there is one Physician [ἰατρός] fleshly and spiritual, begotten and unbegotten, God in the flesh, true life in death, both from Mary and from God, first suffering and then impassible, Jesus Christ, our Lord."[1] A famous document of the early Church, the *Epistle to Diognetus* (end of 2nd c.), says that God "revealed the Savior who is able to save even those things which it was [formerly] impossible to save . . . He desired to lead us to trust in his kindness, to esteem him our . . . Healer."[2] Commenting on the Epistle to the Romans, St Cyril of Alexandria (+444) says that "As in Adam human nature became ill of corruption through disobedience . . . in Christ, it recovers its health."[3]

Such an understanding has biblical roots, since the gospels present to us the mystery of salvation accomplished by our Lord and Savior Jesus Christ through the different miracles that he worked, miracles that healed both the body and the soul. Christ appears both in the gospel and in the mysteries of the Church as the physician, the healer. Christ himself uses the analogy between salvation and healing while saying: *They that be whole need not a physician, but they that are sick . . . for I am not come to call the righteous, but sinners to repentance* (Mt 9.12–13). This also explains the traditional patristic interpretation of the parable of the Good Samaritan (Lk 10.25–37), beginnning with St Irenaeus of Lyons (2nd c.) and Origen (3rd c.), who saw in the Samaritan a figure of Jesus Christ and in the inn a figure of the Church.[4]

---

[1]Ignatius of Antioch, *Epistle to the Ephesians* 7.2 (SC 10:64; *Ignatius of Antioch: The Letters*, PPS 49:32–33).

[2]*Epistle to Diognetus* 9.6 (SC 33:74; translation by the author; cf. the translation in ANF 1:28).

[3]Cyril of Alexandria, *Commentary on the Epistle to the Romans* (PG 74:789b).

[4]Irenaeus of Lyons, *Against Heresies* 3.17.3 (SC 211:336; ANF 1:445) and Origen, *Homily 34 on Luke* (PG 13:1886–88; Origen, *Homilies on Luke, Fragments on Luke*, tr. Joseph

The liturgy of the Orthodox Church adopted this vision. In the prayer of inclination of the Divine Liturgy of Saint John Chrysostom, our Lord Jesus Christ is invoked as *the Physician of our souls and bodies*. The mysteries accomplished by the Church are always directed at healing the body and the soul.[5] For this reason, the Church is concerned not only about the physical illnesses of the body, but also, and most of all, about the illnesses of the soul, which are nothing other than sin. With this in mind, it is not surprising that the monk Job, author of the first Byzantine treatise on the seven sacraments (13th c.), lists under the seventh sacrament the two mysteries of holy unction (εὐχέλαιον) and of repentance (confession of sins),[6] which we shall now study.

The Orthodox Church traditionally applies the *therapeutic* model of the hospital to the sacrament of penitence. Sin is regarded as a spiritual sickness and therefore penance serves as the medicine that brings restoration to wholeness. Canon 102 of the Council in Trullo understands the sacrament of confession in precisely such medical terms, by speaking of diseases, treatment, remedy, patient, physician, and healing:

> For the disease of sin is not simple, but various and multiform, and it germinates many mischievous offshoots, from which much evil is diffused, and it proceeds further until it is checked by the power of the physician. Wherefore he who professes the science of spiritual medicine ought first of all to consider the disposition of him who has sinned, and to see whether he tends to health or (on the contrary) provokes to himself disease by his own behaviour.[7]

Such an understanding of the sacrament of confession can be linked with the sacrament of holy unction, based on the teaching of the holy Apostle James who said, *Is any sick among you? Let him call for the priests*[8] of the church, and let them pray over him, anointing him with oil in the name of the Lord. And the prayer of faith shall save the sick, and the Lord will raise him up. And if he have committed sins, they shall be forgiven him

---

T. Lienhard, S.J., *The Fathers of the Church* 94 (Washington, DC: Catholic University of America Press, 1996), 137–139.

[5]Cf. Symeon of Thessalonica, *De Sancto Euchelæo* 290 (PG 155:525a).

[6]Job Hamartolos, *On the Seven Mysteries of the Church, Cod. 64 Supplementi graeci Parisiensis*, fol. 239, quoted by M. Jugie, *Theologica Dogmatica Christianorum Orientalium*, vol. 3 (Paris, 1930), 17–18.

[7]Joannou, *Discipline générale antique*, 1.1:239–41 (English in NPNF² 14:408).

[8]The Greek word is "presbyters" (πρεσβυτέρους, *presbyterous*), KJV translates *elders*.

(Jas 5.14–15). Confession and holy unction are mysteries of spiritual and physical healing.

1. Confession

1.1.Historical Overview

In the Early Church, baptism was considered the only way to be absolved from sins. For this reason, we still confess *one baptism for the remission of sins* in the Symbol of Faith. For the same reason, in that epoch baptism was often conferred at a very advanced age. It is also the reason why a controversy arose at that time concerning the readmission into the Church of sinners (the so-called *lapsi*, those who had fallen into apostasy). Finally, it was universally accepted that we can reintroduce sinners into the communion of the Church, and thus the mystery of penitence appeared. Saint Symeon of Thessalonica writes that "through penitence, we correct ourselves from our new sins. The gift of penitence was given because, after baptism, the only way to call us to salvation . . . is the confession of sins and the estrangement from evil."[9]

The mystery of penitence is perhaps the most complicated case of sacramental development.[10] Following Archbishop Georges Wagner, we can distinguish three periods in the development of the practice of confession.[11]

First is the classical period, which is closely linked with the canons of the ancient councils and the church fathers. Penitential discipline dealt mostly with major sins: apostasy, murder, and adultery; and since confession dealt with such great sins, it was a very rare event. It had three stages: exclusion from the Church community (excommunication), a period of penance (ἐπιτιμία), and finally, the reintegration of the penitent into the Church community (reconciliation). The power Christ gave to the Church to bind and loose (cf. Mt 16.19) was interpreted precisely as the power to excommunicate and to reconcile. The time of penance (ἐπιτιμία) was

[9]Symeon of Thessalonica, *Dialogue in Christ* 39 (PG 155:179b).
[10]Cf. M. Arranz, "Les prières pénitentielles de la tradition byzantine, 1ère partie," *OCP* 57 (1991): 89.
[11]G. Wagner, "Penitential Discipline in the Oriental Tradition" (in German), *Liturgie et rémission des péchés. Conférences Saint-Serge. 20e Semaine d'Etudes Liturgiques*, A. Triacca, ed. (Rome, 1975), 251–64 [="La discipline pénitentielle dans la tradition orientale," in *La liturgie, expérience de l'Eglise. Etudes liturgiques*, Analecta Sergiana 1 (Paris: Presses Saint-Serge, 2003), 67–80]. See also: J. Erickson, "Penitential discipline in the Orthodox Canonical Tradition," in *The Challenge of our Past* (Crestwood, NY: St Vladimir's Seminary Press, 1991), 23–38.

not regarded as punishment but as therapy. It was a period of trial, during which the Christian had to prove his willingness to reintegrate into the community. This stage had four progressive steps of penance: mourning (πρόσκλαυσις, *prosklausis*), hearing (ἀκρόασις, *akroasis*), prostrating (ὑπόπτωσις, *hyoptōsis*), and standing (σύστασις, *systasis*). Penitents in each of these stages occupied different places in the church building and participated in different parts of the divine service: mourners would stand outside the door of the church, hearers were inside the door of the church in the narthex, prostrators would stand within the door of the nave but attend only the liturgy of catechumens, and finally, standers would stand in the nave for the whole service but not receive Communion.[12] The Divine Liturgy of the *Apostolic Constitutions* (*c.* 380) contains a prayer for the penitents after the prayer for the catechumens and their dismissal. After this prayer the penitents were dismissed,[13] in conformance with the prescription of Canon 19 of the Council of Laodicea (end of 4th c.).[14] At the beginning of this period confession was public, since it implied that sin impaired the relation of the sinner to the entire Church community.

The second period begins with the appearance of the *Kanonarion* attributed to John the Faster, patriarch of Constantinople (582–95), though some scholars think that this document is in fact from the eighth or ninth century. This work is a collection of instructions for confessors, meant to help them to apply the penance (ἐπιτιμία) of the ancient canons in new situations, in a new context: it reduced considerably the length of excommunication, which now often replaced by acts of piety (prostrations, fasting, etc.); it also reduced other penances prescribed by the ancient canons, especially those of St Basil (+379). By the time the *Kanonarion* appeared, confession had already become private and personal, and the secrecy of confession was enhanced. This led to the creation of special "orders" (ἀκολουθίαι, *akolouthiai*) of confession in Byzantium. The oldest ones that are known to us are from the tenth century.

Up to that time, *Euchologia* contained only separate prayers for the penitents,[15] as we can see in the Barberini codex, which contains only two

[12]Cf. Canon 11 of St Gregory of Neocaesarea the Wonderworker (Joannou, *Discipline générale antique*, 2:29; NPNF² 14:602).
    [13]*Apostolic Constitutions* 8.6.3–8.11.6 (SC 336:152–74; ANF 7:483–86).
    [14]Joannou, *Discipline générale antique*, 1.2:138.
    [15]M. Arranz, "Les prières pénitentielles de la tradition byzantine (Les sacrements de la restoration de l'ancien Euchologe constantinopolitain: II-2)," in *OCP* 57 (1991): 87–143; *OCP* 57 (1991): 309–29; and *OCP* 58 (1992): 23–82; J. Getcha, "Une prière pour ceux qui

prayers: one for those who repent (ἐπὶ μετανοούντων, *epi metanoountōn*): *O God our Savior, who by thy prophet Nathan*, and one for those who confess (ἐπὶ ἐξομολογουμένων, *epi exomologoumenōn*): *O Lord our God, who hast given the remission of sins to Peter and the harlot because of their tears*, but no order (ἀκολουθία, *akolouthia*).[16] These prayers ask for God's forgiveness and grace for the penitent undergoing spiritual therapy, which included an abstention from Holy Communion during a certain period of time. We find the same two prayers in *Paris Coislin 213* (1027), as well as a prayer for those who are released from penance (ἐπὶ τῶν ἐξ ἐπιτιμίων λυομένων, *epi tōn ex epitimiōn lyomenōn*): *O deeply compassionate Lord, who art good and the lover of mankind*.[17] Besides these prayers, we find a very large variety of prayers for penitence in the manuscript tradition of the *Euchologion*.[18]

Beginning in the tenth century, we find two types of orders of confession in euchologia: a *presbyteral* type, wherein confession is received by an ordained minister, and a *monastic* type, wherein confession is witnessed by a monk who is not ordained.[19] The second type is much influenced by the *Kanonarion* and confession is made according to a very long, very detailed list of questions. This fact indicates that this type of confession was originally a very rare, exceptional event in the life of the penitent: perhaps before entering a monastery or before monastic tonsure, the postulant had to confess all the sins of his previous life to his sponsor (ἀναδεκόμενος, *anadekomenos*),[20] who was not necessarily a priest. But gradually, through the centuries, the frequency of confession increased.

Later, the power received from Christ to bind and loose (cf. Mt 16.19) was given to the confessor. In the eleventh century, St Symeon the New Theologian states: "Before the monks, the bishops alone by succession from the

se confessent d'un Eucologe slave pré-moghilien: Quelques implications théologiques," *La prière liturgique. Conférences Saint-Serge. 47e Semaine d'Etudes Liturgiques* (Rome: CLV-Edizioni Liturgiche, 2001), 137–49.

[16]*Barberini*, 194–95.

[17]Arranz, Euchologion, 366–367 and 360; Dmitrievsky, *Opisanie*, 2:1022.

[18]Cf. the article by M. Arranz mentioned above, as well as: A. I. Almazov, *Tainaya ispoved' v Provoslavnoi Vostochnoi Tserkvi. Opyt vneshnei istorii: Issledovanie preimushchestvenno po rukopisyam*, 3 vols. (Odessa, 1894).

[19]E. Herman, "Il più antico penitenziale greco," *OCP* 19 (1933): 71–127; A. Raes, "Les formulaires grecs du rite de pénitence," *Mélanges en l'honneur de Mgr Michel Andrieu* (Strasbourg: Palais Universitaire, 1956), 365–72; M. Arranz, "Les formulaires de confession dans la tradition byzantine (Les sacrements de la restoration de l'ancien Euchologe constantinopolitain: II-3)," *OCP* 58 (1992): 423–59, *OCP* 59 (1993): 63–89, 357–86.

[20]It is interesting to note that this is the same term that is used for sponsors in the mystery of baptism.

apostles had the power to bind and loose. This redoubtable function . . . was then transferred to the elect people of God, that is, the monks."[21] By the fifteenth century, confession was received only by an ordained priest. St Symeon of Thessalonica rejects the practice of confession received by an unordained monk and underlines that the confessor has to be a priest since he has to pronounce the prayer of absolution (εὐχή συγχωρήσεως, *euchē synchorēseōs*).[22] The *presbyteral* type of order of confession had a liturgical form (with psalms, litany, and readings of epistle and gospel, etc.), which perhaps seems to indicate that it was at least partially public; this type did not have any examination.[23] But from the twelfth century onwards, this order of confession was influenced by the lists of questions derived from the monastic type, with a particular insistence on carnal sins.

The third period in the history of the practice of confession corresponds to modern times (starting at least in the 18th c.). The characteristic feature of this period, according to Archbishop George Wagner, is the almost complete absence of the application of penance (ἐπιτιμία, *epitimia*).[24] The practice of confession became identified with spiritual direction, and in consequence it became a frequent event in the life of the believer, while remaining entirely private.

1.2. The Order of Confession

Today the practice of confession is private in the Orthodox Church. In some countries (like Russia, Ukraine, Romania) it is compulsory for the faithful to confess before each reception of Holy Communion. Consequently, confession most often takes place immediately before the Divine Liturgy, or on the eve before, after or even during the evening service. In other countries (as in Greece or in much of the Orthodox diaspora), confession is not required before each Holy Communion, and in these places confession takes place apart from the celebration of the Divine Liturgy, at a quieter and more peaceful moment.[25]

[21]Symeon the New Theologian, *Letter on Confession* 11 (Karl Holl, *Enthusiasmus und Bussgewalt beim griechischen Mönchtum* [Leipzig, 1898], 120); quoted by Erickson, "Penitential discipline in the Orthodox Canonical Tradition," 32.

[22]Syméon of Thessalonica, *De sacris ordinationibus* 250 (PG 155:468cd).

[23]M. Arranz, "Les formulaires de confession," II-3, *OCP* 58 (1992): 426–31; J. Getcha, "Une prière pour ceux qui se confessent," 141–43.

[24]Wagner, "La discipline pénitentielle dans la tradition orientale," 79–80. Concerning the contemporary practice of confession, see also: C. Vogel, "La discipline pénitentielle dans l'Église orthodoxe de Grèce," *Revue des Sciences Religieuses* 27 (1953): 374–99.

[25]Concerning the pastoral problems linked with the practice of confession, see our

As Father Alexander Schmemann explained in a famous report: "When the Communion of the entire congregation at each Liturgy, as an act expressing their very participation in the Liturgy, ceased to be a self-evident norm and was replaced by the practice of a very infrequent, usually once-a-year, Communion, it became natural for the latter to be preceded by the sacrament of penance, i.e., confession and reconciliation with the Church through the prayer of absolution."[26] Schmemann emphasized that "it is therefore of paramount importance for us to understand that the transformation of the sacrament of penance into an obligatory condition for Communion not only contradicts Tradition, but obviously mutilates it." While encouraging "a more frequent and, ultimately, regular, Communion," he suggested that "the relationship between the rhythm of confession and that of Communion must be left to the decision of the priest, confession remaining regular, however, and heard not less than once a month."

Our contemporary printed euchologia give an order (*akolouthia*) for confession. We can note some differences in the order between the Greek[27] and Slavonic[28] liturgical books, as shown in the table below:

Table 4.1: The Order of Confession

Greek liturgical books	Slavonic liturgical books
1. Litany	
2. Prayer: *O Lord Jesus Christ, Son of the Living God, the Shepherd and the Lamb*	
3. Trisagion . . . Our Father	1. Trisagion . . . Our Father
4. Psalm 50	2. Psalm 50
5. Troparia: *Have mercy on us, O Lord*	3. Troparia: *Have mercy on us, O Lord*

article: J. Getcha, "Confession and Spiritual Direction in the Orthodox Church," *St Vladimir's Theological Quarterly* 51 (2007): 203–20. On the relation of confession and Holy Communion, see Nenad Milosevic, *To Christ and the Church: The Divine Eucharist as the All-Encompassing Mystery of the Church,* 173–86, and Alexander Schmemann, "Report to the Holy Synod of the Orthodox Church in America," https://oca.org/holy-synod/encyclicals/on-confession-and-Communion.

[26]Schmemann, "Report to the Holy Synod of the Orthodox Church in America."
[27]Cf. *Μικρὸν Εὐχολόγιον* (Athens, 1996), 162–66.
[28]Cf. *Trebnik* (Moscow: Sretensky Monastery, 2000) 106–28.

118   THE EUCHOLOGION UNVEILED

6. Lord, have mercy (40 times)	4. Lord, have mercy (40 times)
7. Prayer: *O God, our Savior, who by thy prophet Nathan*	5. Prayer: *O God, our Savior, who by thy prophet Nathan*
	6. Other prayer: *O Lord Jesus Christ, Son of the Living God, the Shepherd and the Lamb*
8. Confession	7. Confession (with questioning by the confessor)
9. Prayer: *May God who didst pardon David*	8. Prayer: *O Lord God of salvation of thy servant*
	9. Absolution: *May Our Lord and God Jesus Christ, by the grace and compassion of his love for mankind*
10. Dismissal	10. Dismissal

While the Greek liturgical books prescribe a litany at the beginning, the Slavonic liturgical books start directly with the Trisagion. The prayer: *O Lord Jesus Christ, Son of the Living God, the Shepherd and the Lamb* appeared in the tenth century, not in Constantinople, but in the periphery, and since then it has known a tremendous popularity in the manuscript tradition, as a prayer both before and after confession, most likely because of its reference to Christ's promise in Matthew 18.18: "Whatsoever ye shall bind on earth shall be bound in heaven: and whatsoever ye shall loose on earth shall be loosed in heaven."[29] The prayer uses the classical phrase, made up of three verbs for the remission of sins: remit, forgive, and pardon (ἄνες, ἄφες, συγχώρησον), found in the *Horologion* at the service of the Typika. In some manuscripts, it is identified as a prayer of absolution before Communion, most likely because of the reference to the Lamb of God who takes away the sins of the world (cf. Jn 1.29). This prayer is said before the Trisagion according to the Greek liturgical books, while according to the Slavonic books it is said after the prayer: *O God, our Savior, who by thy prophet Nathan*, which itself is the ancient prayer for those who repent (ἐπὶ μετανοούντων) found in the Barberini manuscript.[30]

[29]M. Arranz, "Les prières pénitentielles de la tradition byzantine (Les sacrements de la restoration de l'ancien Euchologe constantinopolitain: II-2)," *OCP* 57 (1991): 102–09; cf. A. Dmitrievsky, *Opisanie*, 2:202, 234, 379, 427, 472, 485, 504, 524, 579, 636, 654, 665.
[30]*Barberini*, 194–95.

All euchologia suggest that the confession of the penitent is to be introduced by an exhortation from the confessor, who is to stress that the penitent is confessing to God: *Brother, inasmuch thou camest to God and to me . . .* in the Greek liturgical books, and: *Behold, my child, Christ invisibly stands here to hear your confession . . .* in the Slavonic liturgical books. The latter suggest a series of questions inspired by *Kanonarion* that the confessor is to ask the penitent.

The most significant difference between the Greek and the Slavonic liturgical books is the prayer of absolution that we find after the confession of sins. The Slavonic liturgical books give two prayers: The first: *O Lord God of salvation of thy servants*, is a tenth century prayer (originally not from Constantinople, but from the periphery), which asks God to reconcile and reunite the penitent with the Church.[31] Thus it used to be a prayer read at the end of the period of penance.

This prayer is then followed by a prayer that pronounces absolution, in which the confessor declares that he is forgiving and absolving the penitent. This prayer was composed by Peter Moghila, the Metropolitan of Kiev, who was inspired by the *Roman Ritual* of Pope Paul V (1614), and it was introduced into his *Trebnik*, published in Kiev in 1646.[32] Later that century, this prayer of absolution was adopted during the revision of liturgical books undertaken by the Russian Patriarch Nikon.[33] The absolution prayer written by Metropolitan Peter Moghila states:

> *May our Lord and God, Jesus Christ, by the grace and compassion of his love toward mankind, forgive thee, my child, N., all thy transgressions. And I, an unworthy priest, through his power given unto me, forgive thee and absolve thee from all thy sins, in the name of the Father, and of the Son, and of the Holy Spirit. Amen.*[34]

[31]M. Arranz, "Les prières pénitentielles de la tradition byzantine," *OCP* 57 (1991): 114–17; cf. A. Dmitrievsky, *Opisanie*, 2:244, 643.

[32]Peter Moghila, *Euchologion*, 356–57 (the title page of this work gives both *Euchologion* and *Trebnik*; the text may refer to it by either title, but in the footnotes we will use *Euchologion*). Cf. A. Wenger, "Les influences du rituel de Paul V sur le Trebnik de Pierre Moghila," *Mélanges en l'honneur de Mgr Michel Andrieu*, 477–99.

[33]N. Uspensky, "The Collision of Two Theologies in the Revision of Russian Liturgical Books in the Seventeenth Century," in his *Evening Worship in the Orthodox Church* (Crestwood, NY: St Vladimir's Seminary Press, 1985), 191–240, particularly 226–39.

[34]Peter Moghila, Euchologion, 356–57 (*GBN* 1:129).

This prayer contains the words: *I . . . forgive thee and absolve thee,* inspired by the Latin formula *ego te absolvo* (*I absolve thee*). It refers to the power given to the confessor to loose and bind sins in Matthew 16.19 and John 20.23. This prayer replaced an earlier one, which the Slavonic *Trebnik* preserves in the rite of confession and Communion of a sick person.[35] The earlier prayer of absolution in Slavic *Euchologia* before Moghila stated:

> *O Lord our God, who forgavest the sins of Peter and the Harlot through their tears, and didst justify the Publican who acknowledged his own iniquities: Do Thou accept the confession of Thy servant and, as Thou art good, overlook his sins by which he has transgressed against Thee, whether voluntarily or involuntarily, whether by word, deed, or thought, for Thou alone hast the power to remit sins. For Thou art a merciful and compassionate God who lovest mankind, and unto Thee do we send up glory: with Thy Father, who is without origin, and and Thy most holy, good, and life-giving Spirit, now and ever, and unto the ages of ages. Amen.[36]*

This is the ancient prayer for those who confess their sins (ἐπὶ ἐξομολογουμένων) found in the eighth century Barberini codex,[37] and, as just noted, still found in the Slavonic books in the service of Communion for a sick person.[38] We note that this ancient prayer is deprecatory, since the priest declares that God alone can remit sins (referring to Mt 9.6, Mk 2.10, and Lk 5.24), and he presents himself as an intercessor who prays for the remission of sins of the penitent. This ancient prayer reflects a more therapeutic approach, while the prayer of Peter Moghila implies rather a juridical approach.[39]

---

[35]This was not the case in the *Trebnik* of Peter Moghila; see *Euchologion*, 329–30.

[36]J. Getcha, "Une prière pour ceux qui se confessent d'un Euchologe slave pré-moghilien: Quelques implications théologiques," *La prière liturgique. Conférences Saint-Serge. 47e Semaine d'Etudes Liturgiques,* , A. Triacca and A. Pistoia, eds, BEL 115 (Rome, 2001), 137–49; translation in *A Small Book of Needs, compiled by the Brotherhood of Saint Tikhon of Zadonsk, second edition* (South Canaan, PA: St Tikhon's Monastery Press, 2012), 35–36.

[37]*Barberini,* 194–95.

[38]Cf. *Trebnik,* Part 1, Moscow, 1991, p. 127–28.

[39]See my article: J. Getcha, "Une prière pour ceux qui se confessent," 137–49. See also: A. Lossky, "Les prières byzantines de confession: repentir et rémission des péchés par miséricorde divine," *La prière liturgique: Conférences Saint-Serge: 47e Semaine d'Etudes Liturgiques,* 151–163; Id., "'Remettre les péchés': quelques aspects liturgiques et doctrinaux de la confession et de l'absolution," Θυσία αἰνέσεως. *Mélanges liturgiques offerts à la mémoire de l'archevêque Georges Wagner,* J. Getcha and A. Lossky, eds, Analecta Sergiana 2 (Paris: Presses Saint-Serge, 2005), 173–85.

The prayer of absolution found in the contemporary Greek *Euchologion* is different. Like the ancient prayer for those who confess their sins (ἐπὶ ἐξομολογουμένων, *epi exomologoumenōn*), it is also deprecatory:

> God it was who pardoned David through Nathan the Prophet when he confessed his sins, Peter who wept bitterly for his denial, and the Harlot weeping at his feet, the Publican and the Prodigal [son]; may the same God forgive thee all things, through me a sinner, both in this world and in the world to come, and set thee uncondemned before his dread Judgement Seat. Now, having no further care for the sins which thou hast confessed, depart in peace.[40]

This is a twelfth-century prayer,[41] which was later slightly revised by the interpolation of the phrase "through me a sinner."

The service of confession concludes with the usual dismissal.

2. Holy Unction

2.1. Historical Overview

The origin of the practice of anointing the sick, which led to the establishment of the sacrament of holy unction (εὐχέλαιον) goes back to the injunction of the holy Apostle James: "Is any sick among you? let him call for the elders [presbyters] of the church; and let them pray over him, anointing him with oil in the name of the Lord: And the prayer of faith shall save the sick [person], and the Lord shall raise him up; and if he have committed sins, they shall be forgiven him" (Jas 5.14–15). In view of this biblical passage, one can understand how the service of holy unction became a service for the sick, served by several priests (presbyters), not only for the healing of the body but for the remission of sins as well. Saint Symeon of Thessalonica actually sees in these words of Saint James an apostolic practice that was founded by Christ, who "called unto him the twelve, and began to send them forth by two and two; and gave them power over unclean spirits . . . And they cast out many devils, and anointed with oil many that were sick, and healed them" (Mk 6.7–13). Symeon emphasizes that this

---

[40]Translation from *A Small Book of Needs*, 57.

[41]M. Arranz, "Les prières pénitentielles de la tradition byzantine (Les sacrements de la restoration de l'ancien Euchologe constantinopolitain: II-2)," *OCP* 58 (1992): 28–31; cf. A. Dmitrievsky, *Opisanie*, 2:472, 643, 654.

sacrament is given to those who repent, for the healing of the body and the soul of the sick.[42]

The anointing of the sick is already attested in the early Church. Some patristic sources, such as Origen (3rd c.),[43] St John Chrysostom (4th c.),[44] and St Cyril of Alexandria (5th c.)[45] refer to it by mentioning St James' words (Jas 5.14–15).[46] Liturgical and canonical documents such as the *Apostolic Tradition*[47] and the *Apostolic Constitutions*[48] from the end of the fourth century, and the *Testament of the Lord* (5th c.),[49] even give us the texts of the prayer used to bless the oil for the anointing of the sick. The ancient *Euchologion of Serapion* (4th c.) also gives a prayer over the oil for the sick.[50] These sources indicate that the anointing of the sick was performed with a single prayer in the early Church;[51] this is indicated also by the etymology of the name of the sacrament, εὐχέλαιον (*euchelaion*): prayer (εὐχή, *euchē*) for the oil (ἐλαίον, *elaion*).

The earliest manuscript of the Byzantine *Euchologion*, the Barberini codex, does not provide such a developed service as the one found in our contemporary euchologia. It contains only five prayers: three prayers over a sick person (εὐχὴ ἐπὶ ἀρρώστου, *euchē epi arrōstou*)—*O Holy Father, Physician of souls and bodies . . . O God mighty and merciful . . .* and *O Lord,*

[42]Symeon of Thessalonica, *Dialogue in Christ* 56 (PG 155:204bc).
[43]Origen, *Homily 2 on Leviticus* (SC 286:110; Origen, *Homilies on Leviticus 1–16*, tr. Gary Wayne Barkley, The Fathers of the Church Series 83 [Washington, DC: Catholic University of America Press, 1990], 47–48).
[44]John Chrysostom, *On the Priesthood* 3.6 (SC 272:154; PPS 1:74).
[45]Saint Cyril of Alexandria, *On Worship in Spirit and in Truth* 6 (PG 68:644).
[46]Paul Meyendorff, *The Anointing of the Sick*, Orthodox Liturgy Series 1 (Crestwood, NY: St Vladimir's Seminary Press, 2009), 31–61. See as well: T. Chronz, *Die Feier des Heiligen Öles nach Jerusalemer Ordnung. Mit dem Text des slavischen Codex Hilferding 21 der Russischen Nationalbibliothek in Sankt Petersburg sowie georgischen Übersetzungen palästinischer und konstantinopolitanischer Quellen. Einführung. Edition. Kommentar*, Jerusalemer Theologisches Forum, Band 18 (Münster: Aschendorff Verlag, 2012); Nenad Milosevic, *To Christ and the Church*, 105–24.
[47]*Apostolic Tradition* 5 (SC 11:33–34; PPS 54:90–92).
[48]*Apostolic Constitutions* 8.29 (SC 336:232; ANF 7:494).
[49]*Testament of the Lord* 1.25 (translated in P. Meyendorff, *The Anointing of the Sick*, 33–34, and more recently in *The Testament of the Lord: Worship & Discipline in the Early Church*, translated, with Introduction and Notes by Alistair C. Stewart, PPS 58 [Yonkers, NY: St Vladimir's Seminary Press, 2018], 103, where the section is designated 1.24).
[50]*Euchologion of Serapion*, Prayer 33 (translated in Meyendorff, *The Anointing of the Sick*, 35).
[51]I. Phountoulis, Ἀκολουθία τοῦ εὐχελαίου, Κείμενα Λειτουργικῆς 15 (Thessalonica, 1978), 5.

Lord all-holy . . . —and two over the oil for a sick person (εὐχὴ ἐπὶ ἐλαίου ἀρρώστου, *euchē epi elaiou arrōstou*): *O Lord, who through thy mercy and compassion* . . . and *O Lord great in mercy and rich in goodness. . . .*[52] Nothing is said about how the anointing was actually done.

In *Coislin 213* (1027), we find holy unction performed by seven priests on seven consecutive days in connection with the Divine Liturgy.[53] The service takes place "in the temple of the house" (ἐν τῷ ναῷ τῆς οἰκίας, *en tō naō tēs oikias*). This is commonly understood as a domestic church, but perhaps it could be interpreted also as a chapel located near the house. Such small chapels still exist in Greece today. Of the seven priests, the one who is going to serve the Divine Liturgy serves the prothesis. Then, he gives the blessing: *Blessed is our God*, and Psalm 50 is said. The priest takes the oil, pours it into a new lamp, and after saying: *Let us pray to the Lord*, he says the prayer: *O Lord, in thy mercy and compassion* (the fourth prayer of the Barberini manuscript). This is repeated by each one of the seven priests. Then the priest who served the prothesis begins the Divine Liturgy. After the Trisagion, following the prokeimenon: *I said, Lord have mercy on me*, comes the epistle with the injunction of St James (Jas 5.10–16), then the Alleluia with the verse *Look down on me and have mercy on me*, and the gospel reading that describes Christ sending his apostles to anoint the sick to heal them (Mk 6.7–13). The Communion hymn is: *I will receive the cup of salvation*. After the prayer behind the ambo, the priests go the house of the sick person, singing the troparion: *As thou hast a fountain of healings*. The priests, starting from the one who served the Divine Liturgy, say the prayer: *O Holy Father, Physician of souls and bodies* (the first prayer in the Barberini codex). Then they anoint the sick person and all those present in the house, by making the sign of the cross on the forehead, the breast, and the hands. Troparia are sung during the anointing: *As ye have a fountain of healings . . . O holy unmercenaries . . . The grace of healings. . . .* The sign of the cross is made with the holy oil on each door of the house and the kitchen. This general anointing is followed by a gospel reading (Lk 19.1–10), the litany, and the dismissal. After the dismissal, the priests return to the

[52]*Barberini*, 192–94. Cf. G. Filias, *Les prières pour les malades et sur l'huile de l'onction dans l'Euchologe Barberini grec 336* (Athens, 1997). [Without specification of source for individual items, translations of the elements of this service are derived from *The Great Book of Needs*, 1:189–236, while translations of elements not found in the contemporary rite are the author's own. For a translation of the contemporary rite in modern literary English, see Paul Meyendorff, *The Anointing of the Sick*, 113–184.—Ed.]

[53]A. Dmitrievsky, *Opisanie*, 2:1017–19.

chapel of the house while saying: *I will bless the Lord at all times* (Ps 33), and the bread (antidoron) is broken and distributed. This order is repeated for seven days. During Great Lent, the Divine Liturgy was replaced by the Liturgy of Presanctified Gifts.

A similar rite is described in *Sinai gr. 973* (12th c.).[54] This rite prescribes that seven priests gather to serve Vespers, Pannychis with a special canon, and Matins with a special canon. After Matins, the seven priests serve the Divine Liturgy in seven different churches "in the name of Archangel Michael"; this is likely owing to the Byzantine tradition that the Archangel Michael was the angel who came down at the pool of the Sheep Gate (cf. Jn 5.4).[55] Then the seven priests gather in one church where a rather complicated "order of the holy oil" takes place.

The priest who served in that church says: *Blessed is our God,* while he mixes holy water from Theophany with wine and oil in an empty lamp. The same is done by each one of the seven priests for his own lamp. Then the deacon intones the litany. When the deacon has said: *That he will deliver him,* the priest says the prayer: *For thou art a great and wondrous God, thou keepest thy covenant and thy mercy unto them that love thee.* The priest then makes the sign of the cross with his fingers over the oil and says the prayer: *Let this oil, O Lord . . .* Then the deacon continues the litany: *Help us, save us,* adding special petitions. Then the priest says the prayer: *O God, great and most-high, who art worshiped by all creation.*

This is followed by the Trisagion, the Our Father, and Psalm 50. Then the first antiphon is sung: *Blessed is the man,* with the refrain: *Help me, O Lord.* This is followed by the penitential troparia: *Have mercy on us, O Lord.* Then the first priest intones the litany, at the end of which he says the prayer: *O Lord our God, who art enthroned on the Cherubim.* This priest then takes the wick from the lamp, makes the sign of the cross with it three times over the holy oil, and lights it.

This action is followed once again by the Trisagion, the Our Father, and Psalm 50. Then the second antiphon is sung: *O Lord my God, in thee have I hoped,* with the refrain: *Through the intercessions.* Other penitential troparia are then sung. Then the second priest says the litany with the prayer: *O Lord, in thy mercy and compassion* (the fourth prayer in the Barberini codex). This

---

[54]A. Dmitrievsky, *Opisanie,* 2:101–09.
[55]In the *Pentecostarion,* the canon at Matins for the Sunday of the Paralytic invokes Saint Michael the Archangel.

priest then takes the wick from the lamp, makes the sign of the cross with it three times over the holy oil of his lamp, and then lights it.

This sequence of Trisagion, Our Father, Psalm 50, antiphon with refrain, prayer, and blessing with the lamp wick, is repeated by the remaining priests (even if there are only two or three).

The third antiphon is: *I will hear thee, O Lord*, with the refrain: *Thou hast heard me, O Lord*, and the third prayer is: *Send forth, O Lord, the richness of thy mercy on the fruit of this olive-tree*; the fourth antiphon is: *The Lord is my shepherd*, with the refrain: *Have mercy on me, O Lord*, and the fourth prayer is: *Have mercy on me, O Lord*; the fifth antiphon is: *Judge me, O Lord*, with the refrain: *Help me, O Lord*, and the fifth prayer is: *O Lord great in mercy and rich in goodness* (the fifth prayer of the Barberini manuscript); the sixth antiphon is: *I have hoped in thee, O Lord*, with the refrain: *Deliver us, O Lord*, and the sixth prayer is *O Lord, in thy mercy and compassion* (the fourth prayer of the Barberini codex); the seventh antiphon is: *Waiting, I waited for the Lord*, with the refrain: *Hear me, O Lord,*[56] and the seventh prayer is: *O Good One, most merciful, most compassionate, Creator, King.*

And when each one has completed the prayers to be said and lit his lamp, the seven priests concelebrate the Divine Liturgy, with the first priest or igumen presiding. At the antiphons, the Typika and the Beatitudes are sung. The pericope for the epistle is James 5.10–16 and that for the Gospel is Mark 6.7–13. At the Great Entrance, the priests walk by the sick person (which means that he is in the church, attending the Divine Liturgy). The Communion hymn is: *I will receive the cup of salvation.* And the Divine Liturgy continues as usual until: *Blessed be the name of the Lord.*

At that point, Psalm 50 is said once again, and the first priest says the prayer: *O Lord our God, who in thy mercy and compassion.* Then, after the exclamation, the priest takes the wick from the lamp, makes the sign of the cross with it three times over the holy oil, and extinguishes it. All the other priests do the same, one after the other. Each time Psalm 50 is said, and a different prayer is said. The second priest says: *O Holy Father, Physician of souls and bodies* (the first Barberini prayer); the third prays: *Lord Almighty, holy king, O God*; the fourth priest says: *O Lord our God, Master of all*; the fifth prays: *O Physician of our souls and bodies*; the sixth: *O our God, the God who saveth and hast mercy*; and the seventh prays: *O holy Father, Physician of souls and bodies* (the first Barberini prayer). Then a prayer attributed to

---

[56]*Sinaï gr.* 973, fol. 79v.

St John the Theologian is read: *O King invisible, incomprehensible, inconceivable, uncircumscribed,* and after it the priests chant the troparion to the Archangel Michael and to the unmercenary physicians. Each priest anoints the the sick person, by making the sign of the cross over forehead, the nostrils, the chin, the neck, the two ears, and the two hands, while saying the prayer: *O Holy Father, Physician of souls and bodies* (the first Barberini prayer), while the troparion to the unmercenary physicians is being sung. All the people present are also anointed. Then the sick person receives Holy Communion, which is followed by Psalm 33: *I will bless the Lord,* and the dismissal of the Divine Liturgy. The sick man is then escorted to his house with the chanting of Psalm 50 and troparion. At the house, the bed, the walls, and the doors are anointed.

In the thirteenth century, the order of holy unction was abbreviated and simplified, and later it became disconnected from the eucharistic context. Nevertheless, the practice of having it performed by seven priests remained, and this fact gave rise to the popular name ἑπταπάπαδον (*heptapapadon*— literally, service "of the seven priests") in Greek, or, in the Slavic languages, соборование (*soborovanie*—service of the "gathering," from the word собор (*sobor*) meaning either gathering, council, or cathedral). In the fourteenth century, this mystery came to be celebrated as we have it in our contemporary liturgical books; it still contains prayers already present in the eighth-century Barberini manuscript, in *Coislin 213* (1027), and in *Sinai gr. 973* (12th c.). The seven readings of the epistle and of the gospel and the seven prayers said by seven priests, who perform seven anointings (one after each sequence of epistle, gospel, and prayer) are vestiges of the former practice, when Divine Liturgies were served over seven days by seven priests. Commenting on this service at the end of the fourteenth century, Saint Symeon of Thessalonica says, "Holy oil has been transmitted as a sacred celebration and an image (*typos*) of the divine mercy, for the purification and the sanctification of those who desire to be delivered from their sins." According to him, "It grants the remission of sins and healing from sickness, and sanctification."[57] But he sees only a symbolic meaning for having seven priests performing it, and he agrees, that it could be performed only by three priests in the case that seven priests cannot be found, or "if needed by less than three, but everything must always be said as transmitted."[58]

---

[57]Symeon of Thessalonica, *Dialogue in Christ* 40 (PG 155:179d).
[58]Symeon of Thessalonica, *Dialogue in Christ* 283 (PG 155:517b).

As witnessed by *Coislin 213* (1027) and *Sinai gr. 973* (12th c.), the custom was to anoint not only the sick person, but all the people present. This is the origin of the Lenten practice of celebrating the mystery of holy unction for all the members of the church; this practice was already attested in *Coislin 213* (1027). According to that manuscript, the mystery was celebrated on the first Saturday of Great Lent and on Lazarus Saturday.[59] The most common contemporary practice (at least, in the Greek tradition) is to serve it on Holy Wednesday afternoon, in spite of the fact that this rite is not prescribed by contemporary printed *Typika*. Even so, the practice of serving it on Holy Wednesday is linked with the themes of the hymns in the Triodion for that day, which recall the gospel reading at Vespers on that evening, Christ's anointing by the sinful woman (Mt 26.6–16). St Symeon of Thessalonica takes this passage as a basis to declare that Christ himself received holy unction to heal human nature, to which he was hypostatically united.[60] Thus, in the Orthodox Church, holy unction was always considered a mystery of healing, administered for the sick at particular times, and once a year for sinners. It never became "extreme unction" as it did in the West in the Middle Ages, except during the time of Metropolitan Peter Moghila (17th c.), who, under Latin scholastic influence, considered that holy unction ought to be served only for sick persons close to death.[61] St Symeon of Thessalonica criticized this Latin practice, underlining that the mystery of holy unction is for the healing of the sick, since the Apostle James writes that the prayer of the presbyters "will raise them up" (Jas 5.15).[62]

2.2. *The Order of Holy Unction*

The order of holy unction, as given in our contemporary printed euchologia, is composed of two parts; the first is the vestige of the hymns and prayers said at the Matins service, and the second, of the readings and prayers said at the seven Divine Liturgies. Theoretically, it ought to be celebrated by seven priests. The order is as follows:

[59] A. Dmitrievsky, *Opisanie*, 2:1018.
[60] Symeon of Thessalonica, *Dialogue in Christ* 56 (PG 155:204d).
[61] Peter Moghila, *Euchologion*, 1:445–47.
[62] Symeon of Thessalonica, *Dialogue in Christ* 56 (PG 155:204d).

Table 4.2: The Order of Holy Unction

I. Matins Service

1. Usual Beginning (Trisagion through Our Father)
2. Psalm 142
3. Little Litany
4. Alleluia and Troparia: *Have mercy on us, O Lord . . .*
5. Psalm 50
6. Canon, with the acrostic: *Psalm of the prayer of the oil by Arsenius*
7. Stichera of the Praises
8. Trisagion prayers through Our Father, and Troparion

II. Holy Unction

1. Litany
2. Prayer of the oil: *O Lord, who through thy mercy and compassion . . .*
3. Troparia
4. 1st Epistle (Jas 5.10–16), Gospel (Lk 10.25–37), litany, and 1st prayer: *O Thou who art without beginning . . .*, then the anointing by the first priest, with the prayer of anointing: *O Holy Father, Physician of souls and bodies . . .*
5. 2nd Epistle (Rom 15.1–7), Gospel (Lk 19.1–10), litany, and 2nd prayer: *O God, great and most high*, then the anointing by the second priest, with the same prayer of anointing
6. 3rd Epistle (1 Cor 12.27–13.8), Gospel (Mt 10.1, 5–8), litany, and 3rd prayer: *O Master almighty*, then the anointing by the 3rd priest with the same prayer of anointing
7. 4th Epistle (2 Cor 6.16–7.1), Gospel (Mt 8.14–23), litany, and 4th prayer: *O good Lord and Lover of mankind*, then the anointing by the 4th priest with the same prayer of anointing
8. 5th Epistle (2 Cor 1.8–11), Gospel (Mt 25.1–13), litany, and 5th prayer: *O Lord our God, who chastenest and again healest . . .*, then the anointing by 5th the priest with the same prayer of anointing
9. 6th Epistle (Gal 5.22–6.2), Gospel (Mt 15.21–28), litany, and 6th prayer: *We thank Thee, O Lord our God*, then the anointing by the 6th priest with the same prayer of anointing
10. 7th Epistle (1 Thess 5.14–23), Gospel (Mt 9.9–13), litany, and 7th prayer: *O Master, Lord our God, Physician of souls and bodies . . .*, then the anointing by the by the 7th priest with the same prayer of anointing

11. Final prayer, with the open gospel book held over the head of the sick person: *O Holy King, deeply compassionate and greatly merciful . . .*

[12. Litany]

13. Idiomela

14. Dismissal

The service takes place either in a church (as was formerly the norm), or in a house, or in a hospital. On a table, we put an icon of Christ and a burning lamp containing oil with wine. The lamp is usually set in a bowl containing grains of wheat. There is also a tradition to light seven candles; one of these is extinguished after each of the seven series of readings, prayers, and anointings.

The first part is quite simple. We recognize the structure and the major elements of a Matins service: Trisagion, Psalm 142 (from the Six Psalms), the litany, the Alleluia and troparia, Psalm 50, the canon, the Praises, the final Trisagion and troparion.

The second part is composed of a litany, a prayer to bless the oil (which is contained in a lamp, in which it is mixed with wine according to the practice of the Great Church of Christ[63]): *O Lord, in thy mercy and compassion* (the fourth prayer of the Barberini *Euchologion*), the troparia, a series of seven epistle and gospel readings, each pair followed by a specific prayer said by each one of the seven priests, then an anointing by each of the seven priests in turn, with the same prayer of anointing.

The first readings are directly related to the sacrament: the Epistle of James (5.10–16), and the parable of the Good Samaritan (Lk 10.25–37), classically interpreted by the church fathers as presenting Christ the Savior as the Physician of souls and bodies. This gospel reading is also closely linked with the sacrament because of the aural play on the words *mercy* (ἔλεος, *eleos*) and *oil* (ἐλαίον, *eleon*), as they are pronounced in Koine and modern Greek. The other gospel readings are narratives related either to the remission of sins or the healing of the sick: Zaccheus (Lk 19.1–10), the mission of the apostles to heal the sick (Mt 10.1–8), the healing of Peter's mother-in-law and of the demoniacs (Mt 8.14–24), the parable of the ten virgins (Mt 25.1–13), the healing of the Cananite woman's daughter (Mt 15.21–28), and the dinner with Matthew the Publican (Mt 9.9–13).

[63]Slavic *Euchologia* replace wine with water, but of course mixing oil and wine is biblical; see, e.g., Lk 10.34.

The first prayer is a compilation of two ancient prayers. In its second part: *For thou art a great and wondrous God, who keepest thy covenant and thy mercy unto them that love thee*, which corresponds to the prayer after the litany in *Sinai gr. 973* (12th c.), the first priest asks God to grant him and his concelebrants the grace to accomplish the Mystery of the Anointing. The second prayer is the ancient prayer found after the litany in the same Sinai manuscript, and the third prayer is the third prayer of anointing in the Sinai codex. The fourth prayer corresponds to the fifth prayer of the Barberini manuscript, and the sixth prayer is the second prayer found there, while the seventh prayer corresponds to its first prayer.

After each of the prayers proper to each of the seven series, as each priest anoints the sick person, he says the prayer of unction: *O holy Father, Physician of souls and bodies*, which is the first prayer over a sick person (εὐχὴ ἐπὶ ἀρρώστου) in the Barberini codex, and is also found for the second anointing in *Sinai gr. 973* (12th c.). In each of the seven anointings the priest makes the sign of the cross with oil on the forehead, the nostrils, the cheeks, the lips, the breast, and both sides of the hands. This procedure is repeated seven times, each time by a different priest, after he has read the gospel and the proper prayer. This is a vestige of the practice of anointing the sick during seven consecutive days at the Divine Liturgy, with each of the seven Liturgies served by a different priest.

When the series of seven readings, prayers, and anointings has been completed, the first priest says the final prayer: *O Holy King, deeply compassionate and greatly merciful, Lord Jesus Christ*, while the holy gospel book is held open over the head of the sick person by the other concelebrating priests, thus showing through this ritual action—as it is expressed by the final prayer—that it is not the priest who is placing his hand over the head of the sick person, but Christ himself who is placing his *mighty and powerful hand, which*, the priest says, *is in this, thy holy gospel*. The final prayer is a deprecatory absolution prayer, in which the priest prays for the remission of the sins of the sick person. It is of great significance that in this final prayer, the priest does not pray at all for the recovery of the sick person, but only for the remission of his sins.

For emergency use, in a hospital or at a home, some euchologia present an abbreviated form of the service of holy unction.[64] Although there

[64]For an example, see Meyendorff, *The Anointing of the Sick*, 175–84. This service is inspired by a service found in a 14th–15th century Slavonic manuscript—Moscow

are some variants among them, basically the service begins with the usual beginning and the litany, followed by prayer of the oil: *O Lord, in thy mercy and compassion*. . . . Then the first readings are read, followed by the litany. Then the priest says the first prayer: *O Thou who art without beginning*, and then anoints the sick person, making the sign of the cross with oil on the forehead, the nostrils, the cheeks, the lips, the breast, and both sides of the hands, while saying the prayer of anointing (*O holy Father, Physician of souls and bodies*). The dismissal then follows.

Theological Academy N° 85, ff. 242–49—described by A. Golubtsov, "Ob obryadovoi storone tainstva eleosvyashcheniya," *Pribavleniya k izdaniyu tvorenii svyatykh ottsov v russkom perevode za 1888 god*. 42.3 (1888): 113–30 (see especially 118).

CHAPTER FIVE

The Mystery of Marriage

1. Historical overview

Before it became a sacrament of the Church, marriage was a social institution. In antiquity, it was arranged by the parents while the bride and groom were still very young. Girls would be betrothed in childhood. It would be concluded by the *stipulatio* of the parents, and very often accompanied by a contract and by presenting the earnest, or pledge (ἀρραβών, *arrabōn*), to the bride; and very often a ring was offered as the pledge. The earnest or the ring served as a kind of contract manifesting the engagement. The marriage usually took place later, when the bride reached the age of twelve. The marriage ceremony was a social feast in the decorated house of the bride, with a banquet, music, and dances; the bride and the bridegroom would wear crowns, usually made of flowers or of leaves. At the end of the banquet, the bride would be taken to the house of her husband. Often, special ceremonies would take place in the nuptial chamber.[1] It was in this civil context that Christian marriage developed.

Marriage, as a social feast, appears many times in the holy Scriptures, especially in the New Testament. It is used by the synoptic gospels in the parables as an image of the kingdom of God (cf. Mt 22.1–14). According to the Gospel of John, our Lord Jesus Christ performed his first miracle, his first sign, at a wedding in Cana of Galilee (Jn 2.1–11). Some church fathers, such as Saint Cyril of Jerusalem, saw in the transformation of water into wine a sign of the Eucharist: the transformation of the wine into the blood of Christ.[2] Such a eucharistic interpretation correlates with the eucharistic theme of the Gospel of John, which speaks later of the heavenly Bread (Jn 6.22–59). But the mystery of the Eucharist consists not only in the transformation of the earthly elements—the bread and the wine—into the body

---

[1]Cf. K. Ritzer, *Le mariage dans les Églises chrétiennes du Ier au XIe siècle* (Paris: Cerf, 1970), 71–77.

[2]Cf. Cyril of Jerusalem, *Mystagogical Homilies* 4.2 (SC 126:136; PPS 57:112–13).

and blood of Christ, but also in the transformation of a human assembly into the Body of Christ, which is the Church. Saint Paul, when narrating the establishment of the Eucharist (1 Cor 11.23–26), comes to speak of the mystical body of Christ (1 Cor 12.12–30), in which Christ is the head and we are the members. In another epistle, Saint Paul compares this mystery of the Church to the mystery of marriage: *This is a great mystery, but I speak concerning Christ and the Church* (Eph 5.32).

Saint Symeon of Thessalonica, in speaking of marriage, says that God, as Creator, established and blessed marriage. For this reason, the Word of God became incarnate and came to the wedding of Cana in Galilee, in order to bless marriage through his presence. But Symeon says that this happened as well in order to signify that Christ, as the heavenly Bridegroom, desired our souls, and for this reason he became incarnate, offered himself freely in sacrifice, and through his pure blood betrothed himself to us, his pure Church.[3] Because of this analogy between the mystery of the Church and the mystery of marriage, Saint John Chrysostom speaks of the union of the spouses in marriage as the establishment of a "small Church" or a "domestic Church."[4]

Since it is a social institution, Christian marriage ought to be blessed by the Church. For this reason, Christians who want to marry ought to ask the blessing of their bishop, so that their marriage might become the foundation of a Christian family. In his epistle to Polycarp, Saint Ignatius of Antioch says: "It becomes men and women too, when they marry, to unite themselves with the consent of the bishop, that the marriage may be after the Lord and not after concupiscence. Let all things be done to the honor of God."[5] But during the first seven centuries, Christian marriage took place during a family feast,[6] to which a priest would be called. Church fathers, such as Saint John Chrysostom, criticized some licentious morals at wedding feasts, and because of that licentious behavior, some canons required that the clergy leave before the arrival of comedians and prostitutes.[7] Since

[3]Symeon of Thessalonica, *Dialogue in Christ* 47 (PG 155:192cd).
[4]John Chrysostom, *Homily 20 on Ephesians*, 6 (PG 62:143; NPNF¹ 13:148); cf. N. Widok, "Christian Family as Domestic Church in the Writings of St. John Chrysostom," *Studia Ceranea* 3 (2013): 167–175.
[5]Ignatius of Antioch, *Epistle to Polycarp* 5.2 (SC 10:150; Ignatius, *The Letters*, PPS 49:102–103).
[6]Cf. the narrative of Socrates Scholasticus, *Ecclesiastical History* 4.23 (PG 67:509c; NPNF² 2:106).
[7]John Chrysostom, *Homily 12 on the Epistle to the Colossians* 4 (PG 62:387; NPNF² 62:318); Canons 53 and 54 of the Council of Laodicea (end of 4th c.) (Joannou, *Discipline générale antique*, 1.2:151–152; NPNF² 14:156–57).

marriage was celebrated during a banquet, the Church prohibited its celebration during Lent.[8] It is in that social context that an ecclesial, liturgical ceremony developed over time. Among Christian families, the presence of a bishop or of a priest at the wedding ceremony was important. At that time the betrothal and the marriage were two separate civil ceremonies that occurred at two different moments in the life of the bride and the groom. Saint John Chrysostom mentions in his homilies the earnest (ἀρραβών, *arrabōn*) presented by the bridegroom to the bride at the betrothal.[9] The father would crown the bride and the groom in that context. Saint Gregory the Theologian mentions the singing of Psalm 127 at such marriage celebrations.[10] Saint John Chrysostom is the first to reinterpret the usage of wedding crowns in a Christian context, saying that they show the victory of the spouses over carnal pleasures, over lust.[11]

Thus, the liturgical ceremony of marriage developed from the participation of the priest in a family feast,[12] and through this participation, the secular elements of the wedding feast were incorporated into the liturgical rites.[13] In the eighth and ninth centuries, the betrothal and the crowning by the priest were still celebrated separately, but the first was the engagement for the second. Thus, Canon 98 of the Council in Trullo (691–692) considers as adultery a marriage between a man and a woman betrothed to a different, living man.[14] Beginning with the legislation of Leo III (717–741), which was later confirmed by the Novel 89 of Leo the Wise (886–912), the liturgical blessing of marriage by the Church became an obligation in the Byzantine Empire, and marriage became a subject not only for civil legislation but also

---

[8]Canon 52 of the Council of Laodicea (Joannou, *Discipline générale antique*, 1.2:151; NPNF[2] 14:156).

[9]John Chrysostom, *Homily on the Captive Eutropius* 2.13 (PG 52:408; NPNF[1] 9:261).

[10]Gregory the Theologian, *Letter 231, to his friend Eusebius* (PG 37:374bd).

[11]John Chrysostom, *Homily 9 on the First Epistle to Timothy* 2 (PG 62:546; NPNF[1] 13:437).

[12]Cf. K. Ritzer, *Le mariage dans les Églises chrétiennes du Ier au XIe siècle*, 138–141, 191–213.

[13]Cf. G. Radle, *The History of Nuptial Rites in the Byzantine Periphery*, Excerpta ex Dissertatione ad Doctoratum (Rome: Pontificio Istituto Orientale, 2012); id., "The Historical Development of Byzantine Rites of Marriage as Evidenced by Sinai Gr. 957," *OCP* 78 (2012): 133–148; id., "The Nuptial Rites in Two Rediscovered First-Millennium Sinai Euchologies," *Rites and Rituals of the Christian East* (Paris: Peeters, 2014), 303–315; A. Pentkovsky, "Le cérémonial du mariage dans l'euchologe byzantin du XIe-XIIe siècle," in A. M. Triacca, A. Pistoia, *Le mariage* (Rome: Edizioni Liturgiche, 1994), 259–287.

[14]Joannou, *Discipline générale antique*, 1.1:235.

for canon law.[15] Eventually, the age for betrothal and marriage was post-poned from childhood (around 7 years) to child-bearing age (or puberty), and therefore, it became natural for both ceremonies to take place one after the other. Nevertheless, by the end of the eleventh century, according to Novel 24 of Alexius I Comnenus, the two ceremonies were not to be celebrated on the same day.[16] According to our contemporary practice, they are celebrated together. As a matter of fact, a decree of the Holy Synod of Russia in 1775 required that they be celebrated together,[17] and the law in Greece prohibits priests from performing them separately.[18]

The first mention of a betrothal celebrated by a priest is found in the eighth century in the *Chronology* of Theophanes, which mentions the betrothal of Leo, the son of Constantine V, with Irene. The Barberini *Euchologion* contains only two prayers for betrothal (περί μνηστείας, *peri mnēsteias*), which are still used today.[19] The first prayer: *O God eternal,* is followed by a prayer of inclination: *O Lord our God who hast espoused the Church as a pure virgin from among the nations.* The tenth-century euchologion manuscript *Sinai 958* contains an "Ecclesiastical Canon for a Betrothal" (εἰς μνήστρα, *eis mnēstra*).[20] The priest, standing at the holy doors of the iconostasis, receives the ring from groom and places it on the holy table. The deacon chants a litany with special petitions for the couple, and this is followed by the two prayers just noted, said by the priest. The priest then takes the ring and gives it to the groom, who in turn gives it to the bride; he kisses her forehead as she kisses his right hand. This rite still reflects the betrothal as the earnest (ἀρραβών, *arrabōn*) given by the groom for his bride. Then, the priest gives them Communion from the Presanctified Gifts. The practice of having two

---

[15]Cf. K. Ritzer, *Le mariage dans les Églises chrétiennes du Ier au XIe siècle,* 166–168; P. L'Huillier, "Novella 89 of Leo the Wise on Marriage: An Insight into its Theoretical and Practical Impact," *Greek Orthodox Theological Review* 32/2 (1987):153–162.

[16]Cf. K. Ritzer, *Le mariage dans les Églises chrétiennes du Ier au XIe siècle,* 184 and 195.

[17]P. Evdokimov, *Sacrement de l'amour* (Paris, 1980), 254; in English, *The Sacrament of Love* (Crestwood, NY: St Vladimir's Seminary Press, 1985), 183.

[18]Charter of the Church of Greece, Article 49 in G. Papathomas, *L'Église de Grèce dans l'Europe unie* (Katerini, 1998), 636. In case the betrothal were to be celebrated without the crowning, the ceremony would be considered invalid and the priest would be suspended for a year, have his salary cut in half, and he might go to prison for a year. See also: C. Vogel, "Fiançailles, mariage et divorce dans les pays de religion orthodoxe grecque," *Revue de Droit canonique* 4 (1954): 298–328.

[19]*Barberini,* 185. Cf. G. Baldanza, "Il rito del matrimonio nell'Euchologio Barberini 336: analisi della sua visione teologica," *Ephemerides Liturgicae* 4–5 (1979): 316–351.

[20]A. Dmitrievsky, *Opisanie,* 2:27–28.

Orarion

Sticharion

Clergy Vestments, Deacon

Plate 1

Phelonion

Epigonation
(Palitsa)

Sticharion

Epitrachelion
(Stole)

Clergy Vestments, Priest

Plate 2

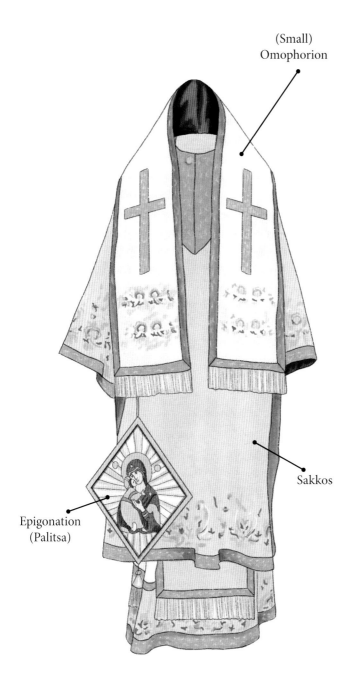

(Small)
Omophorion

Sakkos

Epigonation
(Palitsa)

Clergy Vestments, Bishop

Plate 3

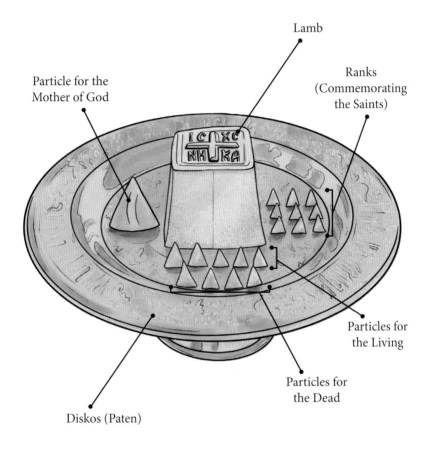

Lamb

Ranks
(Commemorating
the Saints)

Particle for the
Mother of God

Particles for
the Living

Particles for
the Dead

Diskos (Paten)

Prothesis (Proskomedia)

Plate 4

Cassock

Plate 5

Rason (Ryasa)

Plate 6

Kamilavkion with
Epanokamilavkion (Klobuk)

Paramantion (Paraman)

Mandyas

Plate 7

Analabos (Great Schema, in the Greek use)

Plate 8

rings at the betrothal first appeared in the eleventh century. *Coislin 213* prescribes a golden ring for the bride, and a silver (or iron) ring for the groom; the bishop places the bride's ring on the groom's right hand, and the groom's on the bride's right hand, and then the couple exchange the rings. At that point, the bishop unites their right hands.[21] The exchange of the kiss is not present in the euchologia mentioning the exchange of two rings.

The Barberini *Euchologion*, after the two prayers for the betrothal (περὶ μνηστείας, *peri mnēsteias*), gives only one prayer for marriage (εἰς γάμους, *eis gamous*): *O Holy God, who didst form man from the dust*, which is preceded by a litany by the deacon. It is followed by the crowning of the spouses, and after this the priest unites their right hands. The priest gives the peace and then reads the prayer of inclination: *O Lord our God, who in thy saving providence.* Then a third prayer is said over the common cup: *O God who hast created all things by thy might.*[22] The Barberini codex then prescribes that the priest give the spouses "the lifegiving Communion." For this reason, some have interpreted the common cup of the Barberini manuscript as a eucharistic cup. The prayer of inclination mentions the presence of Christ in Cana of Galilee. The common cup refers to this presence and to the miracle of the water changed into wine, and the Communion with the Presanctified Gifts manifests the realization in the Eucharist of that of which the miracle in Cana was a sign. We shall see below that in most manuscripts, the common cup follows the reception of the Eucharist, and therefore it has to be distinguished as a separate rite.

According to another manuscript, *Sinai gr. 957* (9th or 10th c.), the service of crowning is preceded by a prayer for the blessing of the nuptial chamber.[23] The service of crowning itself is the same as in that in the Barberini codex, with this difference: the prayer over the common cup is found after the Communion of the spouses with the Presanctified Gifts, and after the dismissal of the service. Perhaps this prayer was said over a common cup during the wedding banquet, as is done in the Armenian tradition.[24] After the prayer of the common cup, we find in this manuscript the prayer for the removal of the crowns. This rite took place not in the church, but in the nuptial chamber, where the crowns were hung over the nuptial

---

[21]Arranz, *Euchologion*, 325; Dmitrievsky, *Opisanie*, 2:1016.

[22]*Barberini*, 185–187.

[23]Dmitrievsky, *Opisanie*, 2:4–5.

[24]A. Pentkovsky, "Le cérémonial du mariage dans l'Euchologe byzantin," in *Le mariage: XLᵉ semaine d'études byzantines* (BEL 77) (Rome, 1994), 259–288, at 264.

bed.[25] They were usually left there until the eighth day, when the priest came again to the nuptial chamber in order to take them away and to read a special prayer for the "Dismissal of the Nuptial Chamber" (εὐχὴ εἰς λύσιν παστοῦ γάμου) with its prayer of inclination of the head.[26]

In *Sinai gr. 958* (10th c.), its "Ecclesiastical Canon for Marriage" prescribes that the priest and the deacon stand in the sanctuary, and that the crowns be placed on the holy table as well as the holy chalice containing the Divine Communion.[27] The priest blesses the bride and the groom who stand before the holy doors, and then the deacon says the litany. The priest then says the eighth-century prayer: *O Holy God, who didst form man from the dust,* and two other prayers; the third of these prayers is the contemporary first prayer: *O God most pure and the Fashioner of all creation.* Then the priest makes the sign of the cross three times over the heads of the couple and crowns them saying: *Thou hast set upon their heads crowns of precious stones* (cf. Ps 20.4). Then the priest says two other prayers, which were followed by a different prokeimenon: *Thou hast crowned them with glory and honor; O Lord, our Lord, how excellent is thy name in all the earth* (cf. Ps 8.5 and 9); the reading of a different epistle, Hebrews 12.28–13.8, which stresses that: *Marriage is honorable in all, and the bed undefiled; but whoremongers and adulterers God will judge* (Heb 13.4); a different Alleluia verse: *Thou hast given him his heart's desire* (cf. Ps 20.3), and the usual gospel reading about the Wedding in Cana of Galilee (Jn 2.1–11). The readings are immediately followed by a Communion rite introduced by the Lord's Prayer. After giving the peace, the priest reads the prayer of inclination of the head known to us: *O Lord our God, who, in thy saving providence, didst vouchsafe by thy presence in Cana of Galilee,* to which he adds the pre-Communion prayer from the Divine Liturgy of Saint John Chrysostom: *Attend, O Lord Jesus Christ, our God, out of thy holy dwelling place.* The deacon then intones: *Let us attend,* and the priest says: *The presanctified Holy Things for the holy,* and then he gives the spouses Holy Communion from the Presanctified Gifts, as the communion hymn is sung: *I will receive the cup of salvation* (Ps 115.4). Then he reads a different prayer over the common cup, and in this he asks that the power of the Holy Spirit grant the grace of oneness of mind. The priest then gives the common cup to the groom first, then to the

---

[25]For an example, see the *Euchologion* manuscript of the *Metochion of the Holy Sepulcher in Constantinople 8 (182)* of the 15th century, in Dmitrievsky, *Opisanie,* 2:465.

[26]Dmitrievsky, *Opisanie,* 2:5.

[27]Dmitrievsky, *Opisanie,* 2:28–31.

bride, and then again to the groom who finishes it—signifying that no one else could drink from their common cup. The priest unites their hands, and dismisses them in peace. After this service, the manuscript contains a prayer to remove the crowns from the heads of the newlyweds, and a prayer for the dismissal of the nuptial chamber.

Coislin 213 (11th c.) gives the rite of crowning immediately following the rite of betrothal.[28] The priest, with incense, leads the couple to the middle of the church, with Psalm 127 as an entrance hymn: *Blessed is everyone that feareth the Lord.* The manuscript states that this service is intended "for emperors and others," thus suggesting that this was initially an imperial rite which was later extended to other lay people.[29] The crowning is followed by the rite of the common cup. A particularity in this manuscript is that the common cup is of crystal, and it is broken once the bridegroom and the bride have drunk from it, thus showing that only the two spouses can partake of their common life.[30] The tradition of breaking a cup of crystal is probably a secular tradition that was imported from the wedding banquet into the liturgy.[31] After the service of crowning, we find a special prayer for the dismissal of the nuptial chamber.

A little further on in the same manuscript, for the first time, we find in an euchologion a special prayer for a second marriage.[32]

The troparia and the procession of the service of crowning appear for the first time in a fifteenth-century manuscript, *Patmos 690*, in which the procession goes from the church where the marriage was celebrated to the nuptial chamber of the spouses. It prescribes that the best men hold the crowns as they go to the nuptial chamber and as the clergy sing the troparia: *O Holy martyrs*; *Glory to thee, O Christ God*; and a theotokion. When the procession arrives to the doors of the nuptial chamber, the priest says additional prayers for the nuptial chamber, and the dismissal takes place there.[33]

According to Orthodox Tradition, given that the sacrament of marriage is modeled on the mystery of the union of Christ and his Church, Orthodox Christians should enter into only one marriage. Second weddings were never encouraged by the Church, but were permitted only through

[28]Arranz, *Euchologion*, 326; Dmitrievsky, *Opisanie*, 2:1016.

[29]A. Pentkovsky, "Le cérémonial du mariage dans l'Eucologe byzantin," 275.

[30]In some locations this was still observed in the 1900s (e.g., among the Italo-Albanians), but it is not widespread.

[31]A. Pentkovsky, "Le cérémonial du mariage dans l'Eucologe byzantin," 264.

[32]Arranz, *Euchologion*, 332; Dmitrievsky, *Opisanie*, 2:1017.

[33]Dmitrievsky, *Opisanie*, 2:652.

oikonomia. Canon 7 of the Council of Neo-Cesarea (314) forbade a priest to participate in a second wedding ceremony,[34] and Saint John Chrysostom is the author of a treatise on the single marriage, in which he expresses reluctance about a second wedding.[35] In the eighth century, Saint Theodore the Studite is shocked by the fact that in his time those contracting second marriages were receiving the blessing of a priest and were even crowned.[36] A third marriage has been allowed only since the third wedding of the Byzantine Emperor Constantine V (741–775), as the fourth marriage of the Byzantine Emperor Leo VI the Wise (886–912) was condemned by the Synod of Constantinople of 920, which authorized a third marriage only in special cases and prescribed that people contracting a second marriage must be excluded from Communion for four or five years.[37] Somewhere at the end of the fourteenth century or at the beginning of the fifteenth, Saint Symeon of Thessalonica, while commenting on the Communion in the Presanctified Gifts which was given first at the crowning service and was then followed by the rite of the common cup, says, "We do not give the Holy Gifts to those who cannot receive Communion because of their situation, such as bigamists and others. They partake only of the common cup in sign of partial sanctification, community, and unity in the blessing of God."[38]

2. The Betrothal

Table 5.1: The Order of the Betrothal

---

1. Opening blessing: *Blessed is our God,* and litany
2. First prayer: *O God eternal . . .*
3. Second prayer (of inclination): *O Lord our God, who hast espoused the Church as a pure virgin from among the nations . . .*
4. Betrothal

---

[34]Joannou, *Discipline générale antique,* 1.2:78.
[35]John Chrysostom, *On Not Entering a Second Marriage* (Greek title: Περὶ μονανδρίας; SC 138:160–200).
[36]Theodore the Studite, Letter 1.50, PG 99:1089–1096.
[37]G. A. Rhalles and M. Potles, *Syntagma,* vol. 5 (Athens, 1855), 3–10. Cf. K. Ritzer, *Le mariage dans les Églises chrétiennes du Ier au XIe siècle,* 165–166; J. Getcha, "L'idéal du mariage unique exclut-il la possibilité d'un remariage ? La position de l'Église orthodoxe face au divorce," *Revue d'éthique et de théologie morale "Le Supplément"* 228 (2004): 275–306.
[38]Symeon of Thessalonica, *Dialogue in Christ,* 282 (PG 155:513a).

5. Third prayer: *O Lord our God, who didst accompany the servant of the Patriarch Abraham*

[6. Litany]

[7. Dismissal]

The service of the betrothal (ἐπὶ μνηστείας, τοῦ ἀρραβῶνος, обручение; *epi mnēsteias, tou arrabōnos, obruchenie*) is served in the narthex (according to the *Euchologion*, after the Liturgy). There the priest welcomes the bridegroom, who stands on the right side, and the bride, who stands on the left. The rings were already placed on the holy table. The priest makes the sign of the cross over the head of the groom and of the bride three times, and gives them lighted candles. After the opening blessing: *Blessed is our God*, the deacon says the litany, in which we pray

- *that there may be granted unto them children for the continuation of the race*

- *that there may be sent down upon them perfect and peaceful love and assistance*

- *that they may be preserved in oneness of mind and steadfast faith*

- *that they may be blesed with a blameless life, and*

- *that the Lord our God may grant unto them an honorable marriage and a bed undefiled.*

The priest then says the two prayers attested already in the eighth century: *O God eternal*, and: *O Lord our God, Who hast espoused the Church as a pure virgin from among the nations*. Next comes the actual betrothal with the exchange of rings. The priest takes the golden ring (for the bride), and blesses the couple, making the sign of the cross over their heads three times, saying: *The Servant of God, N., is betrothed to the handmaid of God, N., in the Name of the Father, and of the Son, and of the Holy Spirit*. Then he puts the golden ring on the right hand of the groom. The same is repeated with the silver ring for the groom, which the priest puts on the right hand of the bride. Then the best man exchanges their rings. The priest says then the third prayer: *O Lord our God, who didst accompany the servant of the Patriarch Abraham*, which recalls the symbolism of the ring and of the right hand in the Holy Scriptures. The euchologia, which present the service of betrothal as a separate ceremony, give as a conclusion a litany and a dismissal, which today are usually omitted since the betrothal is commonly celebrated together with the service of crowning.

3. The Crowning

Table 5.2: The Order of the Crowning

---

1. Entrance Psalm 127: *Blessed are all they that fear the Lord . . .*[39]
[consent]
2. Opening blessing: *Blessed is the Kingdom,* and litany
3. First prayer: *O God most pure and Fashioner of all creation . . .*
4. Second prayer: *Blessed art thou, O Lord our God . . .*
5. Third prayer: *O Holy God, who didst form man from the dust . . .*
6. Crowning
7. Prokeimenon, Apostle, Alleluia, Gospel
8. Litany
9. Prayer: *O Lord our God, who, in thy saving providence, didst vouchsafe by the presence in Cana of Galilee . . .*
10. Litany of Supplication
11. Our Father
12. Prayer of inclination (of the common cup): *O God who hast created all things by thy might . . .*
13. Common cup
14. Troparia: *Rejoice, O Isaiah; O holy martyrs; Glory to thee, O Christ God,* and procession
15. Removal of the crowns
16. Prayer: *O Lord our God, who didst come to Cana of Galilee . . .*
17. Prayer of inclination: *May the Father, and the Son, and the Holy Spirit . . .*
18. Dismissal

The service of crowning (τοῦ στεφανώματος, τοῦ γάμου, венчание; *tou stephanōmatos, tou gamou, venchanie*) begins with the entrance of the couple, who, holding lighted candles, are led by the priest from the narthex to the middle of the nave as Psalm 127: *Blessed are all they that fear the Lord,* is

---

[39]Ps 127 from *GBN* 1:162.

being sung. The presence of this psalm at wedding ceremonies is ancient,[40] and it is included because of its reference to childbearing: "Thy wife shall be as a fruitful vine on the sides of thy house, thy sons like young olive shoots around thy table. . . . And thou shalt see the sons of thy sons" (Ps 127.3–6).

After the psalm, before the beginning of the service of crowning properly speaking, the Slavic *Euchologia* prescribe the exchange of consent by the bridegroom and bride. The priest inquires of the bridegroom: *Do you, N., have a good and unconstrained will, and a firm intention to take unto yourself this woman, N., whom you see here before you?* Bridegroom: *I have, reverend Father.* Priest: *You have not promised yourself to any other bride?* Bridegroom: *I have not promised myself, reverend Father.* The Priest then asks the bride: *Do you, N., have a good and unconstrained will, and a firm intention to take unto yourself this man, N., whom you see here before you?* Bride: *I have, reverend Father.* Priest: *You have not promised yourself to any other man?* Bride: *I have not promised myself, reverend Father.* This dialogue was introduced, in the vernacular language, by the Metropolitan of Kiev Peter Moghila in his *Euchologion*,[41] under the influence of the exchange of consent at the beginning of the service of marriage in the *Rituale* of Paul V.[42] According to Latin (scholastic) theology, it is by the consent of the spouses that the link of marriage is established by them, and in this sense, they are, in that view, the ministers of the sacrament. This view was quite revolutionary at that time, not only because, according to the Orthodox Tradition, the minister of the sacrament is always the priest who is an icon of Christ, the High-Priest of all sacramental actions, but also because the expression of the consent of the spouses represents an evolution of marriage from the ancient practice by which marriages were arranged by the parents during the childhood of the bride and groom.

Greek euchologia follow the manuscript tradition in not providing any exchange of consent between the spouses. There is a very rare exception in *Sinai gr. 973* (12th c.), where we find a kind of rite of consent. The parents gave the right hand of their respective children to the attendants of the couple (παράνυμφοι, *paranymphoi*), who then gave them to the priest, who made the sign of the cross over them and united them saying three times:

[40]Gregory the Theologian mentions its being sung at wedding feasts (*Letter 231* [PG 37:374bd]), and *Coislin 213* (11th c.) mentions it as an entrance hymn between the betrothal and the crowning (cf. Arranz, *Euchologion*, 326 and Dmitrievsky, *Opisanie*, 2:1017).
[41]Peter Moghila, *Euchologion* (Kiev, 1646), 1:405.
[42]Paul V, *Rituale Romanum* (Rome, 1625), 210–211.

"since he consents, and you consent," as all responded "Yes, if God wills."[43] At the very end of the fourteenth century, Saint Symeon of Thessalonica required that the spouses sign a legal contract between themselves in front of witnesses before their marriage.[44] Other manuscripts from the fifteenth and sixteenth centuries, as well as the printed euchologia of Venice of the sixteenth century, presented an exchange of consent at the beginning of the service of betrothal, which is perhaps more logical. This is the practice still observed by the Byzantine-rite Churches united with Rome.[45]

After the opening blessing: *Blessed is the Kingdom* (as for the Divine Liturgy), the deacon says the litany, in which we pray

- *that this marriage may be blessed as was that in Cana of Galilee*

- *that there may be granted unto them chastity, and fruit of the womb as is expedient for them*

- *that they will be made glad with the sight of sons and daughters*

- *that there may be granted unto them the acquisition of fair children, and a blameless life*

Although the crowning usually follows immediately upon the betrothal, the opening blessing and the litany must always be said, since they begin a rite different from the betrothal.

The priest then says three prayers: 1) *O God most pure and Fashioner of all creation*; 2) *Blessed art thou, O Lord our God*; and 3) *O Holy God, who didst form man from the dust*. The third prayer is the most ancient one.[46] After the three prayers, the priest crowns the bridegroom and the bride. The crowns are made of myrtle or olive tree leaves (in the Greek practice), or of metal with precious stones and a small icon—of Christ for the bridegroom and of the Theotokos for the bride (in the Russian practice). The priest takes the crown of the bridegroom, touches his forehead and then the bride's forehead, then makes the sign of the cross over them saying: *The servant of God, N., is crowned for the servant of God, N., in the name of the Father, and of the Son, and of the Holy Spirit*. This is done three times. And he puts the

[43]Dmitrievsky, *Opisanie* 2:96.
[44]Symeon of Thessalonica, *Dialogue in Christ* 276 (PG 155:505cd).
[45]Dmitrievsky, *Opisanie* 2:420, 488, 633, 903. Cf. Ritzer, *Le mariage dans les Église chrétiennes du Ier au XIe siècle*, 211–213; A. Raes, "Le consentement dans les rites orientaux," *Ephemerides Liturgicae* 47 (1933): 36–47, 249–259.
[46]*Barberini*, 186.

crown over the head of the bridegroom. In the Russian practice, the crowns are held by the couple's attendants. Then the priest takes the crown of the bride, and does the same. And after he has placed the crowns over their heads, the priest blesses them three times saying: *O Lord our God, crown them with glory and honor* (Ps 8.6). According to the monk Job, author of the first Byzantine treatise on the seven sacraments (13th c.), through the priest's blessing with the crowns over the heads of the spouses, the Holy Spirit descends on them and unites them into one flesh.[47]

The rite of the crowning is followed by biblical readings. The reader intones the verses of the prokeimenon: *Thou hast set upon their heads crowns of precious stones. They asked life of thee and gavest it them* (cf. Ps 20.4–5).[48] The first reading is from the Epistle of Saint Paul to the Ephesians (5.20–33), in which Saint Paul insists that the relation between the bridegroom and the bride in the Christian marriage should be modeled on the relation between Christ and his Church: "This is a great mystery, but I speak concerning Christ and the Church" (Eph 5.32). This Christocentric view is the foundation of the Orthodox understanding of the mystery of marriage. Unfortunately, the final words of the epistle ("the wife must respect/fear/ φοβῆται [*phobētai*] her husband") are often misinterpreted today, and in consequence, the reading is often challenged. One must remember that the Byzantine tradition knew an alternate reading, as we said before in speaking of the rite found in the euchologion manuscript *Sinai gr. 958*: a passage from the Epistle to the Hebrews (12.28–13.8), which states, "Marriage is honorable in all, and the bed undefiled: but whoremongers and adulterers God will judge" (Heb 13.4). After the singing of Alleluia, with the verse: *Thou, O Lord, shall keep us and preserve us* (Ps 11.8), comes the gospel reading, which relates the miracle at the wedding in Cana of Galilee (Jn 2.1–11), a fundamental narrative for both the theology and the symbolism of the mystery of marriage.

The readings are followed by the litany chanted by the deacon, which itself is followed by the ancient prayer of inclination: *O Lord our God, who in thy saving providence,*[49] which is said by the priest in between the Augmented

---

[47]Job Hamartolos, "On the Seven Mysteries of the Church," in Chrysanthos of Jerusalem (ed.), Συνταγμάτιον (Tergoviste, 1715), 130, quoted in M. Jugie, *Theologica Dogmatica*, 3:502.

[48][*The Great Book of Needs*, 1:169, presents this in the masculine singular, while common musical settings in the OCA give it as quoted.—*Ed.*]

[49]*Barberini*, 186.

Litany and the Litany of Supplication that are intoned by the deacon. The Litany of Supplication concludes with the recitation of the Lord's Prayer, the granting of the peace, and the contemporary prayer of inclination, which is the ancient prayer of the common cup: *O God who hast created all things.*[50] Then the priest gives the common cup, first to the bridegroom and then to the bride, and each drinks from it three times.

The rite of the common cup is then followed by the procession three times around the table on which the gospel book is placed, while the proper troparia are chanted: *Rejoice, O Isaiah; O holy martyrs;* and *Glory to thee, O Christ God.* According to the Russian practice, the attendants follow the spouses, holding the crowns over their heads. As we have noted before, this is a vestige of a procession from the church to the nuptial chamber where in former times the priest would come to remove the crowns and hang them over the nuptial bed.[51] This ancient practice is reflected also in the removal of the crowns immediately after the procession. Taking the crown of the bridegroom, the priest says: *Be exalted, O bridegroom, like unto Abraham; and be blessed, like unto Isaac; and be multiplied like unto Jacob, walking in peace and doing, in righteousness, the commandments of God.* And taking that of the bride he says: *And you, O bride, be exalted like unto Sarah; and be glad, like unto Rebekah; and be multiplied, like unto Rachel. Rejoice in your husband, keeping the terms of the law, for so is God well pleased.* The priest then says the prayer: *O Lord our God, who didst come to Cana of Galilee,* and after giving the peace, he says the prayer of inclination: *May the Father, and the Son, and the Holy Spirit,* which is a blessing from the Trinitarian God. This final prayer is followed immediately by the dismissal.

We find in our euchologia, after the service of the crowning, two prayers for the removal of the crowns on the eighth day: 1) *O Lord our God, who blessest the crown of the year,* and 2) *Thy servants having met in concord, O Lord.* This is a vestige of the rite of the removal of the crowns from the nuptial chamber on the eighth day, where they had been hanging over the nuptial bed since the day of the wedding.[52]

---

[50]*Barberini,* 187.
[51]Cf. Dmitrievsky, *Opisanie,* 2:652, 465, and 5.
[52]Dmitrievsky, *Opisanie,* 2:5, 343, 831.

4. Second Marriage

Table 5.3: The Order of a Second Marriage

1. Opening blessing: *Blessed is our God*, usual beginning prayers and troparion of the day
2. Litany
3. Prayer: *O God eternal* (= first prayer of the betrothal)
4. Prayer of inclination: *O Lord our God, who hast espoused the Church as a pure virgin from amomg the nations* . . . (from the betrothal)
5. Betrothal
6. Penitential prayer: *O Master Lord, our God* . . .
7. Prayer of inclination: *O Lord Jesus Christ, Word of God* . . .
8. Prayer: *O Holy God, who didst form man from dust* . . . (= third prayer of the crowning)
9. Crowning
10. Prokeimenon, Apostle, Alleluia, Gospel (same as at the crowning)
11. Litany
12. Prayer: *O Lord our God, who in thy saving providence didst vouchsafe by the presence in Cana of Galilee* . . .
13. Litany of supplication
14. Our Father
15. Prayer of inclination (of the common cup): *O God who hast created all things* . . .
16. Common cup
17. Troparia: *Rejoice, O Isaiah; O holy martyrs; Glory to thee, O Christ God*, and procession
18. Removal of the crowns
19. Prayer: *O Lord our God, who didst come to Cana of Galilee* . . .
20. Prayer of inclination: *May the Father, and the Son, and the Holy Spirit* . . .
21. Dismissal

A second marriage may be celebrated only with the written dispensation of the local bishop. The service for the second marriage found in our contemporary euchologia, which is most commonly used only when both spouses are contracting a second (or third) wedding, is a combination of the service of betrothal with the service of crowning with a few particular ancient elements. It begins with the opening blessing: *Blessed is our God*, just as the in the betrothal at a first marriage. (This is different from the opening of the crowning service which starts with the opening blessing of the Divine Liturgy: *Blessed is the Kingdom*). This opening blessing is followed by the usual beginning prayers, the troparion of the day and the litany by the deacon. The priest then reads the first, ancient, prayer of betrothal: *O God eternal*, with its prayer of inclination: *O Lord our God, who hast espoused the Church as a pure virgin from among the nations*. Then the actual betrothal with the exchange of rings takes place, exactly the same way as described in the service of the betrothal at a first marriage.

The betrothal is followed by a penitential prayer: *O Master, Lord our God*, and its prayer of inclination: *O Lord, Jesus Christ, Word of God*. In the first prayer the priest asks God, who forgave Rahab the harlot and accepted the repentance of the Publican, to grant the couple *remission of iniquities, cleansing of sins, and forgiveness of transgressions, whether voluntary or involuntary*, as in the second he implores God to *cleanse the transgressions of [his] servants, for, unable to bear the burden and the heat of the day, and the burning of the flesh, it is better to marry in the Lord than to burn* (recalling the words of Saint Paul in 1 Corinthians 7.9). We must remember that although crowning had been authorized for those entering a second marriage as early as the eighth century, the manuscript tradition of the *Euchologion* testifies to the existence of a special service, without the crowning, consisting only of penitential prayers.[53]

After the penitential prayers, the priest reads the third, most ancient, prayer of the service of crowning: *O Holy God, who didst form man from the dust*. It is followed by the rite of crowning, performed in the usual way. The prokeimenon, the epistle reading, the Alleluia, and the gospel reading and the rest of the service is exactly the same as the regular service of crowning.

5. Mixed Marriages

Issues related to marriage and its impediments were raised in 1961 by the first Pan-Orthodox Conference of Rhodes that registered them among the themes to be discussed by the future Holy and Great Council of the Orthodox Church.[54] The first Pre-conciliar Pan-Orthodox Conference of Chambésy

---

[53]Cf. Dmitrievsky, *Opisanie*, 2:1017, 215, 366, 443, 636, 715–716, 742–743, 861.
[54]List of themes, III.G and VIII.B. Cf. V. Ionita, *Towards the Holy and Great Synod of the*

in 1976 retained the matter of marriage and its impediments among the ten subjects on the agenda of the Holy and Great Council. The text on the impediments to marriage was discussed and agreed on at the Second Pre-conciliar Pan-Orthodox Conference of Chambésy in 1982, which stated the following concerning mixed marriages (in paragraph 7):

> Concerning mixed marriages contracted between Orthodox and non-Orthodox, on the one hand, and between Orthodox and non-Christians, on the other hand:
>
> i. Marriage between Orthodox and non-Orthodox is forbidden according to canonical *akribeia*. Nevertheless, it can be performed by dispensation and love on condition that the children resulting from this marriage will be baptized and brought up in the Orthodox Church. The local Orthodox Churches may take decisions concerning the use of economy in given cases and for particular pastoral needs.
>
> ii. Marriage between Orthodox and non-Christians is absolutely forbidden by canonical *akribeia*. Nevertheless, the local Orthodox Church can decide regarding such marriage, and make use of economy for the Orthodox partner, keeping in mind the particular pastoral needs.[55]

The document was then discussed again and reformulated with the title, "The Sacrament of Marriage and its Impediments," by the Synaxis of the Primates of the Orthodox Churches in Chambésy in January 2016. It was discussed once more and finally approved by the Holy and Great Council of the Orthodox Church in June 2016. The Council declared, concerning mixed marriages, in paragraph II, 5 of that document:

> Concerning mixed marriages of Orthodox Christians with non-Orthodox Christians or non-Christians:
>
> i. Marriage between Orthodox and non-Orthodox Christians is forbidden according to canonical *akribeia* (Canon 72 of the Quinisext Ecumenical Council).
>
> ii. With the salvation of man as the goal, the possibility of the exercise of ecclesiastical *oikonomia* in relation to impediments to marriage must be considered by the Holy Synod of each autocephalous Orthodox

---

Orthodox Church. *The Decisions of the Pan-Orthodox Meetings since 1923 until 2009*, Studia Œcumenica Friburgensia 62 (Basel: Friedrich Reinhardt Verlag, 2014), 127, 130.

[55]Ibid., 154–155.

Church according to the principles of the holy canons and in a spirit of
pastoral discernment.

   iii. Marriage between Orthodox and non-Christians is categorically
forbidden in accordance with canonical *akribeia.*

As a result of this decision, while the ecclesial celebration of a marriage
between an Orthodox Christian and a non-Christian has to be categorically excluded, a marriage between an Orthodox Christian and a Christian
from another confession is possible by the principle of *oikonomia* with the
permission of the Holy Synod of each autocephalous Orthodox Church. In
practice, all the autocephalous Orthodox Churches, with the exception of
the Church of Georgia, allow marriages between an Orthodox Christians
and non-Orthodox Christians when they are celebrated in the Orthodox
Church. According to the statistics of the Archdiocese of America of the
Ecumenical Patriarchate, approximately two of every three marriages (66%)
conducted in the churches in North America over the past several decades
have been categorized as inter-Christian and inter-Church.

A marriage between an Orthodox Christian and a non-Orthodox Christian can be celebrated only with the written dispensation of the local bishop,
after the non-Orthodox Christian spouse has produced his certificate of
baptism.[56] It is important to note that for a Roman Catholic wishing to
remain in good standing in that Church while marrying an Orthodox
spouse, the marriage must be the first, or any previous marriage must be
annulled by the Roman Church; should the person in question decide to
convert to Orthodoxy, this matter becomes far less pressing.

6. Marriage within the Divine Liturgy

In the eighteenth century, Saint Nicodemus the Hagiorite, in his commentary on Canon 13 of the Counil in Trullo, published in *The Rudder,* wished
to emphasize the sacramental value of marriage by linking it to the Divine
Liturgy. He wrote: "Before the Divine Liturgy begins, let [the couple] be
crowned, and once this has been done, let the Divine Liturgy begin. When
it has been completed, let them come and partake of the divine mysteries."[57]

---

[56]See the statement of the Holy and Great Council of the Orthodox Church regarding
mixed marriages, II.5. Note that in Greece, for any marriage at all the priest must have the
written blessing of the bishop.

[57]Cf. Nenad Milosevic, *To Christ and the Church: The Divine Eucharist as the All-
Encompassing Mystery of the Church,* 97.

The eucharistic revival of the 20th century raised the question of the link of the sacrament of marriage with the Eucharist. In consequence, some attempts have been made to incorporate the celebration of marriage within the context of the Divine Liturgy of an ecclesial community.

Nevertheless, it should be remembered that historically marriage was rarely celebrated within the Divine Liturgy. For instance, according to the description of the imperial wedding by Emperor Constantine VII Porphyrogenitus in his Book of Ceremonies, the bride and the bridegroom did not attend the Divine Liturgy. According to this description, they went to the church of the imperial palace for the rite of betrothal, after which they left the church as the patriarch began to serve the Divine Liturgy. Then, at the end of the Divine Liturgy, the imperial couple came back to the church for the rite of crowning.[58] Therefore, in Byzantium, the bridegroom and the bride were the only ones to receive Holy Communion from the Holy Gifts that had just been sanctified at the immediately preceding Divine Liturgy. This is the reason why the most common and widespread practice was to give Communion from Presanctified Gifts at the end of the service of crowning. This ceased to be the practice when the reception of Holy Communion became rare among Orthodox Christians, and also because of the increasing number of second (or even third) marriages, which excluded Orthodox Christians from Communion for a period of time, as we noted at the end of our historical introduction to this sacrament.[59]

In 1971, the Orthodox Church of Greece published an *Archieratikon* that contains a marriage service linked with the Divine Liturgy.[60] The order is as follows: At the end of the doxology and after the dismissal of Matins, while the bishop is standing on his throne, the couple is brought forward and the betrothal is performed, as indicated in the *Euchologion*. The Divine Liturgy then begins with the usual opening blessing, followed by the litany, in which special petitions are added. The three prayers of the crowning service are said by the bishop and intercalated before each of the three antiphons. Instead of the third antiphon, when the third prayer has been said, the Little Entrance takes place, followed by the troparia and the kontakion. Then the couple approach the solea as the bishop comes out to perform the rite of crowning. The Trisagion is then sung, followed by the prokeimenon and the biblical readings. After the litany, the bishop says aloud the forth

[58]Constantine Porphyrogenitus, *Book of Ceremonies*, 1.41.4 (PG 112:465a).
[59]Symeon of Thessalonica, *Dialogue in Christ*, 282 (PG 155:513a).
[60]*Archieratikon*, 113–115.

prayer: *O Lord our God, who in thy saving providence.* Then the usual order of the Divine Liturgy follows. At communion time, the couple receive Holy Communion first among the faithful. After the Ambo Prayer, the rite of the common cup takes place, followed by the procession with the troparia and the dismissal.

Fr John Meyendorff, in the eighth chapter of his book, *Marriage: An Orthodox Perspective,*[61] made a similar proposal for the celebration of marriage within the Divine Liturgy. He suggests that the betrothal be served, as indicated in the *Euchologion,* the evening before the marriage ceremony. The actual marriage should be celebrated the next day during the Divine Liturgy, which would beginn with the usual opening blessing. This would be followed by the litany, in which special petitions would be added. The three prayers of the crowning service would be intercalated before each of the three antiphons. After the third antiphon, the rite of crowning would take place, then the Little Entrance, the Trisagion, the biblical readings and the usual order of the Divine Liturgy. After Communion, the rite of the common cup would take place, then the procession with the troparia and the removal of the crowns. Finally, the regular dismissal of the Divine Liturgy would take place.

The liturgist Ioannis Phountoulis proposed a different pattern. After the dismissal of Matins, the betrothal is performed in the narthex with only the two ancient prayers: *O God eternal,* and its prayer of inclination: *O Lord our God, who hast espoused the Church as a pure virgin from among the nations.* (The third, more recent, prayer—*Lord our God, who didst accompany the servant of the patriarch Abraham*—is omitted). The priest then introduces the couple into the middle of the church, or up to the solea, while Psalm 127 is chanted. The Divine Liturgy then begins with the usual opening blessing and the litany. After the litany, the priest says the ancient prayer: *O Holy God, who didst form man from the dust.* (The two more recent prayers: *O God most pure and the Fashioner of all creation* and: *Blessed art thou, O Lord our God,* are omitted). Then the priest crowns the bridegroom and the bride as prescribed, and blesses them, saying: *O Lord our God, crown them with glory and honor.* After this, he says the entrance prayer and the entrance takes place, followed by the troparia and the Trisagion. The readings of the day and of marriage are read, followed by the litany and the prayer: *O Lord our God, who by thy saving providence.* Then the Cherubic hymn is sung,

---

[61]John Meyendorff, *Marriage: An Orthodox Perspective,* 42–43.

followed by the usual order of the Divine Liturgy. After the Ambo Prayer, the priest comes to the solea or to the middle of the church to bless the common cup and give it to the newlyweds to drink, and the procession with the troparia and the prayers for the removal of the crowns takes place. Then the comes the usual end of the Divine Liturgy, with *Blessed be the name of the Lord* and the dismissal.[62]

The celebration of marriage within the Divine Liturgy is not possible unless both spouses can participate in Holy Communion (for example, in the case of a mixed marriage or in the case of a second marriage, since neither a non-Orthodox person, nor an Orthodox person entering a second marriage can receive Communion during the Divine Liturgy).

[62]Ioannis Phountoulis, *Λειτουργική, Α΄, εἰσαγωγή στη Θεία λατρεία* (Thessalonica, 1993), 297–298. On this subject, see also Nenad Milosevic, *To Christ and the Church: The Divine Eucharist as the All-Encompassing Mystery of the Church*, 97–101.

CHAPTER SIX

Monastic Tonsure

1. Historical Overview

Monastic tonsure has often been considered a sacrament by Byzantine authors. Job Hamartolos considers it the sixth sacrament in his *Treatise on the Seven Sacraments* written in the thirteenth century,[1] while Metropolitan Joasaph of Ephesus mentioned it as the ninth of ten mysteries he enumerated in the tenth century.[2] At the turn of the fourteenth and fifteenth centuries, although Saint Symeon of Thessalonica did not mention monastic tonsure in his list of the seven sacraments,[3] he spoke of it as a sacrament when considering the mystery of repentance[4] and believed that it grants grace,[5] while he considered marriage as a simple ceremony in which grace is not transmitted.[6]

The first description of and commentary on monastic tonsure is found in the sixth chapter of the *Ecclesiastical Hierarchy* of Pseudo-Dionysios (5th c.), where all the elements of the rite are already present. The rite takes place in front of the altar. The candidate stands in front of the priest, who asks the candidate if he is willing to renounce to his previous life, reminds him of the rules of a perfect life, and tonsures the candidate once he has affirmed his commitment. The tonsure is in the form of a cross, and the three divine Persons are named. Then the newly tonsured monk is vested in his new clothes.[7]

---

[1]Job Hamartolos, *On the Seven Mysteries of the Church, Cod. 64 Supplementi graeci Parisiensis*, fol. 239, quoted by M. Jugie, *Theologica Dogmatica Christianorum Orientalum*, 3:17–18.

[2]Joasaph, Metropolitan of Ephesus, *Canonical Answers* 47, Alexander I. Almazov, ed. (Odessa, 1903), 38.

[3] Symeon of Thessalonica, *Dialogue in Christ* 33 (PG 155:177b).

[4]Symeon of Thessalonica, *Dialogue in Christ* 52 (PG 155:197a–d)

[5]Symeon of Thessalonica, *Dialogue in Christ* 269 (PG 155:492b).

[6]Symeon of Thessalonica, *Dialogue in Christ* 281 (PG 155:509d–512a).

[7]Pseudo-Dionysius the Areopagite, *On the Ecclesiastical Hierarchy* 6.2 (PG 3:533b; Liubheid, 245–6).

From the second half of the eighth century, we have the witness of the Barberini codex, in which we find different prayers for those men and women who wish to take the monastic schema (habit) and two orders for the angelic schema, one for the "little habit" and one for the schema.[8] The first takes place in front of the sanctuary "after the order of the troparia," referring most probably to the troparia sung at the Divine Liturgy after the Little Entrance, to which the troparion: *The door of repentance has been opened*,[9] is added. The candidate prostrates himself in front of the doors of the sanctuary. The deacon says a litany in which he prays particularly for the candidate to be tonsured. It is followed by three prayers: *O Lord, God of truth*; *O Master, Lord Jesus Christ, our God*; and: *Thou, who hast established a celestial army*. The second order begins, "after the first prayer," with a litany in which the deacon prays particularly for the candidate to be tonsured. This is followed by two prayers of the schema: *Thou who art, O Master, Lord, our God*, and: *O Lord, God of our salvation*, interspersed by a litany of the deacon. Then we find a prayer for the eighth day for taking off the koukoulion. After that, the Barberini manuscript gives, for each of the eight days, proper prokeimena and Alleluia verses, as well as readings of the epistle and gospel. These elements suggest that the newly tonsured monk remained in the church for eight consecutive days, during which special readings were done at the Divine Liturgy. One can see here an analogy with the eight days the neophytes spent in the church after their baptism and the ablutions that were made on the eighth day. Indeed, the monastic tonsure has often been regarded allegorically by the church fathers as a "second baptism,"[10] and for this reason, Saint Symeon of Thessalonica says that "he who becomes a monk receives a second baptism, is purified from his sins, and becomes a son of light."[11]

In *Coislin 213* (1027) we find a "prayer for the one wishing to wear the mantion (μαντίον)."[12] It consists of a prayer: *O Lord, our God, who hast established as worthy of thee those who have left all worldly things*, which

[8]*Barberini*, 177, 220–234.
[9][This troparion is in Tone 4, Ἤνοικται ἡ θύρα τῆς μετανοίας (*Ēnoiktai hē thyra tēs metanoias*); it is different from the troparion in Tone 8 found in Matins in the Triodion, Τῆς μετανοίας μοι πύλας (*Tēs metanoias moi pylas*), *Open to me the doors of repentance*, with which it seems to have been confused in the translation of the text of the codex (*Barberini*, 367).—Ed.]
[10]Cf. C. Vuillaume, "La profession monastique, un second baptême?" *Collectanea Cisterciensia* 53 (1991): 272–292.
[11]Symeon of Thessalonica, *De Pœnitentia* 270 (PG 155:493a).
[12]Dmitrievsky, *Opisanie*, 2:1028.

is found in the Barberini codex as the prayer for the one who wishes to take the monastic schema.[13] In the Coislin manuscript, this prayer is followed by a prayer of inclination: *O Lord our God, the hope and refuge of all who put their hope in thee.* Then the candidate is tonsured crosswise and is vested with the "mantion," as the priest says: *Our brother, N., takes the pallion (παλλίον), the pledge of the great and angelic schema, let us say for him: Kyrie, eleison.* Then the assembly kisses the brother as Psalm 118 is said. This rite is followed in the manuscript by the order of the pro-schema of monks (ἀκολουθία τοῦ προσχήματος τῶν μοναχῶν; *akolouthia tou proschēmatos tōn monachōn*).[14] The tonsure is preceded by the questions by the priest: *Dost thou come to Christ of thine own will?* as we find them in the contemporary rite of the Little Schema. It is then followed by the prayer *We give thanks to thee, O Christ our God.* This rite is followed by the hymnography for the Great Schema (kathisma hymns, a canon, a kontakion, and stichera), which we still find today. Next comes "The order that takes place for the holy and Great Schema."[15] This rite provides three antiphons for the Divine Liturgy. During these antiphons, the one who wishes to receive the schema goes up to the holy doors, and falls down to the ground and does not get up until the end of the antiphons. Then, once the special troparia are sung, the priest asks the one who wishes to receive the Great Schema: *Why art thou come, brother, falling down before the holy altar?* This is followed by the same catechesis found in contemporary euchologia. And that is followed by another catechesis. After that comes the prayer: *O thou who art, Master almighty, most high King of glory*, and the prayer of inclination: *O holy Lord of Hosts*; both of these are found in the contemporary rite of the Great Schema.

Next the candidate is brought into the sanctuary by the priest, who holds him by the hand. After the candidate makes prostrations, he kisses the holy gospel book on which a pair of scissors has been laid, and the hand of the priest, who says to him: *Behold, Christ stands here invisibly.* Then, the priest says to him: *Take up the scissors and give them to me.* And when he has given him the scissors, the priest says: *Behold, thou receivest them from the hand of Christ.* And taking up the scissors from his hand the priest says: *Blessed is God*, and tonsures him crosswise, saying: *Our brother is tonsured.* ... Then the brothers come to the diakonikon (sacristy) and tonsure him, saying Psalm 118. The priest reads the prayer of the Trisagion (from the Divine

---

[13] *Barberini*, 177.
[14] Dmitrievsky, *Opisanie*, 2:1028.
[15] Dmitrievsky, *Opisanie*, 2:1028–1034.

Liturgy) as the deacon intones the litany. This is followed by the Trisagion, the prokeimenon, the reading of the epistle, Alleluia, and the reading of the gospel. Then the brothers bring the tonsured monastic, who is wearing the tunic (κολόβιον, *kolobion*), to the middle of the holy doors. After the reading of the gospel, three antiphons are sung. Then, the tonsured monastic is vested in the sanctuary with the outer garment (ἱμάτιον, *imation*), the koukoulion, the analabos (ἀνάλαβος), the pallion (παλλίον), the belt (λῶρος, *lōros*), and the sandals; with each item the priest says: *Our brother, N., is clothed.* . . . Then further troparia are sung, and these are followed by the prayer by the priest: *O Lord, our God, who art faithful in thy promises,* and the prayer of inclination: *O Lord our God, lead thou thy servant.* Then the deacon brings the gospel book out of the sanctuary, and the brethren kiss first the book of the holy gospels and then the newly tonsured monk as troparia are sung. The deacon intones the litany, and the Divine Liturgy continues normally. The rite is followed by the prayer for removing the koukoulion.[16] As it appears from this manuscript, the two first rites were only preliminary steps and a pledge for the monastic tonsure into the holy and Great Schema.

In the thirteenth to fourteenth century the notion of "first schema" (τοῦ πρώτου σχήματος, *tou prōtou schēmatos*) appears, as is witnessed in the euchologion manuscript *Sinai gr. 971* (13th to 14th c.).[17] This rite takes place after the Little Entrance of the Divine Liturgy, and it is very similar to our contemporary rite of the "Little Schema." The tonsured monk is vested only with the pallion, as the priest says: *Our brother, N., takes the pallion* (παλλίον), *the pledge of the great and angelic schema; let us say for him: Kyrie, eleison.* In the same manuscript, immediately after the "first schema," we find the order for the great and angelic schema.[18] This takes place at the Divine Liturgy, after the regular antiphons (Typika and the Beatitudes), and it starts with three special antiphons and the troparia, as in the contemporary rite. The rite is similar to the one found in *Coislin 213* (11th c.), which seems to be the prototype. Some manuscripts, including this one, prescribe different rites for monks and for nuns,[19] while others, such as the fourteenth-century *Vatopedi 133 (744)*, indicate that the same rite is used for both monks and nuns, with the difference that male monastic saints are invoked for the tonsure of a monk and female monastic saints are invoked for the tonsure of a nun.[20]

At the end of the fourteenth century to the beginning of the fifteenth century, Saint Symeon of Thessalonica mentions only one tonsure. He says that the candidate is presented in front of the holy doors, because "he is not yet numbered among the angels and the angelic men."[21] He says that he takes his vows in the form of questions and answers,[22] and then he is tonsured crosswise in the name of the Holy Trinity, because "by the Trinity he is sanctified and by the means of the cross he is shown to be dead to the world."[23] For Symeon, "the elements of the monastic schema are seven, as the number of vestments of the bishop, and they also witness to the most perfect life, with the number of gifts of the Holy Spirit."[24] These are the seven elements of the angelic schema: 1) the tunic (χιτῶνα, *chitōna*)—in exchange of his nudity due to sin; 2) the pallion (παλλίον)—which signifies the protection of God; 3) the koukoulion (κουκούλιον)—signifying the illumination by the grace of God; 4) the analabos (ἀνάλαβος)—sewn of leather, having crosses in front, behind, and on the sides of the shoulders, signifying crucifixion to the world; 5) the belt (ζώνη, *zōnē*)—which signifies the mortification of the flesh; 6) the sandals (σανδάλια, *sandalia*)—to step on bad thoughts and to walk on the evangelic way; and 7) the mandyas (μανδύας, *mandyas*)—which enrobes him as a whole since he is enrobed by the power of God.[25]

According to Saint Symeon, "as baptism is one and single, so also the schema of monks. . . . And if we call the schema little and great, these are not two, but one is the great and perfect. For the little one is a betrothal and a preface of the great one, and it was devised by certain later fathers on account of the infirmity of men."[26] In his thirteenth-century treatise on the seven sacraments, Job Hamartolos says that "the monastic schema advances from the less to the more perfect; from that of the Little Schema and so-called rasophore to the holy schema of the tonsure, and from this again to the great angelic schema, as it is called."[27]

---

[20]Cf. Dmitrievsky, *Opisanie*, 2:276–277.
[21]Symeon of Thessalonica, *Dialogue in Christ* 267 (PG 155:489d-492a).
[22]Symeon of Thessalonica, *Dialogue in Christ* 270 (PG 15:492d-493b).
[23]Symeon of Thessalonica, *Dialogue in Christ* 271 (PG 155:493c).
[24]Symeon of Thessalonica, *Dialogue in Christ* 55 (PG 155:204a).
[25]Symeon of Thessalonica, *Dialogue in Christ* 273 (PG 155:497b-500a).
[26]Symeon of Thessalonica, *Dialogue in Christ* 20 (PG 155:104cd).
[27]Job Hamartolos, *On the Seven Mysteries of the Church*, 134.

The contemporary practice appeared in the fifteenth century; this practice distinguishes three degrees of monasticism that are reflected in three different rites, with many variants among the manuscripts: 1) the order for the rasophore, when the candidate receives the tunic (χιτῶνα, *chitōna*) and the kamilavkion (καμηλαύκιον); 2) the order for the first schema, that is of the mandyas, or of the stavrophore, when the candidate receives the tunic (χιτῶνα), the pallion (παλλίον), the belt (ζώνη, *zōnē*), the kamilavkion (καμηλαύκιον), and the sandals (σανδάλια, *sandalia*); 3) the order of the great and angelic schema, when the candidate receives the tunic (χιτῶνα), the pallion (παλλίον), the analabos (ἀνάλαβος), the koukoulion (κουκούλιον), the belt (ζώνη), the mandyas (μανδύας), and the sandals (σανδάλια, *sandalia*).[28]

The manuscript tradition of the orders for monastic tonsure is quite complicated, not only because of a large variety of practices, but also because of an evolution in the terminology linked with the evolution of the monastic vestments. As an example: the old pallion (παλλίον) was identified with the "mantion" (μαντίον) in *Coislin 213* (11th c.),[29] with the mandyas (μανδύας) in *Saint Panteleimon 604* (15th c.),[30] and with the paramantion (παραμάντιον, *paramantion*) in *Saint Sabbas 568* (16th to 17th c.).[31] The interpretation of the terms of the monastic garments was still being discussed in the eighteenth century, as one can see from the dissertation on the monastic habit by Saint Nicodemus the Hagiorite.[32] According to St Nicodemus, stavrophores (monks of the Little Schema) wore the cassock instead of the tunic (χιτῶνα); the rason, an over-garnment reaching to the ankles and having wide sleeves, instead of the pallion (παλλίον); the belt (ζώνη); and the sandals (σανδάλια). He denies that the old pallion (παλλίον) should be interpreted as the square of a fabric with the depiction on the cross on it, often called the paramantion (παραμάντιον—this is worn on the back and has cords passing over both shoulders, and these are tied in front). He states that the one who wants to wear this item should wear it "without a blessing, just as he wears the kamilavkion and the epanokamilavkion (veil)."[33]

[28]Dmitrievsky, *Opisanie*, 2:371, 384–388, 505–511, 558–564.

[29]Dmitrievsky, *Opisanie*, 2:1028.

[30]Dmitrievsky, *Opisanie*, 2:559.

[31]Dmitrievsky, *Opisanie*, 2:945.

[32]Nicodemus the Hagiorite, *Concerning the Schema of Monks and their Garments*, in *Exomologetarion*, II (Athens, 1900), 156–163; English translation in N. F. Robinson, *Monasticism in the Orthodox Churches* (London: Cope and Fenwick, 1916), 129–140.

[33]Ibid., 138.

Nicodemus adds that the monks of the Great Schema wear three additional garments: the koukoulion (κουκούλιον); the analabos (ἀνάλαβος—a piece of fabric worn as an apron with the representation of the cross); and the mandyas (μανδύας—a sort of sleeveless cloak).[34]

Printing fixed the rites of the monastic tonsure and brought a certain uniformity. The edition of the Greek *Εὐχολόγιον sive Rituale græcorum* by J. Goar in Paris in 1647 and the edition of the Slavonic *Trebnik* of Peter Moghila in Kiev in 1646 determined the rites of the later editions. In the edition of Goar, we find three orders. First, the order for the rasophore, with two prayers: *We give thanks unto thee, O Lord our God*, and: *Receive thy servant under thy saving yoke*, after which the candidate is tonsured crosswise "in the name of the Father, and of the Son and of the Holy Spirit" and receives the tunic (χιτῶνα, *chitōna*) and the kamilavkion (καμηλαύκιον) from the priest, who says nothing. The second order is that for the Little Schema—that is, of the mandyas, which takes place after the Little Entrance at the Divine Liturgy. The candidate is tonsured crosswise while the priest says: *Our brother, N., is tonsured in the hair of his head in the name of the Father, and of the Son and of the Holy Spirit: let us all say for him, Lord have mercy.* He receives the tunic (ἱμάτιον, *imation*), the belt (ζώνη, *zōnē*), the kamilavkion (περικεφαλαίαν, *perikephalaian*), the pallion (παλλίον), and the sandals (σανδάλια, *sandalia*). The third order, of the Great and Angelic Schema, provides a canon in the second tone with the acrostic: *Grant unto me, O Christ, the gladness of a happy end*, with stichera following. At the Divine Liturgy, after the Little Entrance, the troparion of the day is sung, and this is followed by three special antiphons. Then the candidate is questioned and receives a catechesis. After two prayers by the priest, the candidate is tonsured crosswise, while the priest says: *Our brother, N., is tonsured in the hair of his head, in the name of the Father, and of the Son and of the Holy Spirit: let us all say for him, Lord have mercy.* He then receives the tunic (χιτῶνα), the pallion (παλλίον), the koukoulion (κουκούλιον), the analabos (ἀνάλαβος), the belt (ζώνη, *zōnē*), and the sandals (σανδάλια).[35]

The edition of Moghila follows the same pattern with some particularities.[36] In the first order, that for the rasophore, when the priest tonsures the candidate crosswise, he says: *In the name of the Father, Amen, and of the Son, Amen, and of the Holy Spirit, Amen. Let us all say for him: Lord have mercy.*

[34]Ibid.
[35]Goar, 468–514.
[36]Peter Moghila, *Euchologion*, 891–955.

The candidate then receives the rason (ряса, *ryasa*) and the kamilavkion (камилавка, *kamilavka*) from the priest, who says nothing. The priest then says a prayer in silence: *O holy, good Son of the good Father*, and delivers an exhortation to entrust the rasophore to his elder: *Behold, I entrust to thee before God*.

In the second order, for the Little Schema, that is of the mandyas, the tonsured monk receives the tunic (хитон, власяниця; *chiton, vlasyanitsya*), the paraman (параманъ [*paraman*], from the Greek παραμάντιον [*paramantion*]), the cross, the rason (ряса), the belt (пояс, *poyas*), the mandyas (мантия, *mantiya*), the podkapok (подкáпокъ), the kamilavkion (камилавка), the sandals (сандáлия, *sandaliya*), the prayer rope (вервица, *vervitsa*), a hand cross, and a lighted candle.

In the third order, of the Great Angelic Schema, the candidate is tonsured crosswise while the priest says *Our brother, N., is tonsured, a second time, in the hair of his head, as a sign of his final renunciation of the world, and of everything that is in the world, and for the final restraining of his will and of all fleshly desires, in which to keep himself in silence and perseverance, in the name of the Father, and of the Son and of the Holy Spirit: let us all say for him: Lord have mercy.*" He then receives the tunic (хитон, власяниця), the rason, the great paraman (великий параманъ, *velikii paraman*), the belt (пояс), the koukoulion (кукулъ, *kukul*) with the analabos (аналавъ, *analav*), the mandyas (мантия), the sandals (сандáлия), the prayer rope (вервица), a hand cross, and a lighted candle. The granting of a lighted candle to the newly professed monk is not a novelty introduced by Peter Moghila, since it is found in some older manuscripts, for example, in *Patmos 691* (15th to 16th c.), with the words: *Let thy light so shine before men that they may see thy good works . . .* (Mt 5.16). This same manuscript prescribes that the brotherhood come to the newly professed monk and ask him: *Bless, father. What is thy name?* When the monk answers, the brothers reply: *Mayest thou be saved, monk, N.*[37] This exchange is prescribed by contemporary euchologia at the end of the Divine Liturgy, after the Ambo Prayer.

[37] Dmitrievsky, *Opisanie*, 2:664.

2. The Order for Taking the Rason

Table 6.1: The Order of the Service for Taking the Rason

1. Opening blessing and prayers
2. Penitential troparia: *Have mercy on us*; *O Lord, have mercy on us*; *O blessed Theotokos, open the doors of compassion*
3. First prayer: *We give thanks unto thee, O Lord our God*
4. Second prayer: *Receive thy servant under thy saving yoke, O Master*
5. Tonsure
[6. Prayer: *O holy, good Son of the good Father*]
7. Dismissal
[8. Exhortation to entrust the rasophore to his elder]

The service takes place in front of the holy doors of the iconostasis. After the opening blessing: *Blessed is our God*, and the usual beginning prayers, the penitential troparia are sung. The priest reads two prayers: *We give thanks unto Thee, O Lord our God*, already found in *Coislin 213* (11th c.) for the pro-schema,[38] and: *Receive Thy servant under Thy saving yoke, O Master*. He then tonsures the candidate crosswise with the formula: *In the name of the Father. Amen. And of the Son. Amen. And of the Holy Spirit. Amen.* The candidate then receives the rason and the kamilavkion, in silence. And then the dismissal follows.

According to the contemporary Russian practice, the rasophore receives the klobuk, that is the kamilavkion with the veil fixed to it. The the priest says a further prayer in silence: *O holy, good Son of the good Father*, and then he gives an exhortation for entrusting the rasophore to his elder: *Behold, I entrust to thee before God*.

---

[38]Dmitrievsky, *Opisanie*, 2:1028.

3. The Order of the Little Schema

Table 6.2: The Order of the Service of the Little Schema

---

1. Troparion: *Make haste to open thy fatherly arms unto me*
2. Catechesis, including questions and answers
3. First prayer before the tonsure: *Therefore, may the All-compassionate and greatly merciful God*
4. Second prayer before the tonsure: *O Lord our God, who hast decreed*
5. Prayer of inclination: *O Lord our God, the hope and refuge*
6. Tonsure
7. Vesting
8. Prayer: *O Lord our God, do thou lead thy servant*
   [if the order does not take place within the Divine Liturgy, then:
9. Litany
10. *As many as have been baptized into Christ, have put on Christ*
11. Reading of the Epistle and Gospel
12. Litany
13. Presentation of the hand cross and the candle, and the kiss
14. Dismissal]

The order of the Little Schema (this is the same for all candidates, both monks and nuns, with the use of the appropriate nouns and pronouns), takes place within the Divine Liturgy, in front of the holy doors of the iconostasis, after the Little Entrance and the singing of the troparia and the kontakia of the day; this is the order found in the eighth-century Barberini *Euchologion*.[39] After the last kontakion, the troparion, *Make haste to open thy fatherly arms unto me* (from the service for the Sunday of the Prodigal Son in the Triodion), is sung. During that troparion, the brother to be tonsured, wearing only a white tunic or shirt, is brought by the ecclesiarch from the narthex to the holy doors, and he makes several prostrations on the way: as he enters into the nave, in the middle of the nave, and in front of the holy doors. According to the Russian practice, the one to be tonsured is brought by his elder and the ecclesiarch. After making the last prostration, he usually crawls up to the priest as the elder and the ecclesiarch cover him with their mandyas, or, in any case, he falls to the ground and remains prostrate on the floor.

[39]*Barberini*, 177, 220–234.

The priest begins to read the catechesis on monastic life, which includes several questions which the candidate must answer. According to the Russian practice, the priest, after reading the introduction of the catechesis, raises the candidate from the floor and starts asking him questions, to which the candidate responds by formulating the vows of stability, chastity, obedience and poverty. After reading the long catechesis, the priest asks the candidate once more whether he acknowledges all these things and whether he agrees to hold fast his vows. After the candidate's positive response, the priest reads the first prayer before the tonsure: *Therefore, may the all-compassionate and greatly merciful God.* The priest then reads a second prayer, laying the book on the bowed head of the candidate: *O Lord our God, who hast decreed*, found in the Barberini *Euchologion* as the prayer for one who wishes to take the monastic schema.[40] It is followed by the prayer of inclination: *O Lord our God, the hope and refuge*, found in *Coislin 213* (11th c.).[41]

The rite of tonsure follows these prayers. The priest places the scissors on the book of the holy gospels, and says to the candidate: *Take up the scissors, and give them to me.* The candidate takes them, and gives them to the priest while kissing his hand. This is done thrice. Then the priest, after reminding the candidate that he received the scissors from the hand of Christ himself, takes the scissors and says: *Blessed is God, who willeth that all men should be saved and come to the knowledge of the truth, who is blessed unto the ages of ages* (cf. 1 Tim 2.4), as at the end of the pre-baptismal rites. Then the priest cuts the hair of the candidate crosswise saying: *Our brother, N., is tonsured in the hair of his head, in the name of the Father, and of the Son and of the Holy Spirit: let us all say for him, Lord have mercy.* The usage is to give the new monastic a new name at this point. The brethren sing three times: *Kyrie, eleison.* According to the Russian practice (instituted by Peter Moghila), the formula for the tonsure is: *Our brother, N., is tonsured in the hair of his head, as a sign of his renunciation of the world, and of everything in the world, and for the restraining of his will and of all fleshly desires, in the name of the Father, and of the Son, and of the Holy Spirit: let us all say for him, Lord have mercy.*

The tonsure is followed by the vesting. For each garment that the newly tonsured monastic receives, the priest says: *Our brother, N., is clothed with* . . . and the brethren respond each time by singing three times: *Kyrie, eleison.*

[40]*Barberini*, 177.
[41]Dmitrievsky, *Opisanie*, 2:1028.

According to the Greek practice, the priest gives the newly tonsured monastic the cassock, the belt, the kamilavkion with the epanokamilavkion (veil), the rason, and the sandals. According to the Russian practice, the priest gives the newly tonsured the cassock, the rason, the belt, the mandyas, the klobuk, the sandals, the prayer rope, the hand cross, and the lighted candle, with the proper words. Finally, the priest says: *Our brother, N., has received the betrothal of the great and angelic schema, in the name of the Father, and of the Son, and of the Holy Spirit. Let us say for him, Lord have mercy.* And the brethren respond each time by singing three times: *Kyrie, eleison.*

The vesting is followed by a final prayer: *O Lord our God, do thou lead thy servant*, mentioned in *Coislin 213* (11th c.).[42] After this prayer, the regular order of the Divine Liturgy continues, with the exclamation of the priest for the Trisagion: *For thou art holy, O our God*, the Trisagion, and the biblical readings. In the Greek practice, after the readings, the priest presents the hand cross and the candle to the newly tonsured monastic, with the words: *The Lord said: If any man will come after me, let him deny himself, and take up his cross, and follow me* (Mt 16.24), and: *The Lord said: Let thy light so shine before men, that they may see thy good works and glorify thy Father who is in heaven* (Mt 5.16).[43] (In the Russian practice, these are given at the end of the vesting). After the Ambo Prayer, the brethren sing the sticheron: *Brethren, let us understand the power of the mystery*, during which they exchange a kiss with the newly tonsured monastic, asking: *What is thy name, brother?* and after receiving the answer, they reply: *Mayest thou be saved in the angelic rank.* Then the dismissal of the Divine Liturgy takes place.

If the order does not take place within the Divine Liturgy, then, after the final prayer, the deacon says the litany, and this is followed by the singing of *As many as have been baptized into Christ, have put on Christ* (as for baptism), the readings of the epistle and gospel, and the litany. Then, in the Greek practice, the priest presents the hand cross and the candle to the newly tonsured monastic, and after this comes the exchange of the kiss, and the final dismissal.

4. The Order of the Great and Angelic Schema

Before the tonsure, at Matins, a special canon found in the *Euchologion* is chanted, with the acrostic: *Grant unto me, O Christ, the gladness of a happy*

---

[42]Dmitrievsky, *Opisanie*, 2:1034.
[43]Goar, 480–481.

end, as well as special stichera. The order of the great and angelic schema also takes place during the Divine Liturgy, after the Little Entrance, after the singing of the troparia appointed for the day. The candidate to·be tonsured into the great angelic schema lays aside his head covering and sandals, makes three prostrations in the middle of the church and stands there.

Table 6.3: The Order of the Great and Angelic Schema

1. Antiphons and troparia
2. Catechesis, including questions and answers
3. First prayer before the tonsure: *Therefore, may the all-compassionate and greatly merciful God*
4. Second prayer before the tonsure: *O Master Almighty*
5. Prayer [of inclination]: *O holy Lord of hosts*
6. Tonsure
7. Vesting
8. Troparia: *Put on the robe of salvation; My soul shall rejoice in the Lord*
9. Prayer: *O Lord our God, who art faithful in thy promises*
10. Prayer of inclination: *O Lord our God, do thou lead thy servant*
[if the order does not take place within the Divine Liturgy, then:
11. Litany
12. *As many as have been baptized into Christ, have put on Christ*
13. Reading of the Epistle and Gospel
14. Litany
15. Presentation of the hand cross and the candle, and kiss
16. Dismissal]

During the singing of the special antiphons, the candidate to be tonsured goes up to the holy doors. According to the Russian practice, he falls to the ground and remains prostrate on the floor as the special troparia are sung. The priest then begins to read the catechesis on monastic life, which includes several questions to which the the candidate responds by formulating the vows of stability, chastity, obedience, and poverty. After reading the long catechesis, the priest asks the candidate once more whether he acknowledges all these things and whether he agrees to hold fast his vows. After the positive answer of the candidate, the priest reads the first prayer before the tonsure: *Therefore, may the all-compassionate and greatly merciful*

God. The priest then makes the sign of the cross thrice over the head of the candidate and reads a second prayer facing toward the east: *O Master Almighty.* This is followed by the former prayer of inclination: *O holy Lord of Hosts.* Both prayers are found in *Coislin 213* (11th c.).[44]

These prayers are followed by the rite of the tonsure. The priest places the scissors on the gospel book and says to the candidate: *Take up the scissors, and give them to me.* The candidate takes them, and gives them to the priest while kissing his hand. This is done thrice. Then, the priest, after reminding the candidate that he received the scissors from the hand of Christ himself, takes the scissors and says: *Blessed is God, who willeth that all men should be saved and come to the knowledge of the truth, who is blessed unto the ages of ages* (cf. 1 Tim 2.4), as at the end of the pre-baptismal rites. Then the priest cuts the hair of the candidate crosswise saying: *Our brother, N., is tonsured in the hair of his head, in the name of the Father, and of the Son and of the Holy Spirit: let us all say for him, Lord have mercy.* The usage is to give a new name to the newly tonsured monastic at this point. The brethren sing three times: *Kyrie, eleison.* According to the Russian practice (instituted by Peter Moghila), the formula for the tonsure is: *Our brother, N., is tonsured, a second time, in the hair of his head, as a sign of his final renunciation of the world, and of everything in the world, and for the final restraining of his will and of all fleshly desires, in which to keep himself in silence and perseverance, in the name of the Father, and of the Son and of the Holy Spirit: let us all say for him: Lord have mercy.*

The tonsure is followed by the vesting. For each garment that the newly tonsured monastic receives, the priest says: *Our brother, N., is clothed . . .* , and the brethren respond each time by singing three times: *Kyrie, eleison.* According to the Greek practice, the priest gives the newly tonsured monastic the cassock, the rason, the koukoulion, the analabos, the belt, the sandals, and the mandyas. According to the Russian practice, the priest gives the newly tonsured monstic the cassock, the rason, the great paraman, the belt, the koukoulion with the analabos, the mandyas, the sandals, the prayer rope, the hand cross, and the lighted candle, each with the proper words. Finally, the priest says: *Our brother, N., has received the great and angelic schema, in the name of the Father, and of the Son, and of the Holy Spirit. Let us say for him, Lord have mercy*; and the brethren respond each time by singing three times: *Kyrie, eleison.*

[44]Dmitrievsky, *Opisanie*, 2:1032.

The vesting is followed by troparia: *Put on the robe of salvation,* and: *My soul shall rejoice in the Lord,* and these are followed by a final prayer: *O Lord our God, who art faithful in thy promises,* and a prayer of inclination: *O Lord our God, do thou lead thy servant,* mentioned in *Coislin 213* (11th c.).[45] After this prayer, the regular order of the Divine Liturgy continues, with the exclamation of the priest for the Trisagion: *For holy at thou, O our God,* the Trisagion and the biblical readings. In the Greek practice, after the readings, the priest presents the hand cross and the candle to the newly tonsured monastic, with the words: *The Lord said: If any man will come after me, let him deny himself, and take up his cross, and follow me* (Mt 16.24), and: *The Lord said: Let thy light so shine before men, that they may see thy good works and glorify thy Father who is in heaven* (Mt 5.16).[46] (In the Russian practice, these items were already given at the end of the vesting). After the Ambo Prayer, the brethren sing the sticheron: *Brethren, let us understand the power of the mystery,* and exchange a kiss with the newly tonsured, asking: *What is thy name, brother?* and after they receive the answer, they reply: *Mayest thou be saved in the angelic rank.* Then the dismissal of the Divine Liturgy takes place.

If the order does not take place within the Divine Liturgy, then, after the final prayer, the deacon says the litany, and this is followed by the singing of *As many as have been baptized in Christ, have put on Christ* (as for baptism), the readings of the epistle and gospel, and the litany. Then, in the Greek practice, the priest presents the hand cross and the candle to the newly tonsured monastic, and after this comes the exchange of the kiss, and the final dismissal.

We find in the *Euchologion* a prayer for laying aside the koukoulion on the eighth day: *O most-merciful Lord, who by the taking of the angelic schema.*[47] This is a vestige of an old practice, witnessed by the Barberini *Euchologion,* according to which the newly tonsured monk remained in the church for eight consecutive days, by analogy with the eight days the neophytes spent in the church after their baptism and the ablutions that were made on the eighth day.[48]

---

[45]Dmitrievsky, *Opisanie,* 2:1034.
[46]Goar, 513–514.
[47]Goar, 519–520.
[48]*Barberini,* 226–227.

CHAPTER SEVEN

The Mystery of Death

1. Historical Overview

In the fifteenth century, Metropolitan Joasaph of Ephesus mentioned the funeral rites "over those who have fallen asleep in a sacred way" as the seventh of ten mysteries he enumerated.[1] A millennium earlier, Pseudo-Dionysios (5th c.) dedicated a whole chapter of his *Ecclesiastical Hierarchy* to the funeral ceremonies, among his commentaries on the different sacramental rites.[2] But the first mention of prayers and rites for the departed is found in the *Apostolic Constitutions*, compiled around the year 380.

The *Apostolic Constitutions* make a clear distinction between the Christian approach to the dead and the Judaic approach: the dead bodies are no more considered as impure and no purification is required after touching a dead body. Moreover, this work encourages Christians to gather in cemeteries to read the sacred books and to sing psalms in honor of the martyrs, the saints, and the brothers who are buried there. It also prescribes the singing of psalms for the funeral of the dead, and that the remains of the departed are not to be despised.[3] Furthermore, it describes the prayer for a departed Christian conducted at the first hour of the night, in what might suggest a kind of vigil. The deacon prays: *For the rest of N., so that God, the lover of mankind, may receive his soul, forgive him all voluntary or involuntary sin, be propitious and favorable to him, and admit him into the dwelling of the pious dead, who rest in the bosom of Abraham, Isaac, and Jacob, with all those who have been pleasing to him from the beginning, and have fulfilled his will, where there is neither sickness, nor sorrow, nor sighing.* Then the bishop prays for the departed to the *God of Abraham, the God of Isaac, and the God of Jacob . . . not the God of the dead but of the living,* that he will *forgive him if he has*

---

[1]Metropolitan Joasaph of Ephesus, *Canonical Answers* 47, ed. A. Almazov (Odessa, 1903), 38.

[2]Pseudo-Dionysios the Areopagite, *Ecclesiastical Hierarchy* 7 (PG 3:552d–565c; Luibheid, 249–251).

[3]*Apostolic Constitutions* 6.30 (SC 329:388–392; ANF 7:464).

committed any voluntary or involuntary sin, and to admit him to a place *where there is no sickness, nor sorrow, nor sighing*.[4] The *Apostolic Constitutions* also mention the prayer for the departed on the third day, because of the resurrection of Christ; on the ninth day, in memory of the departed and of those who are still alive; on the fortieth day, in imitation of the people of Israel who mourned Moses; and on the anniversary of the death, in memory of the departed.[5]

In his description of the funeral ceremonies, in the framework of a communal liturgy, Pseudo-Dionysios, in his *Ecclesiastical Hierarchy*, mentions psalmody, biblical readings, and prayers. He also makes a distinction between the funeral of a clergyman and that of a layman or that of a monk. If the departed belonged to the clergy, his body is placed at the foot of the altar table, while if he was a layman or a monk, his body is placed in front of the doors of the sanctuary. The "prayer of thanksgiving" is then said, an expression that indicates that the Eucharist was celebrated. Passages from Holy Scripture about the resurrection of the dead are read, and psalms related to the same topic are sung. After the dismissal of the catechumens, the names of the departed are proclaimed, and the bishop says a prayer over the body of the departed person.[6] The prayer asks for the forgiveness of all the faults committed by the departed for which human weakness is responsible, and to establish him *in the light and place of the living, in the bosom of Abraham, Isaac, and of Jacob, where sickness, sorrow, and sighing are unknown*.[7] Then the bishop gives the last kiss to the dead person, and the whole assembly does the same. After the kiss of peace, the bishop pours oil over the body, which is then buried in the ground next to other departed Christians of the same dignity. Pseudo-Dionysios compares the anointing of the dead with the anointing of the catechumen: in the rites of Christian initiation, the anointing with oil preceded baptism, and signified that the catechumen was exchanging his old garment for a new one and was called to spiritual warfare; now, at the funeral, oil is poured out at the end of the ceremony to testify that the deceased had struggled throughout his life until the final victory.[8]

---

[4] *Apostolic Constitutions* 8.41 (SC 336, 256–258; cf. ANF 7:497–498).

[5] *Apostolic Constitutions* 8.42 (SC 336, 258–260; cf. ANF 7:498).

[6] Pseudo-Dionysios the Areopagite, *Ecclesiastical Hierarchy* 7 (PG 3:556bd; Luibheid, 251–252).

[7] Pseudo-Dionysios the Areopagite, *Ecclesiastical Hierarchy* 7 (PG 3:560ab; cf. Luibheid, 253–254).

[8] Pseudo-Dionysios the Areopagite, *Ecclesiastical Hierarchy* 7 (PG 3:564d–565a; Luibheid, 256–257).

The Barberini *Euchologion* does not contain a funeral service properly speaking, but only different prayers that ought to be said for the burial of a layman, of a clergyman, and of a monastic.[9] Among them, we find the famous prayer that is still used today: *O God of spirits and of all flesh*, which asks the Lord to *give rest* [to the departed] *in a place of brightness, in a place of green pasture, in a place of repose, whence sickness, sorrow, and sighing have fled away*, and to forgive *every sin committed by him whether by word or deed or thought*.[10] This prayer is most probably a very ancient one, developing the same idea as the one found in the *Apostolic Constitutions*, and perhaps the one referred to by Pseudo-Dionysius. Some ascribe it to Saint Basil the Great.[11] It is followed by a prayer of inclination of the head: *O Lord, O Lord*, which corresponds to the prayer known today as *Lord of hosts, who art the joy of the afflicted*, in the funeral of a priest.

These two prayers are found also in *Coislin 213* (1027), which in addition contains a prayer and a prayer of inclination for a departed priest: *We give thanks to thee, O Lord our God*, which is still used today for the funeral of priest, though not as a prayer of inclination; a prayer for a departed deacon, a prayer for a departed child: *O Lord, who guardest infants in this present life*, a prayer for a departed monk: *O Lord our God, who in thy wisdom hast molded man from earth*, as well as other prayers.[12] These prayers were inserted into the regular liturgical services of the ecclesial community, as suggested by the witness of the *Apostolic Constitutions*. In Constantinople, the asmatic service of the Pannychis (a type of all-night vigil) was chosen for the prayers for the departed. It was a service structured by three antiphons, each of them followed by a litany of the deacon and a prayer of the priest. The contemporary Byzantine-rite services for the departed are still much influenced by the ancient Pannychis.[13]

The euchologion manuscript *Sinai gr. 973* (12th c.) gives a complete order for the departed.[14] It starts with the Trisagion and the litany, including the special petitions for the departed known to us today. At the conclusion of

[9]*Barberini*, 235–238.

[10]*Barberini*, 235.

[11]Vitaliano Bruni, *I funerali di un sacerdote nel rito bizantino secondo gli eucologi mano-scritti di lingua greca* (Jerusalem: Franciscan Printing House, 1972), 157.

[12]Dmitrievsky, *Opisanie*, 2:1012–1013; Arranz, *Eucologio*, 309–315.

[13]M. Arranz, "Les prières presbytérales de la Pannychis de l'ancien euchologe byzantin et la Panikhida des défunts II," *OCP* 41 (1975): 119–139, at 138.

[14]Dmitrievsky, *Opisanie*, 2:110–111.

the litany, the priest said the two prayers for the departed found in the Barberini *Euchologion*: *O God of spirits and of all flesh*, and: *O Lord, O Lord*.

Another euchologion manuscript, *Sinai 963* (also 12th c.), gives a complete order for a departed monk.[15] It consists of Psalm 118, followed by the Six Psalms, Alleluia in the second tone, the troparia: *Remember, O Lord, as as thou art good, thy servant*, and: *Have mercy on me, O God*, the canon, the Praises, the stichera of the tone, the Beatitudes, and the readings of the epistle and of the gospel. Psalm 118 is followed by the Evlogetaria, called "troparia of the undefiled" (τροπάρια τοῦ Ἀμώνου).[16] The litany contains the special petitions for the departed we know today, and it is followed by the prayer: *O God of spirits and of all flesh* from the Barberini *Euchologion*. *Sinai 963* also provides the series of stichera prosomoia for the eight tones, now attributed to St John of Damascus and still used today in the funeral of a layman. It gives the prokeimenon: *His soul shall abide amid good things* (ἐν ἀγαθοῖς, *en agathois*), the epistle reading from Romans 14.6–9 and the gospel reading from John 5.24–30. Then troparia: *Remember, O Lord, as thou art good* are sung, and these are followed by the Trisagion and the "troparia of the Trisagion," then the stichera for the last kiss (τελευταῖος ἀσπασμός, *teleutaios aspasmos*). Then follows the prayer for a departed priest or monk: *We give thanks to thee O Lord our God*, found also in *Coislin 213*, and a prayer of inclination: *O good God and Lover of mankind*. After that comes a series of stichera according to the eight tones for departed monks. These are followed by the kontakion for the departed: *With the saints give rest* and its ikos: *Thou only art immortal*, still used today in the funeral services. Finally we find a canon for a departed monk in tone 6.

The euchologion manuscript *Sinai gr. 990* (14th c.) gives another order for the funeral of a layman.[17] It starts with the troparion: *The narrow way*, and other troparia; these are followed by a litany, a canon, a prokeimenon, the readings of the epistle and the gospel, then the prosomoia for the last kiss, and the litany with special petitions for the departed, with the concluding prayer: *O God of spirits and of all flesh*, found in the Barberini *Euchologion*.

The euchologion manuscript *Dionysiou 450* (1408) contains another order for the funeral of a layman.[18] This starts with Psalm 118 with refrains,

[15]Dmitrievsky, *Opisanie*, 2:135–139.
[16]Ps 118 is known as "The Undefiled" or "The Blameless" (ὁ Ἄμωμος, *ho Amōmos*) from its first line, Blessed are the undefiled (or blameless) in the way.
[17]Dmitrievsky, *Opisanie*, 2:326.
[18]Dmitrievsky, *Opisanie*, 2:390–391.

followed by the Evlogetaria: *The choir of saints*. We find then the kathisma hymns: *Give rest, O our Savior*, the litany, an antiphon, the Beatitudes, an idiomelon,[19] the prokeimenon: *Blessed is the way*, the reading of the epistle from 1 Corinthians 15.20–28, and the usual reading of the gospel from John 5.24–30, followed by the troparia for the last kiss. After that the priest commemorates the departed and pronounces the dismissal. For the burial, the Trisagion is sung, and the troparia: *With the souls of the righteous departed*. When the departed person is put into the grave, the priest pours oil from a lamp over his body, and then says the litany and the prayer for the departed: *O God of spirits and of all flesh*, and the dismissal concludes the service.

The same manuscript contains a service for the funeral of a priest.[20] After Psalm 118 and the Evlogetaria, the priest commemorates the departed. Three antiphons are sung, each followed by a litany, then the Beatitudes with troparia, the kontakion: *With the saints give rest*, the prokeimenon: *Blessed is the way*, and the reading of the epistle from 1 Corinthian 15.47–57, and the regular reading of the gospel from John 5.24–30, the troparia for the last kiss, and the dismissal.

The euchologion manuscript *Saint Sabbas 369* (15th c.) contains a service for the funeral of a child.[21] After the usual beginning and Psalm 90, we find the troparia: *O thou, who with wisdom profound*, and then the canon for a departed child, still found today in the Slavonic printed euchologia for the funeral of a child. This is followed by the stichera for the Praises and the same prokeimenon and epistle and gospel readings found in the contemporary Russian practice, then the litany with the prayer: *O Lord, who guardest infants in this present life*, the Trisagion, the troparia: *Remember O Lord as thou art good*; *O thou, who with wisdom profound*, and the dismissal.

The fifteenth-century manuscript *Euchologion* of the Constantinopolitan *Metochion of the Holy Sepulcher 8 (182)* contains another service for the funeral of a monk,[22] similar to the one contained in our contemporary euchologia. It consists of the usual beginning, the troparia: *Remember, O Lord, as thou art good, thy servant*, and Psalm 90, followed by Alleluia and the troparia: *O thou, who with wisdom profound* and: *We have thee as a wall*

[19]An idiomelon is a hymn that has its own proper melody, a melody that is not used for any other hymn.
[20]Dmitrievsky, *Opisanie*, 2:391–392.
[21]Dmitrievsky, *Opisanie*, 2:451.
[22]Dmitrievsky, *Opisanie*, 2: 478–481.

and a haven, then Psalm 118 concluding with the Evlogetaria, the litany
with the special petitions for the departed, the antiphons (*anabathmoi*), the
Beatitudes, the prokeimenon, and the readings of the epistle from Romans
14:6–9 and of the gospel from John 6.40–44, the litany with the prayer: *We
give thanks to thee, O Lord our God*, that was found in *Coislin 213*, and the
stichera for the last kiss. The Trisagion is then said, a litany and a prayer for
monks and priests: *The great and just high priest Jesus Christ.* The remains
are placed in the grave as the Trisagion is being chanted, and as the grave
is being sealed the troparia are sung. The litany is said once more, with the
prayer over the grave: *Remember, O Lord God*, the troparia: *Remember, O
Lord, as thou art good; With all the saints; We have thee as a wall and a haven;
Kyrie, eleison* 100 times, and the dismissal.

The variety of services for the departed ceased in the seventeenth century, thanks to printing. The *Euchologion* of Jacques Goar, published in
Paris in 1647, gives three distinct services—one for the funeral of laymen,[23] another for the funeral of monks,[24] and the third for the funeral of
priests,[25] as well as three distinct hymnographic canons for departed men,[26]
women,[27] and children.[28] The Slavonic printed edition of the *Trebnik* of
Peter Moghila, printed in Kiev in 1646, contains exactly the same services
as the Goar *Euchologion*: the funeral of laymen considered to be "according to the order of Saint Sophia of Kiev and of the Lavra of the Caves,"[29] of
children,[30] of priests,[31] and of monks.[32] These became the standard order
for the funeral services still used today, although the contemporary Greek
editions have introduced several simplifications and abbreviations, as we
shall see below.

[23]Goar, 525–538.
[24]Goar, 544–557.
[25]Goar, 561–580.
[26]Goar, 583–587.
[27]Goar, 588–592.
[28]Goar, 592–597.
[29]Peter Moghila, *Euchologion*, 1:585–626.
[30]Peter Moghila, *Euchologion*, 1:629–627.
[31]Peter Moghila, *Euchologion*, 1:652–696.
[32]Peter Moghila, *Euchologion*, 2:956–976.

2. The Funeral of a Layman

Table 7.1: The Order of the Funeral of a Layman, Part 1—The Lity [λιτή] or Trisagion for the Departed

---

1. Opening blessing and usual beginning prayers
2. Troparia: *With the souls of the righteous departed*
3. Litany
4. Prayer for the departed: *O God of spirits and of all flesh*
5. Dismissal
6. Memory eternal

The funeral used to begin in the house of the departed with a brief service often called the "Lity for the Departed" or the "Trisagion." In today's circumstances, this service often takes place in a hospital, in a morgue, or in a funeral home. The departed is placed in his coffin. According to the Russian practice, a headband depicting Christ, the Theotokos, and the Forerunner, with the inscription of the Trisagion, is placed on his forehead.

This very brief service is composed of the troparia for the departed, the litany with special petitions for the departed, and the ancient prayer for the departed found in the Barberini *Euchologion*. Then, the remains of the departed are transferred to the church where the funeral takes place. During the transfer of the remains, the Trisagion is sung.

Table 7.2: The Order of the Funeral of a Layman, Part 2—The Funeral Service Proper

---

Greek books[33]	Slavic books[34]
1. Opening blessing: *Blessed is our God*	1. Opening blessing: *Blessed is our God*
	[2. Psalm 90]
2. Psalmody = Psalm 118 (in three parts, each followed by a Little Litany, prayer for the departed and exclamation)	3. Psalmody = Psalm 118 (in three parts, each followed by a Little Litany, prayer for the departed and exclamation)

---

[33] *Μικρὸν Εὐχολόγιον* (Athens, 1996), 236–256.
[34] *Trebnik*, vol. 1 (Moscow, 1991), 168–204.

3. After the third part, Evlogetaria:
Blessed art thou, O Lord;
The choir of saints

4. Kontakion:
With the saints give rest

5. Idiomela of
Saint John Damascene

6. Beatitudes with troparia

7. Prokeimenon, Apostle,
Alleluia, Gospel

8. Litany and prayer for the
departed: *O God of spirits and*
of all flesh

[9. If a bishop is presiding, he
reads the prayer of absolution]

10. Dismissal

11. Memory eternal

12. Last kiss and stichera prosomoia

---

4. After the third part, Evlogetaria:
Blessed art thou, O Lord;
The choir of saints

5. Kathisma hymn: *Give rest, O our*
Savior

[6. Psalm 50]

7. Canon attributed to
Theophanes—3rd, 6th and 9th
ode followed by a Little Litany,
prayer for the departed and
exclamation.

After the 6th ode, kontakion:
With the saints give rest

8. Idiomela of
Saint John Damascene

9. Beatitudes with troparia

10. Prokeimenon, Apostle,
Alleluia, Gospel

11. Litany and prayer for the
departed: *O God of spirits and*
of all flesh

[12. Last kiss and stichera
prosomoia]

13. Trisagion and troparia: *With the*
souls of the righteous departed

14. Litany and Prayer for the
departed: *O God of spirits and of*
all flesh

[15. If a bishop is presiding,
he reads the prayer of absolution]

16. Dismissal

17. Memory eternal

The funeral service in the church begins, after the opening blessing and the reading of Psalm 90, with the singing of Psalm 118, divided into three parts, with refrains: *Alleluia* for the first and third portions; *Have mercy upon thy servant* for the second portion. One can recognize here the influence of the asmatic service of Constantinople, where Psalm 118 used to be the antiphon for the Sunday Pannychis. Each part is followed by a Little Litany, a prayer for the departed and exclamation. The third part is concluded by the Evlogetaria for the Departed, sometimes called in the manuscripts "troparia of the undefiled," as we explained in the historical introduction at the beginning of this chapter. These troparia were modeled on the Evlogetaria of the Resurrection, which appeared in Jerusalem in the ninth century in the service of Holy Saturday, and which are now sung at Matins every Sunday.[35] Then, the Little Litany of the third part is followed by the kathisma hymn: *Give rest, O our Savior.*

After Psalm 50, a canon attributed to Theophanes, a ninth-century Constantinopolitan hymnographer, is sung. After the third, sixth, and ninth odes, a Little Litany is said, with the prayer for the departed, followed by proper hymns. In practice, the canon is often abbreviated. In the Russian practice, only the heirmoi and the refrain: *Give rest, O Lord, unto the soul of thy servant*, are usually sung. According to the practice of the Church of Greece, the canon is omitted, and only the kontakion: *With the saints give rest*, is sung immediately after the evlogetaria.

The canon is followed by the eight idiomela, attributed to Saint John of Damascus (8th c.), one in each of the eight tones. These are followed by the troparia on the Beatitudes. Originally all these elements belonged not to the Constantinopolitan cathedral rite, but to the Palestinian monastic rite that was introduced in Constantinople in the ninth century and was synthesized with the cathedral rite in the twelfth century by the *Typikon* of the Evergetis monastery.

This hymnography is followed by the biblical readings. The prokeimenon: *Blessed is the way*, already attested in the later manuscript tradition, introduces the reading of the Apostle from 1 Thessalonians 4.13–18, wherein St Paul writes, "we believe that Jesus died and rose again, even so them also, which sleep in Jesus will God bring with him." The Alleluia and the reading of the Gospel from John 5.24–30 follow. In that gospel pericope we read that those who believe in Christ "have passed from death unto life." The readings are normally followed by the litany and the prayer for the departed, although these are often omitted at this point.

According to the printed euchologia, the prosomoia are sung during the ceremony of the last kiss (τελευταῖος ἀσπασμός), already mentioned in the *Ecclesiastical Hierarchy* of Pseudo-Dionysios.[36] For practical reasons—

---

[35]See our first volume: J. Getcha, *The Typikon Decoded*, 111–112.
[36]The citations are found above, in the Historical Overview.

essentially to gain time—the rite of the last kiss is often postponed until after the dismissal of the funeral service, as the table above shows the situation in the contemporary Greek printed euchologia.

Then, according to the printed text, the Lity for the Departed (Trisagion) is served again. The contemporary Greek practice omits this. The printed euchologia state then that if a bishop is presiding, he reads a special prayer of absolution for the departed. In the contemporary Russian practice, this prayer is read even if a priest is presiding at the funeral, and usually the text of the prayer is printed on a sheet of paper which is then put into the hands of the departed. Then the dismissal takes place, and *Memory eternal* is sung.

At the cemetery, the Lity for the Departed (Trisagion) is chanted one more time, the same way as it was done at the house (or other venue). At the end, oil from a lamp is poured over the remains of the departed, and the grave is then covered. As we have seen, the rite of pouring oil over the body of the departed is already attested by Pseudo-Dionysius, who compares this rite with the anointing of the catechumens: as new life was given in baptism, now the departed is passing through death from this earthly life into eternal life.[37]

3. The Funeral of a Layman during Bright Week

The funeral service is slightly different when it occurs during paschal (bright) week, since paschal hymnography is added. In the house, the Lity (Trisagion) is served as follows:

Table 7.3: The Order of the Funeral during Bright Week, Part 1—The Lity or Trisagion for the Departed

Greek books[38]	Slavic books[39]
1. Opening blessing and usual beginning prayers	1. Opening blessing and usual beginning prayers
2. *Christ is risen* (thrice) and *Jesus is risen from the tomb*	2. *Christ is risen* (thrice) and Paschal Verses

---

[37]Cf. Pseudo-Dionysios the Areopagite, *Ecclesiastical Hierarchy* 7 (PG 3:564d–565a; Liubheid, 256–257).

[38]*Μικρὸν Εὐχολόγιον*, 260–262.

[39]*Trebnik*, vol. 3 (Moscow, 1984), 277–278.

3. Litany	3. Litany
4. Prayer for the departed: *O God of spirits and of all flesh*	4. Prayer for the departed: *O God of spirits and of all flesh*
	5. *Having beheld the resurrection of Christ*
5. Dismissal	6. Dismissal
6. Memory eternal and Christ is risen	7. Memory eternal and Christ is risen

In the church, the funeral service consists essentially of the paschal canon, which replaces the canon for the departed. The biblical readings are not the regular ones for the departed, but the readings from the Divine Liturgy prescribed for that day of Bright week. Read after the sixth ode of the canon and after the kontakion, they are preceded by: *As many as have been baptized into Christ,* and followed by: *Having beheld the resurrection of Christ.* The prosomoia for the rite of the last kiss are replaced by the stichera of Pascha.

The contemporary Greek practice simplifies the earlier order, which is still followed by the Slavonic printed euchologia. Instead of the paschal canon, the Greek practice prescribes the singing only the katavasiai, and the biblical readings follow after all the katavasiai have been sung, as one can see in the following table:

Table 7.4: The Order of the Funeral during Bright Week, Part 2—The Funeral Proper

Greek books[40]	Slavic books[41]
1. Opening blessing: *Blessed is our God*	1. Opening blessing: *Blessed is our God*
2. *Christ is risen* (thrice)	2. *Christ is risen* (thrice) and the Paschal Verses
3. Litany, prayer for the departed and exclamation	3. Litany, prayer for the departed and exclamation
4. Katavasiai of Pascha, each followed by *Christ is risen* (thrice) and *Jesus is risen from the tomb,* a Little Litany, and the exclamation of the departed	4. Canon of Pascha. 3rd, 6th, and 9th ode are followed by followed by a Little Litany, the exclamation of the departed, and the proper hymn.

[40] *Μικρὸν Εὐχολόγιον* (Athens, 1996), 262–266.
[41] *Trebnik*, vol. 3 (Moscow, 1984), 279–286.

5. Exaposteilarion of Pascha	After the 6th ode: *With the saints give rest*, and: *As many as have been baptized into Christ, have put on Christ*, Prokeimenon, Apostle, Alleluia, Gospel of the day of Bright week followed by: *Having beheld the resurrection of Christ* and: *Jesus is risen from the tomb*, Little Litany, and exclamation of the departed.
6. Prokeimenon, Apostle, Alleluia, Gospel of the day of Bright week	
	5. Evlogetaria: *Blessed art thou, O Lord*; *The choir of saints*
	6. Stichera of Pascha with last kiss
7. Litany and prayer for the departed: *O God of spirits and of all flesh*	7. Litany and prayer for the departed: *O God of spirits and of all flesh*
[8. If a bishop is presiding, he reads the prayer of absolution]	
9. Dismissal	8. Dismissal
10. Memory eternal	9. Memory eternal
11. Last kiss with the doxastikon of the paschal stichera	

4. The Funeral of a Priest

The order for the funeral of a priest[42] is particular and quite complicated, since it is a hybrid service into which elements from various liturgical traditions have been combined.

Before the service, the departed priest is vested in all his priestly vestments, his face is covered by an aër, and the book of the holy Gospels is placed over his breast. The funeral service is served in the church as follows:

Table 7.5: The Order of the Funeral of a Priest

1. Opening blessing: *Blessed is our God*

2. Psalmody = Psalm 118 (in three portions, each followed by a Little Litany, prayer for the departed, and exclamation)

3. After the third section, Evlogetaria: *Blessed art thou, O Lord*; *The choir of saints*

---

[42]Goar, 561–580 = *Trebnik*, 3:184–252.

4. Kathisma hymns: *Give rest, O our Savior*

5. Antiphon 1

6. Prokeimenon 1, Apostle 1 (1 Thess 4.13–17), Alleluia, Gospel 1 (Jn 5.24–30) and prayer 1: *O Master Lord our God*

7. Troparion, Psalm 22, Kathisma hymn (Sedalen)

8. Prokeimenon 2, Apostle 2 (Rom 5.12–21), Alleluia, Gospel 2 (Jn 5.17–24) and prayer 2: *We give thanks unto thee, O Lord our God*

9. Antiphon 2, Psalm 23, troparion, Kathisma hymn (Sedalen)

10. Prokeimenon 3, Apostle 3 (1 Cor 15.1–11), Alleluia, Gospel 3 (Jn 6.35–39) and prayer 3: *O Lord of hosts, who art the joy of the afflicted*

11. Antiphon 3, Psalm 83, troparia

12. Prokeimenon 4, Apostle 4 (1 Cor 15.20–28), Alleluia, Gospel 4 (Jn 6.40–47)

13. Beatitudes with troparia

14. Prokeimenon 5, Apostle 5 (Rom 14.6–9), Alleluia, Gospel 5 (Jn 6.48–54)

15. Psalm 50

16. Canon (after the sixth ode, kontakion: *With the saints give rest* with twenty-four ikoi

17. The Praises with stichera

18. Great Doxology (in its Palestinian redaction, read[43])

19. Aposticha of Saint John Damascene

20. *It is good to give praise to the Lord*, Trisagion, and troparia: *With the souls of the righteous departed, give rest, O our Savior*

21. Litany

22. Prayer of absolution[44]

23. Last kiss and stichera prosomoia

24. And taking the body to the grave, the priests sing the heirmoi of the Great Canon

25. Trisagion and troparia: *In the place of thy rest O Lord*

26. Litany and Prayer for the departed: *O God of spirits and of all flesh*

27. Burial

28. Dismissal

---

[43]See *The Typikon Decoded*, 80.
[44]*The Great Book of Needs* 3:320 gives a slightly different order for the last elements of this service.

One can recognize the combination of at least four distinct parts. The service begins as the funeral of a layman with the opening blessing and Psalm 118 (from the Constantinopolitan Pannychis), divided into three parts, each followed by a Little Litany, prayer for the departed, and exclamation. The third part of the psalm is concluded by the Evlogetaria, and the third litany is followed by the kathisma hymn: *Give rest, O our Savior.*

Then, the funeral for a priest continues as a service of three antiphons, which recall the asmatic services of the Constantinopolitan cathedral rite. After the third antiphon, we find the Beatitudes with troparia for the departed, whose origin is not in the Constantinopolitan cathedral rite, but in the Palestinian monastic tradition. Between the antiphons and the Beatitudes are interpolated five biblical readings with proper prokeimena and Alleluia verses. This arrangement recalls the structure of Matins of Great Friday, at which twelve gospel readings are inserted between the antiphons and other hymnography. After each of the first three gospel readings, we find special prayers, which probably originally accompanied the three antiphons: *O Master Lord our God, we give thanks to thee, O Lord our God*, and *O Lord of hosts, who art the joy of the afflicted.* The first of these is found in the Barberini *Euchologion*, where it is considered a prayer for a departed monk.[45] The second is found in *Coislin 213* (1027).[46] The third is also found in the Barberini manuscript.[47]

After the fifth and last gospel reading, we find the third part of the service, which follows the order of Matins in the Palestinian monastic service. It starts with Psalm 50, followed by a special hymnographic canon for the departed priest, followed by the Praises with stichera for the departed priest, the reading of the Great Doxology in its Jerusalem redaction, followed by the aposticha attributed to Saint John Damascene, the psalmic prayer: *It is good to give praise to the Lord*, the Trisagion and the other prayers, the troparia for the departed: *Give rest, O our Savior,* etc., and the litany.

One should note another, fourth, element, placed after the sixth ode of the canon: the kontakion: *With the saints give rest,* is followed by 24 ikoi. We find here an ancient Constantinopolitan kontakion composed of 24 strophes, inserted into a Palestinian-type monastic service.

The final part of the service consists of the prayer of absolution, followed by the rite of the last kiss during the singing of the proper prosomoia. Then,

[45] *Barberini,* 238.
[46] Dmitrievsky, *Opisanie,* 2:1013.
[47] *Barberini,* 235.

according to the printed text, the remains of the departed priest are taken to the grave while the priests sing the heirmoi of the Great Canon of Saint Andrew of Crete (apart from this funeral service, this canon is usually sung during the first and fifth weeks of Great Lent). At the cemetery, the Lity (or Trisagion) for the Departed is sung, and this is followed by the burial and the dismissal.

According to contemporary Greek practice,[48] the funeral of a priest is celebrated in much the same manner as the funeral of a layman. All the troparia of the evlogetaria are sung; this is notable in the Greek practice, because the second and third troparia of the evlogetaria are usually omitted in a funeral for a layman. The prayer for the departed priest: *We give thanks to thee, O Lord our God*, from *Paris Coislin 213*, replaces the usual prayer for the departed: *O God of spirits and of all flesh*.

5. The Funeral of a Monk

The contemporary order for the funeral of monks[49] is relatively simple and similar to the one found in *Metochion of the Holy Sepulcher 8 (182)* of the fifteenth century:[50]

Table 7.6: The Order of the Funeral of a Monk

---

1. Opening blessing: *Blessed is our God*

2. Psalm 90, Alleluia and the troparia: *O thou, who with wisdom profound*, and *We have thee as a wall and a haven*

3. Psalmody = Psalm 118 (in two sections, each followed by a Little Litany, prayer for the departed and exclamation)

4. After the second section, Evlogetaria: *Blessed art thou, O Lord*, and *The choir of saints*

5. Kathisma hymns: *Give rest, O our Savior*

6. Psalm 50

7. Antiphon 1 and stichera of Theophanes

8. Antiphon 2 and stichera

9. Antiphon 3 and stichera

---

[48]Cf. *Μικρὸν Εὐχολόγιον*, 257–259.
[49]Goar, 544–557 = Peter Moghila, *Euchologion*, 2:956–976.
[50]Dmitrievsky, *Opisanie*, 2:478–481.

10. Antiphon 4 and stichera

11. Antiphon 5 and stichera

12. Antiphon 6 and stichera

13. Antiphon 7 and stichera

14. Antiphon 8 and stichera

15. Litany and prayer for the departed: *O God of spirits and of all flesh*

16. Kontakion: *With the saints give rest,* and ikos

17. Beatitudes with troparia

18. Prokeimenon: *Blessed is the way,* Apostle (1 Thess 4.13–17), Alleluia, Gospel (Jn 5.24–30)

19. Litany and prayer: *O God of spirits and of all flesh*

20. Last kiss and prosomoia of Saint John Damascene

21. Troparia: *With the souls of the righteous departed,* etc.

22. Litany and Prayer for the departed: *O God of spirits and of all flesh*

23. Dismissal

[24. Prayer of absolution]

After the opening blessing and Psalm 90, Alleluia is sung with verses followed by the troparia: *O thou, who with wisdom profound,* and: *We have thee as a wall and a haven.* Then Psalm 118 is sung with refrains; the psalm is divided into two sections, and the second section concludes with the Evlogetaria. These are followed by the kathisma hymn: *Give rest, O our Savior,* and this is followed by Psalm 50. Then comes a series of eight antiphons, each followed by a series of stichera. Then the Beatitudes are sung with special troparia. The prokeimenon and the readings of the epistle and of the gospel are the same as those for the funeral of a layman. The litany then follows with the same prayer as that found in the funeral of a layman. Then the rite of the last kiss takes place during the singing of the prosomia attributed to Saint John Damascene. The troparia for the departed: *With the souls of the righteous departed,* etc., are then sung, followed by the litany and the prayer for the departed, and the dismissal. After the dismissal, the prayer of absolution is said by the bishop or the hegoumen, and after that the burial takes place.

6. The Funeral of a Child

The special order of a funeral of child is used for any child who dies before the age of seven. The Lity in the house is the same as for the funeral of a layman, except that the usual prayer for the departed is replaced by the prayer for the departed child: *O Lord, who guardest infants in the present life*, already found in *Paris Coislin 213* (of 1027).[51]

In the church, the order of the service varies, with the Russian practice following a more ancient pattern, and the contemporary Greek practice following a simplified order of the funeral of an adult. The differences are shown in this table:

Table 7.7: The Order of the Funeral of a Child

Greek books[52]	Slavic books[53]
1. Opening blessing: *Blessed is our God*	1. Opening blessing: *Blessed is our God*
2. Psalmody = Psalm 118 (in three parts, each followed by a Little Litany, prayer for the departed child and exclamation)	2. Psalm 90
	3. Troparia: *O thou, who with wisdom profound*, and *We have thee as a wall and a haven*
3. After the third part, Evlogetaria: *Blessed art thou, O Lord*; *The choir of saints*	4. Psalm 50
4. Kontakion: *With the saints give rest*	5. Canon for a departed child
5. Idiomela of Saint John Damascene	(after the 3rd ode, litany and prayer: *O Lord Jesus Christ our God, who hast promised to bestow the Kingdom of Heaven*, and Kathisma Hymn [Sedalen])
6. Beatitudes with troparia	(after the 6th ode, litany and prayer: *O Lord Jesus Christ our God, who hast promised to bestow the Kingdom of Heaven* and kontakion: *With the saints give rest*)
7. Prokeimenon, Apostle (Rm 6.9–11), Alleluia, Gospel (Lk 18.15–17, 26–27)	
8. Litany and prayer for the departed child: *O Lord, who guardest infants in the present life*	(after the 9th ode, litany and prayer: *O Lord Jesus Christ our God, who hast promised to bestow the Kingdom of Heaven*, and exaposteilarion)
9. Dismissal	
10. Last kiss and two special stichera prosomoia	

[51]Dmitrievsky, *Opisanie*, 2:1013.
[52]Μικρὸν Εὐχολόγιον, 272–274.
[53]*Trebnik*, 3:253–276.

6. Exclamation: *For holy art thou, O our God*, and Trisagion

7. Prokeimenon, Apostle (1 Cor 15.39–46), Alleluia, Gospel (Jn 6.35–40)

8. Last kiss and selected stichera prosomoia

9. Trisagion and troparia: *With the souls of the righteous departed*

10. Litany and Prayer for the departed: *O God of spirits and of all flesh*

11. Dismissal

12. Memory eternal

13. Prayer: *O Lord, who guardest infants in this present life*, and burial

According to the Russian practice, after the opening blessing: *Blessed is our God*, Psalm 90 is chanted, and this is followed by the troparia: *O thou, who with wisdom profound*, and: *We have thee as a wall and a haven*. Then Psalm 50 is read, and after it the special canon for a departed child. This canon is found in Greek in the Goar *Euchologion*.[54] After the third ode, the litany is intoned, and it is followed by a special prayer: *O Lord Jesus Christ our God, who hast promised to bestow the Kingdom of Heaven*, and the kathisma hymn. After the sixth ode, the litany is said again, with the same special prayer, then the kontakion for the departed: *With the saints give rest*. After the ninth ode, the litany and the special prayer are said once more, followed by the exaposteilarion. Then the priest exclaims: *For holy art thou, O our God* (which usually precedes the Trisagion at the Divine Liturgy). After this the Trisagion is sung, then the usual prokeimenon and two special readings, of the epistle (1 Cor 15.39–46) and the gospel (Jn 6.35–40). The rite of the last kiss then follows during the singing of selected stichera prosomoia. Then the Lity (Trisagion) follows, with the usual troparia: *With the souls of the righteous departed*, the litany and the usual prayer for the departed: *O God of spirits and of all flesh*. After the dismissal and the singing of *Memory eternal*, the priest says the special prayer for the departed child: *O Lord our*

[54]Goar, 592–597.

God, who guardest infants in this present life, found in *Coislin 213*, and the burial takes place.

According to the contemporary Greek practice, which follows the abbreviated order of the funeral of a layman, the usual prayer for the departed: *O God of spirits and of all flesh*, is always replaced by the special prayer for the departed child: *O Lord our God, who guardest infants in this present life*. The readings are also different from those in the Russian practice: Romans 6.9–11 and Luke 18.15–17.26–27.

7. About Cremation

The Orthodox Church considers death as a "blessed dormition" (κοίμησις). Such a perception of death is based on the biblical view of death, both in the Old Testatment, where death is presented as an eternal repose and a sleep (Sir 46.19, 48.11) and in the perspective of the New Testament, where death awaits resurrection. For this reason, Christ says about the death of Lazarus: "Our friend Lazarus sleeps, but I go that I may wake him up" (Jn 11.11). From a Christian perspective, therefore, death is a temporary separation between the body and the soul, one that lasts only until the final resurrection. For this reason, Saint Paul makes an analogy between the Christian practice of burial and a seed sown in the ground: "So is the resurrection of the dead. The body is sown in corruption, it is raised in incorruption" (1 Cor 15.42).

The Orthodox Church holds the mystery of resurrection at the heart of her spirituality. She also holds a holistic approach to salvation, which includes both the body and the soul. For this reason, she reminds her faithful not only of the immortality of the soul, but also of the resurrection of the body. All the funeral rites of the Orthodox Church imply the presence of the body: the censing of the remains throughout the funeral service, the rite of the last kiss of the departed, the anointing of the remains with oil, and finally, the burial in the grave. The Greek etymology of the word cemetery (κοιμητήριον) means literally "sleeping room." The cemetery (or the ossuary in a monastery) is a liturgical place where liturgical services commemorating the departed are conducted and where, according to both ancient Christian and popular practices, food in memory of the departed is shared. The kolyva, a traditional dish prepared for the funeral and for the commemoration of the departed, consists in a platter of grains of boiled wheat with honey or sweets; it symbolizes both the resurrection of the buried body and the joy of the everlasting life in God's Kingdom.

For this reason, the Orthodox Church rejects categorically the cremation of the body as a funeral practice. In accordance with the rigor (*akribeia*) of her Tradition, the Orthodox Church does not celebrate funerals for people who have chosen to be cremated. Nevertheless, in a spirit of condescension, applying the principle of ecclesiastical *oikonomia*, the Holy Synod of the Ecumenical Patriarchate allows only the celebration of the Lity for the Departed (Trisagion), without kolyva, for those who have been cremated, but not the funeral service.

8. The Funeral for a non-Orthodox Christian

Since the Orthodox Church considers the funeral service as a sacramental action, she celebrates it only for members of the Orthodox Church. Nonetheless, in some pastoral cases, when non-Orthodox Christians do not have the possibility to be buried by their respective priest or pastor because such cannot be found in the area where the burial is to take place, and when in such circumstances the relatives of the departed approach the Orthodox Church for a burial, some solution may be found by applying the principle of ecclesiastical *oikonomia*. According to the decision 1621/343 of March 15, 1891 of Holy Synod of the Church of Greece, a funeral for a non-orthodox Christian is found in the edition of the *Μικρὸν Εὐχολόγιον*. Similarly, according to a decision of the Church of Russia, an order of a funeral for a non-orthodox Christian is also found in the edition of the *Trebnik*. We present both orders in parallel in the following table:

Table 7.8: The Order of the Funeral of Non-Orthodox Christians

Church of Greece[55]	Church of Russia[56]

1. Opening blessing:
    Blessed is our God
	1. Opening blessing:
	    Blessed is our God

2. Psalmody = Psalm 118 (without litany and prayer)	2. Psalm 87

3. Prokeimenon, Epistle,
    Alleluia, Gospel
	3. Psalmody = Psalm 118
	    (without litany and prayer)

[55] *Μικρὸν Εὐχολόγιον* (Athens, 1996), 276.
[56] *Trebnik*, vol. 3 (Moscow, 1984), 342–354.

4. Dismissal	4. After the third part, Evlogetaria:
5. Burial	*Blessed art thou, O Lord,* and
	The choir of saints
	5. Psalm 38
	6. Ikos: *Thou only art immortal*
	7. Prokeimenon, Apostle (Rom
	1.6–9), Alleluia, Gospel
	(Jn 5.17–24)
	8. Last kiss and stichera prosomoia
	9. Dismissal
	10. Burial

One can see that both services, which are extremely simple, do not contain any litany or prayer for the departed, and are composed only of psalmody and biblical readings, with some limited hymnography in the case of the service proposed by the Church of Russia. While the order proposed by the Church of Greece prescribes the usual biblical readings, the order proposed by the Church of Russia suggests different ones (Rom 14.6–9 and Jn 5.17–24).

9. Pannikhida and Lity for the Departed

According to the Tradition of the ancient Church, as witnessed by the *Apostolic Constitutions,*[57] the Orthodox Church commemorates the departed on the third day, on the ninth day, and on the fortieth day of their repose, as well as on the anniversary of their death. On this occasion, either the service of the pannikhida or *mnēmosyno* (μνημόσυνο) or the Lity for the Departed (Trisagion) is served.

The term *pannikhida* comes from the word *pannykhis,* a type of all-night vigil, in the sung office of the Cathedral of Hagia Sophia in Constantinople. This service had a structure of three antiphons, and it influenced today's Byzantine-rite services for the departed.[58] The contemporary pannikhida, as it is served according to the Russian practice, is in fact an abbreviation of the service for the funeral of a layman. It is served in memory of laymen, clergy, and monastics. The order is the following:

---

[57] *Apostolic Constitutions* 8:42 (SC 336:258–260; ANF 7:498).
[58] M. Arranz, "Les prières presbytérales de la Pannychis de l'ancien euchologe byzantin et la Panikhida des défunts," 38.

Table 7.9: The Order of the Pannikhida

1. Opening blessing: *Blessed is our God,* and usual beginning prayers
[2. Psalm 90]
3. Litany and prayer for the departed: *O God of spirits and of all flesh*
4. Alleluia and the troparia: *O thou, who with wisdom profound,* and: *We have thee as a wall and a haven.*
5. Evlogetaria: *Blessed art thou, O Lord,* and *The choir of saints*
6. Little Litany and prayer for the departed: *O God of spirits and of all flesh*
7. Kathisma hymn: *Give rest, O our Savior*
[8. Psalm 50]
9. Canon for the departed—3rd, 6th and 9th ode, each followed by a Little Litany and the prayer for the departed.
After the 6th ode, kontakion: *With the saints give rest,* and ikos
10. Trisagion and troparia: *With the souls of the righteous departed*
11. Litany and prayer for the departed: *O God of spirits and of all flesh*
12. Dismissal
13. Memory eternal

In current practice, the pannikhida is often abbreviated. The prescribed psalms are omitted in most cases. The canon is abbreviated, if not totally omitted. Only the refrains remain (*Give rest, O Lord, the soul of thy servant* and the Glory . . . both now and ever . . .), sung several times, and the heirmoi, sung as a katavasia in place of the [third], sixth and [ninth] ode.

According to the Greek practice, the *mnēmosyno* (μνημόσυνο) takes place toward the end of the Divine Liturgy. After the Ambo Prayer, the Evlogetaria: *The choir of saints,* are sung first, then the kontakion: *With the saints give rest,* and the troparia: *With the souls of the righteous departed,* the litany, the prayer for the departed: *O God of spirits and of all flesh,* and Memory eternal. Then the usual dismissal of the Divine Liturgy takes place.[59]

The Lity for the departed (Trisagion) is usually served at the end of a service (as at the end of Vespers) or separately, usually at the grave. It is identical to the first and last part of the funeral service, served respectively at the house and at the grave of the departed. The order is as follows:

---

[59] *Μικρὸν Εὐχολόγιον* (Athens, 1996), 284.

Table 7.10: The Order of the Lity or Trisagion for the Departed

1. Opening blessing and usual beginning prayers
2. Troparia: *With the souls of the righteous departed*
3. Litany
4. Prayer for the departed: *O God of spirits and of all flesh*
5. Dismissal
6. Memory eternal

CHAPTER EIGHT

Other Major Sacramental Rites

Introduction

In addition to the mysteries in his list of seven sacraments, including the monastic tonsure (baptism, christmation, Communion, priesthood, marriage, holy schema, holy unction, and repentance), Job Hamartolos in the thirteenth century mentions four rites (ἔθιμα, *ethima*): the sanctification of waters, the dedication of a church, the sanctification of holy Myron (Chrism), and the rite of the elevation of the Panagia during the monastic meal on feast days.[1] Metropolitan Joasaph of Ephesus in the fifteenth century, in his list of ten mysteries, also included the sanctification of the divine Myron (τῆς τελετῆς τοῦ θείου μύρου, *tēs teletēs tou theiou myrou*), the dedication of the temple (ἡ καθιέρωσις τοῦ ναοῦ, *hē kathierōsis tou naou*), the funeral rites, and the monastic tonsure.[2]

Nicolas Cabasilas and Symeon of Thessalonica saw in fact in the three episcopal rites of ordination, sanctification of the Myron, and the sanctification of the church, three pillars essential for the life of the Church. Symeon states, "as for the Divine hierurgy we need a bishop or a priest, for the ordination and for the sacred rite of the myron we need a bishop, as well as an altar, which is the temple, since it is on the altar that is celebrated the hierurgy, the ordination and the [sanctification of the] Myron."[3] In other words, for an ordination, a sanctified altar is necessary in addition to the bishop who performs the ordination. And for the sanctification of the altar (and of the church), Holy Myron is necessary, which once again is sanctified by one of the bishops—the patriarch. For the sanctification of the Myron, an altar is necessary. Thus, none of these three rites (ordination, Myron, dedication of the church) can be performed by a priest, but are performed only by a bishop, since he is the head of the local Church.

---

[1]Job Hamartolos, *On the Seven Mysteries of the Church*, fol. 239, in M. Jugie, *Theologica Dogmatica Christianorum Orientalum*, 3:17–18.

[2]Joasaph, Metropolitan of Ephesus, *Canonical Answers* 47, ed. A. Almazov, 38.

[3]Symeon of Thessalonica, *De sacro templo et eius consecratione* 100 (PG 155:305a).

In order to provide a complete overview of the major sacramental rites of the Orthodox Church, we shall describe in this chapter the sanctification of the Holy Myron, the dedication of a church, and the blessing of the water.

1. The Sanctification of Holy Myron (Chrism)

1.1. Historical Overview

The first testimony of the sanctification of the Holy Myron (Chrism) is found in the *Ecclesiastical Hierarchy* of Pseudo-Dionysius, usually attributed to Peter the Fuller (5th c.), according to the testimony of Theodore the Reader.[4] This document does not say on which day of the year this rite took place, but it says that it is performed by the local bishop.[5] Ancient canons also underline that the sanctification of the Myron is an episcopal privilege, and that it was already forbidden to priests to celebrate it. Canon 6 of the council of Carthage (419) states that "the confection of the Chrism (χρίσμα) . . . shall not be accomplished by priests."[6]

According to the Coptic tradition, Theophilus of Alexandria, around 390, established the tradition of sanctifying the Holy Myron once a year, on Great Friday, in connection with the mystery of baptism that took place on the next day during the Paschal vigil.[7] Since no Divine Liturgy is celebrated on Great Friday, the rite was probably soon moved to the previous day, Great and Holy Thursday.

The French Byzantinist L. Petit recognized that because of the lack of sources it is difficult to estabish precisely when the diocesan bishops stopped performing this rite, which became first the privilege of metropolitans, and later the privilege of patriarchs, and finally of the Ecumenical Patriarch.[8]

---

[4]Theodore the Reader, *Ecclesiastical History* (PG 86:208–209); G. Wagner, "La consécration du myron," *La liturgie, expérience de l'Église*, 148–149. Cf. P. Menevisoglou, *Τὸ Ἅγιον Μύρον ἐν τῇ Ὀρθοδόξῳ Ἀνατολικῇ Ἐκκλησίᾳ, ἰδίᾳ κατὰ τὰς πηγὰς καὶ τὴν πράξιν τῶν νεωτέρων χρόνων τοῦ Οἰκουμενικοῦ Πατριαρχείου*, Ἀνάλεκτα Βλατάδων 14 (Thessalonica, 1972), 46.

[5]Pseudo-Dionysius, *Ecclesiastical Hierarchy*, 4.2, 3.2. (PG 3:473, 476b; Liubheid, 224–225, 226–227).

[6]Canon 6, Council of Carthage, in Joannou, *Discipline générale antique*, 1.2:220.

[7]P. Trempelas, *Μικρὸν Εὐχολόγιον*, vol. 1 (Athens, 1950), 301; Menevisoglou, *Τὸ Ἅγιον Μύρον*, 46.

[8]L. Petit, "Du pouvoir de consacrer le saint chrême," *Échos d'Orient* 3 (1899–1900): 1–7, at 2.

The Barberini *Euchologion* merely states that this rite is celebrated on Great Thursday by a bishop, without specifying that this bishop is the patriarch.[9] It is performed after the Anaphora, after the ecphonesis: *And may the mercies of our Great God and Savior,* when the prayer: *Lord of mercy and Father of Lights* is said followed by the prayer of the inclination: *We bow the neck of our heart before thee, O God of all.*[10]

Jacques Goar stated in his edition of the *Euchologion* that the practice that only the Ecumenical Patriarch may sanctify the Holy Myron precedes the times of Patriarch Photius (9th c.), but he does not give any reference. Perhaps this is the case, given that the Eastern Patriarchs took refuge in Constantinople after the Muslim invasions of the eighth century, and started concelebrating with the Ecumenical Patriarch for the sanctification of the Holy Myron. According to Goar, the main reason was merely economical: the diocesan bishops did not have the means to buy the expensive ingredients that were necessary for the confection of the Myron.[11] Symeon of Thessalonica (+1429) says in his commentary on the rite of sanctification of the Holy Myron that it is performed by "the most holy patriarch, surrounded by his clergy, since he is the source of priesthood."[12]

Nonetheless, we have different attestations that Holy Myron was still sanctified during the seventeenth century in Kiev and in Moscow, with the consent of the Ecumenical Patriarchate. The reason seemed to be linked with complaints sent to the Patriarchate concerning the falsification by Poles of vials of Myron sent into Polish Lithuania and Russia during their passage in Little Russia.[13] If we take these testimonies seriously, the Ecumenical Patriarchate granted to the metropolitan of Kiev and to the patriarch of Moscow the right to sanctify the Myron by ecclesiastical economy (κατ᾽ οἰκονομίαν), on the basis of the ancient tradition of the Church when each diocesan bishop had the right to sanctify it, without conferring on them a special authority.[14]

As we saw in Symeon of Thessalonica's narration, by the fourteenth century the Ecumenical Patriarch, as the first (πρῶτος) in the diptychs,

---

[9]*Barberini,* 143.

[10]*Barberini,* 144–145.

[11]Goar, 643.

[12]Symeon of Thessalonica, *De sacro ritu sancti olei* 71 (PG 155:240a).

[13]Petit, "Du pouvoir de consacrer le saint chrême," 5.

[14]Thus, the opinion of certain Russian canonists that the right of sanctifying the Myron is one of the prerogatives of an autocephalous Church has no foundation. Cf. V. Tsypin, *Tserkovnoe pravo* (Moscow, 1994), 207; Menevisoglou, Τὸ Ἅγιον Μύρον, 133–177.

presided at this ceremony, which today, at the Ecumenical Patriarchate, has a pan-Orthodox character through the participation of delegations from various autocephalous Churches, and thus manifests the unity of the Orthodox Church at the universal level.[15] The evolution in the presidency of the rite of sanctification of the Holy Myron goes in parallel with the evolution of primacy in the Church, from the local level through the regional level to the universal level. V. Phidas links it with the ecclesiastical right to ordain, to judge, and to receive appeals.[16]

The Tomos of the Church of Greece (1850), the first modern autocephaly to be proclaimed in the nineteenth century, prescribed that this new Church would receive the Holy Myron from the Ecumenical Patriarchate.[17] In 1879, when Ecumenical Patriarch Joachim III delivered the Tomos of autocephaly to the Church of Serbia, the same condition was imposed.[18] In 1826 the Church of Romania requested from the Ecumenical Patriarchate the right to sanctify the Holy Myron in Bucharest, but this was refused. The Church of Romania did sanctify its Holy Myron in 1882, and this was strongly criticized by Ecumenical Patriarch Joachim III and the Holy and Sacred Synod of the Ecumenical Patriarchate.[19] Nevertheless, Holy Myron is being sanctified today not only at the Ecumenical Patriarchate but also in Moscow, in Belgrade, and in Bucharest.[20]

1.2. Order

On Great Monday, after the Presanctified Liturgy, the patriarch, accompanied by the metropolitans and the clergy, goes to the special building (μυρεψείον, *myrepseion*) where the Holy Myron is to be prepared. He serves the blessing of water and blesses everything that will be used in the preparation of the Holy Myron. The Patriarch intones the opening blessing and usual beginning prayers are recited. The troparion and the kontakion of Pentecost are sung, as well as a special troparion and kontakion for the preparation of the Holy Myron. During that time, the patriarch, assisted

[15]Petit, "Du pouvoir de consacrer le saint chrême," 1–7; Menevisoglou, Τὸ Ἅγιον Μύρον, 183–187.
[16]V. Phidas, *L'institution de la pentarchie des patriarches* [in Greek], vol. 3 (Athens, 2012), 235–244.
[17]Rhalles-Potles, *Syntagma*, Athens, 5:183.
[18]Ἐκκλησιαστικὴ Ἀλήθεια 2 (1881): 155.
[19]Petit, "Du pouvoir de consacrer le saint chrême," p. 6–7.
[20]Menevisoglou, Τὸ Ἅγιον Μύρον, 177. The OCA also sanctifies its own chrism.

by the clergy, pours oil and wine into copper cauldrons, as well as aromatic flowers and plants. The Patriarch then blesses each vessel with the sign of the cross, saying: *In the name of the Father, and of the Son, and of the Holy Spirit. Amen.* Then, holding the trikirion and the dikirion, he lights the fire under each vessel. At that point the reading of the four Gospels begins, and it continues on each of the first three days of Holy Week. The confection of the holy Myron takes place during these three days under the supervision of deacons and appointed specialists. On Great Wednesday, the holy Myron is decanted and cooled. Symeon of Thessalonica connects this rite with the gospel reading of that day, about the prostitute who anointed Christ with precious myrrh.[21] After the Presanctified Liturgy on Holy Wednesday, the Patriarch comes to the building, and after the opening blessing and prayers are said, and a special troparion is sung, he pours into the Myron the fragrances that must be incorporated after the cooking. Then the dismissal takes place, and the Myron is poured into special jars and sealed.

The sanctification of the Holy Myron takes place on Great Thursday. Before the vesperal Divine Liturgy of Saint Basil the Great, the jars are taken in procession from the myrepseion to the church and placed around the prothesis table, as two alabaster vases, one containing the old Myron and one containing the new, are placed on the holy table. During the Great Entrance, walking behind the candles and the deacons holding censers, the Grand Archimandrite bears the alabaster vase containing the old Myron as the Grand Protosyngelos bears the alabaster vase containing the new Myron, and behind them come the priests holding the jars containing the Myron that has just been prepared. They are followed by the clergy holding the diskos and the chalice, as usual. The patriarch meets them at the holy doors of the sanctuary, and he receives first the alabaster vase containing the old Myron, kisses it, and places it on the holy table on the right side. Then he receives the alabaster vase containing the new Myron, kisses it, and places it on the holy table on the left side. Then he receives the holy gifts and places them between the two vases. The priests holding the rest of the jars containing the Myron then enter the sanctuary and place them around the holy table. The Divine Liturgy then continues as usual.

After the completion of the Anaphora, just before the Litany of Supplication before the Our Father, the archdeacon proclaims: *Let us attend!* The Patriarch unseals the alabaster vase containing the new Myron and blesses it

---

[21]Symeon of Thessalonica, *De sacro ritu sancti olei* 71 (PG 155:240c).

three times with the sign of the cross, saying: *In the name of the Father, and of the Son, and of the Holy Spirit. Amen.* And he does the same with each jar containing the new Myron, as the proper troparia are being sung. Then, the archdeacon proclaims: *Let us attend!* And the patriarch once again blesses the new Myron three times with the sign of the cross, saying the same words as before, as the second deacon intones the proper antiphon. Then the third deacon says: *Let us pray to the Lord!* And the patriarch says the prayer of sanctification, kneeling with all the other bishops: *O Lord of mercy and Father of Lights.* The patriarch then says: *Peace be unto all.* The deacon: *Let us bow our heads to the Lord.* And the patriarch says the prayer of inclination: *We bow our head and and heart before thee, O God of all.* These prayers are already found in the Barberini *Euchologion.*[22] Proper troparia are then sung. Then, the patriarch once again blesses the new Myron three times with the sign of the cross, with the same formula. He then covers the jars and blesses the assembly with the trikirion, and the Divine Liturgy continues with the Litany of Supplication and the Our Father.

At the end, when the Holy Gifts are transferred to the prothesis, the Patriarch gives the two alabaster vases to two senior metropolitans, as the priests take up the jars, and thus the newly sanctified Myron is carried in procession to the room where the Holy Myron is stored (μυροθήκη), to the chanting of Psalm 44.

2. The Dedication of a Church

2.1. Historical Overview

The Christian rite of the dedication of a church[23] has its roots in the Jewsih practice recorded in the Old Testament. We know that the Jews celebrated the annual festival of the dedication of the Temple, known today as Hanuk-kah; this feast commemorates the cleansing of the temple of Jerusalem by Judas Maccabeus after Antiochus Epiphanes profaned it in 165 BC (cf. 1 Macc 1–4). We know also that the Romans used to dedicate their cities and temples, and that the ceremonial of these events included processions and

[22]*Barberini,* 144–145.
[23]Cf. our article: J. Getcha, "La dédicace des églises dans le rite byzantin," *Les enjeux spirituels et théologiques de l'espace liturgique: Conférences Saint-Serge. 51e Semaine d'Études Liturgiques* (Rome: CLV-Edizioni liturgiche, 2005), 75–91.

sprinkling. Nevertheless, it seems that the Christian rites have inherited more of the Jewish ritual than of the pagan.[24]

The service of the dedication of churches is intimately linked to the consecration of the altars, which are indispensable for the celebration of the Eucharist, the foundation of the Church. For this reason, the rite of dedication of a church is intimely linked with the celebration of the Divine Liturgy.[25]

In the Apostolic era, the Eucharist was celebrated as part of a meal in the houses of the faithful, and therefore home tables were simply used as altars. Nevertheless, in the New Testament, the Apostole Paul speaks of the "table of the Lord" (τραπέζα Κυρίου—1 Cor 10.21) to designate the eucharistic table, while the Epistle to the Hebrews (13.10) picks up the term *thysiastērion* (θυσιαστήριον), which designated the altar for the offering of sacrifices in the Old Testament (Gen 8.20; Ex 27.3; 2 Chron 14:5). These two terms are still used in the contemporary printed *Euchologion* when it speaks of the altar table in the rite of dedication of a church.

But very soon the early Christians began to celebrate the Eucharist over the relics of martyrs. In the second century, Saint Ignatius of Antioch used the term *thysiastērion* to designate the place of the eucharistic synaxis,[26] and Saint Irenaeus of Lyons uses the same term when he speaks of the eucharistic sacrifice that is to be offered frequently on the altar.[27] Other Fathers also use the term *trapeza* (τραπέζα) to refer to the altar. In any case, they never use the terms *bōmos* (βωμός) or *eskhara* (ἐσχάρα) which were used to designate the sacrificial pagan altar, because the Eucharist is by definition the sacrifice without the shedding of blood, offered once and for all by Christ.

The first mention of the dedication of a church in the patristic literature is found in Eusebius of Caesarea's *Ecclesiastical History*, where he mentions the sanctification of the altar (*thysiastērion,* θυσιαστήριον) of the Basilica of Tyre in the year 314.[28] But it was the dedication of the Church of the Anastasis (also known as the Church of the Holy Sepulcher) in Jerusalem

[24]P. de Puniet, "Dédicace," *DACL* 4.1:374–405, at 376.

[25]Ibid., 380.

[26]Ignatius of Antioch, *To the Ephesians* 5.2 (SC 10 bis: 62; *Ignatius of Antioch: The Letters*, PPS 49:28–31); *To the Trallians* 7.2 (SC 10-bis: 100; *Ignatius of Antioch: The Letters,* PPS 49:60–61). Cf. Henri Leclercq, "Autel," *DACL* 1.2:3155–3189, at 3156.

[27]Irenaeus of Lyons, *Against heresies* 4.18.6 (SC 100:615). Cf. H. Leclercq, "Autel," 3156.

[28]Eusebius of Caesarea, *Ecclesiastical History* 10.2–4 (SC 55:79–81). Cf. H. Leclercq, "Autel," 3156; P. de Puniet, "Dédicace," 375.

in 335 that inaugurated a solemn ritual (*ta enkainia*, τὰ ἐγγκαίνια) which was (and still is) celebrated every year.[29] If we look at Eusebius' description, we can imagine that the dedication of the churches was originally limited to the solemn celebration of the Eucharist for the first time on the new altar. In the third century, Saint Cyprian of Carthage implied that it is the Eucharist that sanctifies the altar, by affirming that among heretics neither baptism nor anointing with oil is valid, since they do not have the Eucharist, without which there cannot exist the altar where the holy Chrism is consecrated.[30]

The ancient custom of celebrating the Eucharist over the relics of martyrs led to the construction of churches over the tombs of martyrs (*martyria*).[31] Thus, some altars were erected over the relics of martyrs, while others had none. But soon holy relics began to be solemnly translated to new churches. One of the first testimonies of such translations of relics is related with the construction of a new church built in Milan in 386. When Saint Ambrose was preparing to dedicate it through the celebration of the Eucharist alone, the Milanese faithful asked him to dedicate it as a Roman basilica. In response to this request, the bishop replied that he would do it gladly, if he could find relics of martyrs. And then the relics of the Milanese martyrs Gervasius and Protasius were discovered and placed in the old basilica, before being solemnly transferred on the next day to the new church and placed under the altar in the Basilica of St Ambrose,where they are still found to this day.[32]

[29]Eusebius of Caesarea, *The Life of Constantine*, 4.45 (PG 20:1195; NPNF² 1:552); Egeria, *Itinerarium*, 48–49 (SC 296:316–318; Egeria, *Diary*, 126–27); Sozomen, *Ecclesiastical History* 2:26 (SC 306:346). Cf. P. De Puniet, "Dédicace," 375. Until the sixteenth century, Byzantines celebrated the anniversary of the dedication of their churches instead of their patronal feast. Cf. M. Lisitsyn, *Pervonachal'ny slavyano-russkii tipikon* (Saint-Petersbourg, 1911), 106–107; V. Prilutsky, *Chastnoe bogosluzhenie v Russkoi tserkvi v XVI v pervoi polovine XVII v.* (Kiev, 1912), 93–100.

[30]Cyprian of Carthage, Letter 70 to Januarius and others 2; *Letter 70* is summarized in PL 4:408, and the text is printed in PL 3:1035-1044, with the relevant section at 1040-1041; an English translation may be found in St Cyprian of Carthage, *The Letters of St. Cyprian of Carthage, Letters 67–82*, ed. Walter J. Burghardt and Thomas Comerford Lawler, trans. G. W. Clarke, vol. 4, Ancient Christian Writers (New York; Mahwah, NJ: Newman Press, 1989), 45–48, at 46–47. Cf. P. De Puniet, "Dédicace," 380.

[31]Cf. Egeria, *Itinerarium*, 19, 22, 23 (SC 296:202, 226, 230, 232; Egeria, *Diary*, 77–81, 86–89).

[32]Ambrosius, *Epist.* 22 (PL 16:1066; Saint Ambrose, *Letters*, trans. Sister Mary Melchior Beyenka, O.P. [Washington: Catholic University of America Press, 1967, 1987, 2001], 376–384 at 376, where it bears the number 61). Cf. P. De Puniet, "Dédicace," 381.

Between the fourth and sixth centuries, we find several attestations of such translations of relics, accompanied by solemn processions with the singing of psalms, during the dedication of new churches in the East, such as the sanctuary of Saint Euphemia in Chalcedon, of the Church of the Holy Wisdom in Constantinople (415), and that of Saint Irene in the same city (551).[33] This practice became widespread in the East, and it favored the transfer of relics or taking fragments from them to be used for the dedication of new churches. This practice somewhat surprised the Romans, who used to keep the relics intact. Thus in 519, when Emperor Justinian requested that Pope Hormisdas of Rome give him some fragments of relics of the holy apostles and the holy deacon and martyr Lawrence, the Pope refused, as he wished to remain faithful to the ancient tradition of keeping intact the bodies of martyrs honored by the Church.[34] After the first iconoclastic crisis, the Seventh Ecumenical Council (Nicea, 787) decided in its seventh canon that a bishop who consecrated a church without relics should be deposed.[35] From that time on, every consecrated altar must have relics.

Undoubtedly under the influence of ancient Jewish rites, the idea that the altar ought to be sanctified or purified before the celebration of the Eucharist spread gradually in the East. The earliest known testimony of the anointing of an altar with oil is found in one of the hymns of St Ephrem the Syrian (4th c.), who writes: "Oil is the staff of old age and the armor of youth; it sustains the sick and it is like a wall of strength; it is one, but manifold in its benefits. It bestows anointing on altars, that they may bear our sacrifice."[36] Later, the anointing of the altar table with Holy Myron became the norm. This anointing imitates the consecration of altars in the Old Testament, and it could be put in parallel with the anointing with Chrism during the Christian initiation rites. One can definitely establish a parallel between the baptism, chrismation, and Eucharist received by a catechumen becoming Christian, and the purification by water, the anointing with Holy Myron, and the celebration of the Eucharist on the new altar table.

[33]Theodore the Reader, *Ecclesiastical History* 2.62 (PG 86:213); *Chronicon Pascale ad annum 415* (PG 92:787–788); Theophanes, *Chronographia* (PG 108:500). Cf. P. De Puniet, "Dédicace," 382.

[34]Hormisdas, *Epist. 64* (PL 63:474–477). Cf. P. De Puniet, "Dédicace," 382.

[35]P.-P. Joannou, *Discipline générale antique*, 1.1:260–261.

[36]St Ephrem of Syria, *Hymn 25 on Oil and the Olive*, strophe 3, in Sancti Ephraem Syri, *Hymni et sermones*, ed. Thomas Joseph Lamy, vol. 2 (Malines: Dessain, 1886), cols 785–792, at cols. 787–788 (parallel Syriac and Latin). Cf. P. De Puniet, "Dédicace," 386.

The use of water for ritual purification was also common among the Jews, as among the Romans. We know, on the other hand, that among Christians holy water was used apart from baptism to sanctify places and objects. Thus, the cleansing of the altar with water was added to its anointing with oil. By extension, the sanctification of the altar led to the sanctification of the interior and exterior walls of the church, which in turn ought to receive as well sprinkling with holy water and anointing with Holy Myron. The first attestation of such sprinkling is found in a letter of Saint Gregory the Great, who affirms that pagan temples converted into churches should be sprinkled with lustral water before an altar table was constructed there and holy relics were placed in it.[37]

The practice of washing the altar on Holy Thursday appeared in the seventh century, as attested by St Isidore of Seville.[38] This practice quickly spread to Constantinople, and from there throughout the Byzantine and Slavic world, with the reception of the Typikon of the Great Church. According to Goar, this rite commemorates the humility manifested by our Lord when he washed the feet of his disciples.[39] This rite of washing the altar first with warm water, then with wine mixed with rose water, was also included in the rite of the dedication of a church.

The eighth-century Byzantine *Euchologion* contains a shorter form of the rite of the dedication than the one in current use.[40] It is composed of two parts: 1) the order of purifying a holy temple and the holy table that is in it (τάξις γινομένη ἐπὶ καθιερώσεως ἁγίου ναοῦ καὶ τῆς ἐν αὐτῷ ἁγίας τραπέζης, *taxis ginomenē epi kathierōseōs hagiou naou kai tēs en autō hagias trapezēs*), which was served on the eve, and 2) the order of dedicating a holy temple that has been purified (τάξις γινομένη ἐπὶ τοῖς ἐγκαινίοις τοῦ ἤδη καθιερωθέντος ἁγίου ναοῦ, *taxis ginomenē epi tois enkainiois tou ēdē kathierōthentos hagiou naou*), served on the day of the dedication.[41] These two parts were later united in a single service served on the day of dedication itself, before the celebration of the Divine Liturgy. In the contemporary ritual, a vigil precedes on the eve of the dedication of the church.

According to Apostolic Canon 31, Canon 5 of the council of Antioch, and Canon 4 of the Fourth Ecumenical Council, a church cannot be built

[37]Gregory the Great, *Epist.* 11.76 (PL 77:1215).
[38]Isidore of Seville, *De eccles. officiis* 1:28 (PL 83:784).
[39]Goar, 499.
[40]*Barberini*, 156–164
[41]*Barberini*, 156 and 162.

without the consent and the knowledge of the diocesan bishop.[42] For this reason, it became the usage that only the diocesan bishop could perform the dedication of the church. Canon 7 of the Seventh Ecumenical Council, requires that the dedication of a church be celebrated with the deposition of relics of holy martyrs.[43]

2.2. Order

Table 8.1: The Order of the Dedication of a Church

2.2.1. PURIFICATION OF THE HOLY TABLE
[IN ANCIENT TIMES, SERVED ON THE EVE]

[1. Prayer 1: *O Lord God our Savior*

2. Psalm 144: Construction of the holy table)

3. Psalm 22]

4. Prayer 2 (kneeling): *O God who art without beginning and eternal*

5. Great Litany

6. Prayer 3: *O Lord our God, who didst sanctify the streams of Jordan*

7. Psalm 83 and washing with water

8. Psalm 50, from *Sprinkle me with hyssop*, and washing with wine and rose water

9. Unction with Holy Myron—Alleluia

10. Psalm 132

[11. Psalm 131. Vesting of the holy table with the katasarkion]

12. Psalm 92. Vesting of the holy table with the other cloths, the gospel book, and the cross

13. Psalm 25. Censing of the holy table and of the church; the walls and columns of the church are sprinkled with holy water and anointed with Holy Myron

14. Little Litany

15. Prayer 4, of dedication: *O Lord of heaven and earth*

16. Prayer 5, of inclination: *We thank thee, O Lord God of Hosts*; lighting of a candle

17. *Let us depart in peace* [and procession, with troparia, to the nearby church where the holy relics are kept]

---

[42]P. Joannou, *Discipline générale antique*, 2.1:73; 2.2:22 and 108–109.

[43]P. Joannou, *Discipline générale antique*, 2.1:261.

2.2.2. THE DEDICATION, WITH TRANSFER OF THE HOLY RELICS [BEFORE THE DIVINE LITURGY]

1. *For holy art thou, O our God* and Trisagion
2. Prayer 1: *O Lord our God, faithful in thy words*
3. Prayer 2, of inclination: *O Lord our God, through the prayers of the most pure Sovereign Lady, the Theotokos*
4. Transfer of the holy relics to the new church with the singing of troparia
5. In front of the main entrance: *Blessed art thou always, O Christ our God*
6. *Lift up your heads, O ye princes* (Psalm 23.8)
7. Prayer 3: *O God and Father of our Lord Jesus Christ*
8. Prayer 4, of inclination: *O Master, Lord our God* (of the Little Entrance)
9. *The Lord of hosts—he is the King of glory* (Psalm 23.10). Entrance into the church and deposition of the holy relics under the holy table
10. Prayer 5: *O Lord our God, who hast given this glory also unto the holy martyrs that suffered for thee*
[11. Prayer 6: *O Lord our God, who by thy word alone didst create the world,* with the Little Litany
12. Augmented Litany
13. Sprinkling with holy water
14. Dismissal]

III. Divine Liturgy
With special readings: Heb 3.1–4 and Jn 10.22–30 (or Mt 16.13–18) (from the feast of the dedication)

The day before the dedication, the bishop brings three fragments of the relics of martyrs, which are contained in a small reliquary placed on a holy diskos covered by the asterisk and a veil. The diskos is placed on a small table prepared for this purpose, in front of the icon of Christ in the iconostasis, and a lighted candle is placed before the table. The canonical tradition and liturgical texts insist that the relics should be relics of martyrs, since the Church is built on the testimony and the faith confessed by the holy martyrs who were witnesses (*martyres*, μάρτυρες) of Jesus Christ. In the hymnography of the dedication, the martyrs are called *theophores*—God-bearers. According to Saint Nicolas Cabasilas, nothing is better suited to the mysteries of Christ than martyrs, because they have body, spirit, death, and all things in common with Christ.[44] According to the *Euchologion*, these relics ought to be placed in an already existing church that is near the church to be dedicated.

The vigil is served in the presence of these relics. At the vigil, we sing the service of the dedication of the church of the Anastasis in Jerusalem (see the *Menaion*, 13 September), the service of the saint or the feast in whose name the new church is dedicated, and the service of the day.

On the day of the dedication, the bishop arrives at the church to be dedicated, puts on all his liturgical vestments, and, in order to protect them, he covers them with the *savanon* (σάβανον), a white apron with sleeves that covers the vestments from top to bottom and is secured by a belt.

Then the bishop, assisted by his clergy, begins to erect the altar table. The altar is to be square, about one meter (a little over thirty-nine inches) high, and supported on columns. A cavity, intended to receive the relics, is to be prepared either in the table itself, or in one of the columns. The commentaries on the Divine Liturgy state that the altar symbolizes the tomb of Christ.[45]

Once vested, the bishop, without any opening blessing, reads the prayer *O Lord God, our Savior,* in which he prays the Lord to allow him to perform the dedication of the church and to erect its holy table. This prayer is absent from the ancient Byzantine euchologia. After this prayer, the bishop is assisted by the priests (and possibly by a craftsman) to set the altar table (*mensa*) on its columns, on which he has already poured ceromastic—a mixture of pure beeswax, mastic, myrrh, aloe, incense, resin, and aromatic gum, all symbolizing the aromatics brought to the tomb of Christ by Joseph of Arimathea and the myrrhbearing women—while the choir sings Psalm 144, *I will exalt thee, O my God.* Once the holy table has been put together, the choir sings Psalm 22, *The Lord is my Shepherd*, while the clergy clean from the table any ceromastic that has overflowed. These two psalms are also absent from the Barberini *Euchologion.* The first Christian altars were probably made of wood, and the ceromastic was used for a practical reason: to seal the table (*mensa*) to its columns. Since the sixth century, however, the use of stone or marble altars has been common, probably as a vestige of the

---

[44]Nicolas Cabasilas, *Life in Christ* 5.25 (SC 361:32); English translation in Nicholas Cabasilas, *The Life in Christ*, tr. Carmino deCatanzaro (Crestwood, NY: St Vladimir's Seminary Press, 1974), 156.

[45]Cf. Germanus of Constantinople, *Divine Liturgy* 41 (PPS 8:89); Symeon of Thessalonica, *On the Sacred Temple* 136 (PG 155:345d).

celebration of the Divine Liturgy over the tombs of martyrs. For this reason the Byzantine euchologia describe the sanctification of a stone altar.

Once the altar is assembled, the bishop reads the kneeling prayer: *O God who art without beginning and eternal*, an anamnesis of the creation, the ark of the covenant, the temple of Solomon, and the establishment on earth of churches and altars for the offering of the eucharistic sacrifice without the shedding of blood. This prayer also includes an epiclesis that asks for the coming of the life-giving Spirit to fulfill with dignity the dedication of the church and the sanctification of the altar. In the Barberini *Euchologion*, this prayer concluded the Litany of Peace by which the rite of purification of the church began;[46] this positioning recalls the beginning of the baptismal rite, where the prayer for the blessing of the waters also concludes the Litany of Peace. In current practice, this kneeling prayer ends with a litany by the deacon and the bishop's exclamation: *For holy art thou, O our God, who restest upon the precious martyrs who have suffered for thee, and unto thee do we send up glory . . .*

At this point the altar table is washed. The bishop reads the prayer: *O Lord our God, who didst sanctify the streams of Jordan,* for the blessing of the water, wine, and rose water that will be used *unto the sanctification and completion of this thine altar.* The bishop performs a first ablution by pouring lukewarm water on the altar in the form of a cross three times, while saying: *In the name of the Father, and of the Son, and of the Holy Spirit.* The Barberini codex specifies the use of baptismal water,[47] and thus a parallel could be drawn here with the triple immersion in the baptismal font during Christian initiation. The altar is washed with four cloths, while the choir sings Psalm 83, *How beloved are thy dwellings, O Lord of hosts!* The altar is then wiped with four cloths.

After this first ablution, the altar is washed a second time, with an aromatic mixture of wine and rose water, which the bishop pours three times, while saying: *Thou shalt sprinkle me with hyssop, and I shall be made clean; thou shalt wash me, and I shall be made whiter than snow* (Ps 50.7). Then he continues to recite Psalm 50, and the altar is then wiped with four sponges.

After the ablutions, the altar table is anointed with Holy Myron. This anointing is to be compared with chrismation during Christian initiation.

[46]*Barberini,* 157.
[47]*Barberini,* 159.

In the ancient Byzantine practice, the bishop poured the Holy Myron three times, making the sign of the cross while saying: *Alleluia, Alleluia, Alleluia.* It is significant that the ancient *Euchologion* specifies here that it is done "as at the moment of the holy baptism," in reference to the pre-baptismal anointing, when the sanctified oil is poured into the baptismal font. This same *Euchologion* further specifies that the bishop then anoints the table and the columns with his hand. In the current Russian practice, the bishop uses a brush to draw three crosses on the altar table with the Myron, as well as a cross on each of the columns. Meanwhile, the choir sings Psalm 132, *Behold, what is so good or so pleasant, as for brethren to dwell in unity?*

While Psalm 131: *Remember, Lord, David and all his meekness, how he swore an oath unto the Lord,* is being sung, the altar table is covered with the *katasarkion* (κατασάρκιον, срачица), a tablecloth that is a permanent cover for the altar table and that is tied to its columns. The katasarkion symbolizes the shroud that enveloped the body of Christ when it was taken down from the cross and laid in the tomb, and for this reason a depiction of the shroud of Christ is often depicted on this altar cloth. We can also see a parallel with the white baptismal garment of Christian initiation, in which the neophyte is dressed immediately after the triple immersion and chrismation. The Barberini codex does not mention the katasarkion. In contemporary Greek practice, before the katasarkion is placed on the altar, four small squares of cloth with depictions of the four evangelists are glued with ceromastic at each corner of the altar.

Then Psalm 92: *The Lord reigns, he is clothed in majesty*, is sung, while the altar table is covered by its "garments" or inditia (ἐνδύτιον or ἐπενδύτης). The outermost covering of the altar is made of a precious brocade. All the other necessary liturgical objects are then placed on the altar table: the eiliton, the gospel book, the cross, etc. Once the altar is thus adorned, the table of the prothesis is dressed, and the sacred vessels are placed on it. Each covering and each object is sprinkled beforehand with holy water.

Then Psalm 25: *Judge me, O Lord, for I have walked in mine innocence*, is sung. Meanwhile, the bishop censes the altar table, the sanctuary, and the whole church. He (or one of his concelebrants) then sprinkles all the walls with holy water. The Barberini manuscript does not mention the sprinkling with holy water. Then, by means of a reed with a brush at its end, the bishop (or one of his concelebrants) anoints the walls and columns of the church with Holy Myron, while drawing either the monogram of Christ, or a cross.

When the anointing has been done, the deacon says the Little Litany, which concludes with the prayer of dedication said by the bishop: *O Lord of heaven and earth*, in which he asks the Lord to fill with divine glory the church that has been built for his glorification, and to make of its altar table the Holy of Holies on which the eucharistic sacrifice without the shedding of blood is to be offered for the forgiveness of sins. To this prayer is added the prayer of inclination, which gives thanks for the church newly sanctified in order that the eucharistic sacrifice may be offered in it. In the Barberini *Euchologion* this concludes the first part of the dedication, the part that was formerly celebrated on the eve. In current practice, until this point no candles have been lit, but now the bishop himself lights the first candle and places it on the altar table, and from it all the other lamps and candles of the church are lit.

Once the sanctification of the church is completed, the second part of the dedication begins, with the transfer of the relics. The bishop, the clergy, and the faithful go in procession to a nearby church where the relics were placed on the eve, while singing appropriate troparia in honor of the martyrs. The hymnography recalls that *as with fine purple linen, thy Church has been adorned with the blood of thy martyrs,* and that *the universe offers the God-bearing martyrs as the first-fruits of nature to thee, O Lord.* When the procession arrives at the church, the bishop enters the sanctuary. The deacon says the Little Litany, and the bishop says the ecphonesis of the Trisagion, which the choir sings immediately. It is interesting to note that we see here a remnant of the stational liturgy of Constantinople, where it was a frequent practice to begin the liturgy in one church and to continue it, after the singing of the Trisagion and the Little Entrance, in a different church.[48] Indeed, this procession corresponds to the moment of the Little Entrance of the eucharistic liturgy. In the ancient Byzantine practice, the transfer of the relics and their placement under the altar table of the new church was immediately followed by the biblical readings, which marked the beginning of the Divine Liturgy.

After the Trisagion, the bishop says the prayer: *O Lord, our God, faithful in thy words*, in which he prays that the assembly may be able to share the

inheritance of the holy martyrs and that the faithful may become their imi-
tators. This is followed by the prayer of inclination: *O Lord our God, through
the prayers of the most pure Sovereign Lady, the Theotokos,* in which the
bishop asks for the Lord's help to direct *the work of his hands.* Both prayers
are found in the Barberini *Euchologion.*[49]

After the prayer of inclination, the bishop transfers the holy relics from
the old church to the new church; he bears them on the veil-covered diskos,
which he holds over his head. This procession is accompanied by the singing of troparia recalling that the Church was built on the rock of faith, and
asking the Lord to strengthen his Church on the unshakable rock of his
commandments.

In the Russian practice, when the procession arrives at the new church,
it goes around the building three times, while the exterior walls are sprinkled with holy water. The procession stops in front of the closed main doors
of the church, and troparia in honor of holy martyrs are sung. The bishop
places the diskos containing the holy relics on a small table prepared for
this purpose, and says: *Blessed art thou, O Christ our God, always, now
and ever, and unto the ages of ages.* Then Psalm 23.9: *Lift up your head, O
gates,* which used to be sung as a troparion,[50] is now sung in the form of
a dialogue between the bishop, who stands outside the church, and the
chanters, who are inside. The bishop sings: *Lift up your gates, O ye princes,
and be lifted up O eternal gates, and the King of Glory shall enter in* (Ps 23.9).
From the inside, the chanters answer: *Who is this King of glory?* (Ps 23.10a).
The bishop censes the holy relics, and sings the verse of Psalm 23 a second
time, and the chanters respond again with the other verse. The bishop then
says the prayer: *O God and Father of our Lord Jesus Christ,* and, as a prayer
of inclination, the prayer of the Little Entrance: *O Master, Lord our God.*
These prayers are absent from the Barberini *Euchologion.*[51] Then, making
the sign of the Cross on the doors of the church while holding in his hands
the diskos with the holy relics, the bishop answers by chanting: *The Lord
of hosts, he is the King of Glory* (Ps 23.10b). This verse is then repeated by
the choir. These psalmic verses were chosen for the feast of Ascension, to
mark the entrance of the incarnate Son of God into Heaven. Saint Nicolas
Cabasilas, explaining the choice of these verses, says that the bishop must
introduce the holy relics into the new church as if Christ were entering

[49]*Barberini,* 163.
[50]*Barberini,* 164.
[51]Ibid.

in person.[52] This parallel exists between Christ and the martyrs not only because they are witnesses (*martyres*, μάρτυρες) of Christ, but also because they are the bearers of Christ.

The doors of the church are then opened, and the bishop enters holding the diskos with the relics, while the chanters sing the troparion of the dedication of the Church of the Anastasis in Jerusalem. The bishop sets the diskos on the altar table, anoints the holy relics with the Holy Myron, and places them in the reliquary, which is then placed in the slot provided for this purpose under the holy table. Then he reads the prayer for the placing of the relics, which recalls the origin of the translation of the relics: *O Lord our God, who hast given this glory also unto the holy martyrs that suffered for thee.* In this prayer he asks that by the deposition of these relics, the assembly be made worthy to offer, without condemnation, the eucharistic sacrifice without the shedding of blood. This prayer was already present in the Barberini *Euchologion*,[53] and in that document it was followed immediately by the Trisagion and the readings of the Divine Liturgy. The Slavic euchologia add a kneeling prayer, attributed to Saint Kallistos, Patriarch of Constantinople (14th c.): *O Lord our God, who by thy word alone didst create the world*; in this prayer the bishop asks the Lord to send the inheritance of the most Holy Spirit and to grant the remission of sins and all that is necessary for the salvation of those who worked for the construction and consecration of the church.

It should be noted that in the contemporary Greek practice, especially when the slot for the holy relics is found in the table (*mensa*) itself, the transfer of the relics is done at the beginning of the service of the dedication, that is to say before the purification of the altar table, since it is impossible to deposit the relics once the katasarkion has been tied. Nevertheless, we consider that this practice contradicts not only the ancient order of the service, as we have described it, but also its theological meaning. Indeed, the altar must first be cleansed by water and anointed by Holy Myron before the relics can be placed under it and the Divine Liturgy be served, in the same way as baptism and chrismation precede the Eucharist in the rites of Christian initiation.

In the contemporary Russian practice, once the relics have been placed under the altar, the bishop exits the sanctuary and goes to the middle of the

[52]Nicolas Cabasilas, *Life in Christ* 5.26 (SC 361, 32–34; Cabasilas, *The Life in Christ*, 157).
[53]*Barberini*, 164.

church. There he he blesses the four walls of the church with the cross and sprinkles them with holy water, then, after the Augmented Litany intoned by the deacon, the bishop says the dismissal.

When all these rites have been completed, the Divine Liturgy is served, from the beginning. The readings of the patron saint of the church are prescribed, and the readings for the dedication; these are Hebrews 3.1–4, where we read that "he that built all things is God," and John 10.22–26, which mentions the feast of the dedication of the ancient temple of Jerusalem, or Matthew 16.13–18, which mentions Peter's confession that Jesus is the Christ, and Jesus' promise that the church would be founded on that confession, and that the gates of hell would not prevail against it. Usage prescribes that seven liturgies ought to be served on the new altar table (and newly consecrated antimensia).

2.3. *The Sanctification of Antimensia*

The sanctification of antimensia usually takes place at the same time as the sanctification of the altar table, at the dedication of a church. We find in the *Great Euchologion* and in the *Archieratikon* a separate rite for the sanctification of antimensia, a service that in fact is derived from the rite of the dedication of the church.

The word *antimension* comes from the Greek *anti* [ἀντί], "instead of," and the Latin *mensa*, a term that in Latin is used of any sort of table, including the lid of a tomb, and derivatively of the altar erected over the tomb of a martyr, and then also of the altar table. The antimension is a linen (or silk) cloth about 40 x 60cm [16 x 23 inches], and it is actually a portable altar.[54] It symbolizes, just as does the altar, the tomb of Christ, which is usually depicted on it. The antimension first appeared during the second period of Byzantine iconoclasm (815–844), to allow Orthodox priests to celebrate anywhere, since some altars had been desecrated by the iconoclasts.

After the triumph of Orthodoxy in 844, the use of antimensia was reserved for places where there was no consecrated altar. Commenting on

[54]Cf. J. M. Izzo, *The Antimension in the Liturgical and Canonical Tradition of the Byzantine and Latin Churches* (Rome: Pontificium Athenaeum Antonianum, 1975); K. Nikolsly, *Ob antiminsakh Pravoslavnoi Russkoi Tserkvi* (Saint-Petersburg, 1872); S. Pétridès, "L'antimension," *EO* 3 (1899–1900): 193–202; Idem, "Antimension," *DACL* 1.2:2319–2326; A. Raes, "Antimension, tablit, tabot," *POC* 1 (1951): 65–70; J. Salaville, "Antimension," *Catholicisme*, vol. I (Paris, 1948), columns 643–644; M. S. Zheltov and I. O. Popov, "Antimins," *Pravoslavnaya Entsiklopediya*, vol. 2 (Moscow, 2001), 489–492.

Canon 7 of the Seventh Ecumenical Council, which requires that bishops consecrate altars with relics, the canonist Theodore Balsamon (+ *c.* 1196) says that antimensia are sanctified by the bishops at the same time as they dedicate a church, and that the bishops distribute the antimensia to chapels, which are not consecrated.[55]

The antimensia were also used for the celebration of the Divine Liturgy during imperial, military, or missionary journeys, or by solitary monks. Canonical testimonies as late as the eighteenth century say that antimensia are never used on sanctified altars, but they are sent only where there is a necessity, on unconsecrated altars, or on altars whose consecration is uncertain.[56] In our contemporary practice, antimensia are used even though the altar table has been sanctified, but in this case, they are usually without relics. They are thus used instead of the former eiliton (εἰλητόν)—a folded piece of fabric, usually red, intended to collect the crumbs of the sanctified eucharistic bread during the celebration of the Divine Liturgy.[57] In our days, the antimension is considered essential for the celebration of the Divine Liturgy because it bears the signature of the ruling bishop in whose name the Divine Liturgy is being celebrated.

The antimensia are consecrated in the same way as the altar. In the Byzantine practice, they are used instead of cloths to wipe the altar when it has been washed with the water. Once the altar has been washed a second time with wine and rose water, they are used once again to wipe the altar instead of the sponges. They are also anointed: the bishop traces on each one of them three crosses with Holy Myron. The antimensia receive a fragment of relics of holy martyrs, which is placed in a small pocket sewn on the back and fixed with ceromastic. The bishop puts his signature on the antimensia once they have been sanctified. Once the altar is dressed, the antimensia are placed on the altar and remain there for the celebration of seven consecutive Divine Liturgies.

---

[55]Rhalles-Potles, *Syntagma*, 2:372. Cf. Pétridès, "Antimension," 2320.

[56]Salaville, "Antimension," 643; Pétridès, "Antimension," 2321; Prilutsky, *Chastnoe bogosluzhenie v Russkoi tserkvi v XVI v pervoi polovine XVII v.*, 40; Rhalles-Potles, *Syntagma*, 5:114; Miklosich and Müller, *Acta et diplomata græca*, 2:340.

[57]The eiliton, however, is still used with the antimension, to contain and protect it.

3. The Blessing of Water

3.1. Historical Overview

The use of sanctified water is attested by Christian writers of the fourth and fifth centuries.[58] In his homily on the Baptism of Christ, delivered in Antioch in 387, Saint John Chrysostom mentions that Christians gather in the middle of the night for the feast of Theophany and take the water sanctified on that day from the place of their gathering, carry it home in jars, and keep it carefully throughout the year.[59] In the fifth century, Theodore the Reader mentions the intervention of Peter the Fuller (5th c.) in the order of the sanctification of the water by an epiclesis. This sanctification took place in the midle of the night, on the eve of the feast of Theophany.[60] In the sixth century, a pilgrim to Jerusalem from Plaisance, called Antoninus, describes the celebration of Theophany at the Jordan river, where, during the vigil service, after Matins, the clergy descended into the Jordan itself to bless the water, and he mentions that the faithful took the sanctified water home in jars.[61]

At the end of the sixth century, John the Faster, the Patriarch of Constantinople, mentions that the blessed water of Theophany (ἁγίασμα τῶν Φώτων, *hagiasma tōn Phōtōn*) can be received by penitents instead of Holy Communion on the feast of the Nativity of Christ, on Theophany, on Great Thursday and Saturday, on Pascha, and on the feast of the Holy Apostles.[62]

The Barberini *Euchologion* gives us the most ancient order for the blessing of water on Theophany: an Augmented Litany (*diakonika*, starting with: *Let us all say*) with special petitions for the sanctification of the water, a prayer by the priest said in silence (μυστικῶς): *O Lord Jesus Christ, the only-begotten Son*,[63] a prologue: *O Trinity uncreated, consubstantial*,[64] later

---

[58]On the history of the blessing of water, see: F. C. Conybeare, *Rituale Armenorum together with the Greek Rites of Baptism and Epiphany* (Oxford, 1905), 415–421; P. de Puniet, "Bénédiction de l'eau en la fête de l'Épiphanie," *DACL* 2:698–708, at 700–701; M. Vidalis, "La bénédiction des eaux de la fête de l'Épiphanie," *La prière liturgique: Conférences Saint-Serge: XLVIIe Semaine d'Études Liturgiques*, BELS 115 (Rome: CLV-Edizioni liturgiche, 2001), 237–239; N. Denysenko, *The Blessing of Waters and Epiphany* (Farnham, Surrey: Ashgate, 2012), 17–81.

[59]John Chrysostom, *On the Baptism of Christ* (PG 49:365–366).
[60]Theodore the Reader, *Ecclesiastical History* 2:48 (PG 86:208–209).
[61]*Antonini Placentini Itinerarium* 11:4–5 (CCSL 175:135).
[62]John the Faster, *Penitential* (PG 88:1913a).
[63]*Barberini*, 133–134.
[64]*Barberini*, 134.

attributed to Saint Sophronius of Jerusalem, a second prologue: *Blessed is the Lord, the God of Israel,*[65] which is older than the first and is often attributed in the manuscripts to Saint Basil, the prayer of blessing: *Great art thou, O Lord*[66]—recalling the structure of an anaphora—and a prayer of inclination: *Incline thine ear and hear us, O Lord.* The prayer: *Great art thou,* is probably the most ancient, since it is found not only in the Byzantine, but also in the West Syrian, Armenian, and Coptic traditions.[67] The Barberini manuscript then adds another prayer, said at the fountain in the courtyard of the church: *O God, our God.*[68]

The ninth-century *Typikon of the Great Church* gives us some details about the blessing of water in Hagia Sophia. The sanctification of water of Theophany takes place on the Eve (*paramonē*) of the feast, that is on January 5, at the dismissal of the vesperal Divine Liturgy. Instead of saying "let us depart in peace," the deacon said "Wisdom," and then intoned a litany, the patriarch said the prayer of the waters inside the sanctuary, and after the completion of the prayer, he went out to the fountain of the baptistery. The chanters then intoned on the ambo the troparion in the fourth plagal mode (Tone 8): *The voice of the Lord upon the waters,* as all the faithful proceeded to the baptistery. There, the prayer of blessing of water was said. The troparion was followed by three readings chanted on the ambo, most probably during the prayer said in the baptistery: Isaiah 35.1–10, Isaiah 55.1–13, and Isaiah 12.3–6.[69] The *Typikon of the Great Church* refers to a second prayer said in the baptistery, and this might be understood as the prayer for the water used for baptism celebrated on the next day.[70]

Sinai gr. 957 (9th to 10th c.) provides us with further details: the sanctification begins with a litany by the deacon, during which the bishop silently says the prayer attributed to Saint Germanus of Constantinople: *O Lord Jesus Christ,* then a prayer said aloud, including poetic phrases starting with "today" similar to those in the prayer: *Blessed is the Lord, the God of Israel,* of the Barberini *Euchologion.* After this there is a commemoration of the emperor, and then the prayer of inclination: *Incline thine ear and hear us, O Lord,* and then another prayer, said at the font: *O God, our God.*[71]

---

[65] *Barberini,* 135.
[66] *Barberini,* 136–138.
[67] Denysenko, *The Blessing of Waters and Epiphany,* 83–101.
[68] *Barberini,* 138.
[69] J. Mateos, *Le Typikon de la Grande Église,* 1:182–183.
[70] This is what J. Mateos suggests. ibid., 183 n. 3.
[71] A. Dmitrievsky, O*pisanie,* 2:7–8.

Sinai gr. 958 (10th c.) indicates that the blessing of the water takes place at the font, where the liturgical assembly goes in procession while singing the troparion: *The voice of the Lord.* While the deacon intones the litany, the priest silently says the prayer: *O Lord Jesus Christ*, a prayer said aloud: *We glorify thee, O Master all holy*, which includes poetic phrases starting with "today" similar to those in the prayer: *Blessed is the Lord, the God of Israel*, of the Barberini *Euchologion.* After this he says the prayer of blessing: *Great art thou, O Lord*, another prayer: *O God, our God*, and the prayer of inclination: *Incline thine ear, O Lord, and hearken unto us.* Then the priest "illumines" (Greek φωτίζει, that is, he "baptizes") the life-giving cross while singing the troparion of the feast: *When thou, O Lord, wast baptized in the Jordan*, and a second troparion: *The hand of the Baptist trembled.* During the singing of these troparia, the assembly goes back into the church, where a prokeimenon is intoned: *The waters saw thee*, the passages of the Epistle to the Corinthians and the Gospel of Mark are read, then the concluding prayers and dismissal.[72]

Grottaferrata Γ. β. 10 (10th to 11th c.) prescribes a double celebration of the sanctification of the water at Theophany: one on the eve, after the readings according to the ancient practice, and a second one, early in the morning on the day of the feast, after the completion of Matins.[73]

The euchologion manuscript, *Paris Coislin 213* (1027) prescribes the sanctification of the waters after the dismissal of the Divine Liturgy. It mentions the litany by the deacon, during which the priest says the prayer: *O Lord Jesus Christ*, silently, then the prayer of blessing: *Great art thou, O Lord*, aloud, and finally the the prayer of inclination: *Incline thine ear, O Lord, and hearken unto us.* The manuscript also mentions the other prayer, said at the font: *O God, our God.*[74] This order corresponds to the contemporary order given in the Slavic euchologia.

Sinai gr. 991 (14th c.) gives a different service. After the gospel, the deacon intones the Augmented Litany with special petitions. Then the priest first says the prayer: *O Lord Jesus Christ*, then a prayer said aloud: *Blessed art thou, O Lord, the God of our fathers . . . We glorify thee, O Master all holy*, and finally the prayer of inclination: *Incline thine ear, O Lord, and hearken unto us.* Then he immerses the cross in the water while singing Alleluia and

[72]A. Dmitrievsky, *Opisanie*, 2:26–27.

[73]F. C. Conybeare, *Rituale Armenorum together with the Greek Rites of Baptism and Epiphany*, 421.

[74]A. Dmitrievsky, *Opisanie*, 2:999.

the troparion of the feast: *When thou, O Lord, wast baptized in the Jordan,*
thrice. This service concludes with an ancient prologue said as a closing
prayer: *Blessed art thou O Lord God, who dost bless and sanctify us all.*[75]

Sinai gr. 974 (16th c.) indicates that the blessing of the water takes place
at the font, where the liturgical assembly goes in procession while singing
the troparia: *The voice of the Lord; Today the nature of the waters is made
holy; As man thou didst come to the river, O Christ the King; Taking the form
of a servant, O Lord, thou didst come to the voice crying in the wilderness;*
and: *Come, all ye faithful.* The service continues with the reading of two
prophecies from Isaiah, of the Epistle to the Corinthians, and the Gospel of
Mark. The deacon then intones the Augmented Litany: *Let us all say,* with
special petitions, and the priest says the prayer: *O Lord Jesus Christ.* This is
followed by verses: *Glory to God in the highest; O Lord open my lips; Let my
mouth be filled with thy praise;* and a prayer said aloud: *Blessed art thou, O
Lord the God of our fathers, who dost bless and sanctify all things,* a second
prayer said aloud: *O Trinity uncreated, consubstantial*—the first prologue of
the Barberini *Euchologion.* To this prayer the second prologue of that manuscript: *Blessed is the Lord, the God of Israel,* with its poetic phrases starting
with "today," is immediately added, and that is followed by the prayer of
blessing: *Great art thou, O Lord,* and the prayer of inclination: *Incline thine
ear, O Lord, and hearken unto us.* Then the priest immerses the cross in the
water while singing Alleluia and the troparion of the feast: *When thou, O
Lord, wast baptized in the Jordan,* and the service concludes with an ancient
prologue said as a closing prayer: *Blessed art thou, O Lord the God of our
fathers, who dost bless and sanctify all of us.*[76]

The Barberini *Euchologion* does not contain the Small Blessing of Water.
Balsamon (+ after 1195), while commenting on Canon 65 of the Quini-
sext Council in Trullo that prohibits the pagan custom of lighting a fire
in the houses at the beginning of each month, mentions that this practice
was replaced by the Small Blessing of Water, which is an ancient rite of
the Church. He says that the Fathers prescribed the celebration the blessings of water (ἁγιασμοί) at the beginning of each month (καθ᾽ ἑκάστην
ἀρχιμηνίαν).[77] For this reason, some believe that Patriarch Photius may
have introduced this rite in the ninth century, but they provide no references. It is actually only starting in the thirteenth century that liturgical

[75] A. Dmitrievsky, *Opisanie,* 2:330–331.
[76] A. Dmitrievsky, *Opisanie,* 2:676–683.
[77] PG 137:741a; Rhalles-Potles, *Syntagma,* 2:458.

manuscripts contain a service for the Small Blessing of Water (ἁγιασμός). *Patmos 105* (13th c.) gives a such a service for August 1, with many differences in comparison with our current service.[78] In the fourteenth century, Patriarch Philotheos Kokkinos and Metropolitan Cyprian of Kiev revised the text of the Small Blessing of Water for the feast of the Procession of the Cross on August 1.[79] *Sinai gr. 981* (14th c.) gives the troparia in honor of the Theotokos for the Small Blessing of Water served at the beginning of each month.[80] *Sinai gr. 980* and *Thessalonica 29* (both 15th c.) also give such a service to be served on the first day of each month (ἀκολουθία τοῦ ἁγιασμοῦ τῆς νεομηνίας, *akolouthia tou hagiasmou tēs neomēnias*).[81]

3.2. Great Blessing of the Waters on Theophany

Table 8.2: The Order of the Great Blessing of the Waters on Theophany

After the Ambo Prayer:

1. Idiomela of Sophronius of Jerusalem: *The voice of the Lord upon the waters*, etc.
2. Old Testament Readings (Is 35.1–10, Is 55.1–13, and Is 12.3–6)
3. Prokeimenon, Tone 3: *The Lord is my Light and my Savior*
4. Epistle (1 Cor 10.1–4)
5. Alleluia
6. Gospel (Mk 1.9–11)
7. Litany of Peace
8. Priest's prayer: *O Lord Jesus Christ, the only-begotten Son*
9. Prayer of Sophronius of Jerusalem: *Trinity beyond all being, beyond all goodness*
10. Prayer of inclination: *Incline thine ear, O Lord, and hearken unto us*
11. Troparion: *When thou, O Lord, wast baptized in the Jordan*
12. Idiomelon: *Let us sing, O faithful, the greatness of God's dispensation*
13. *Blessed be the name of the Lord* and the dismissal of the Divine Liturgy

---

[78] A. Dmitrievsky, *Opisanie*, 2:165–166.
[79] Job Getcha, *La réforme liturgique du métropolite Cyprien de Kiev* (Paris: Les Éditions du Cerf, 2010), 99–100, 101–104, 227.
[80] A. Dmitrievsky, *Opisanie*, 2:338.
[81] A. Dmitrievsky, *Opisanie*, 2:434, 650.

In current practice, the Great Blessing of the Waters is served twice: on the eve of Theophany, at the end of the vesperal Divine Liturgy of Saint Basil the Great (or Vespers of the feast, when the eve falls on Saturday or Sunday), and on the day of Theophany, at the end of the Divine Liturgy. After the Ambo Prayer, the assembly goes out, with lights and incense, either to the font located in the courtyard or in the narthex, or to a natural body of water, with the celebrant at the front of the procession. The font and the assembly are censed while the chanters sing the idiomela attributed to Saint Sophronius of Jerusalem in Tone 8: *The voice of the Lord upon the waters cries out; Today the nature of the waters is sanctified; As man thou didst come to the river, O Christ the King; Taking the form of a servant, O Lord, thou didst come to the voice crying in the wilderness.* When the idiomela have been sung, the Old Testament prophecies are read (Is 35.1–10; Is 55.1–13; Is 12.3–6); these are already found in the *Typikon of the Great Church* (10th c.).[82] After the readings comes the Prokeimenon in Tone 3: *The Lord is my Light and my Savior; whom, then, shall I fear?* (Ps 26), and the Epistle (1 Cor 10.1–4), which recalls the miracle of the water spreading from the rock, from which the people of Israel drank in the desert (Ex 17.6), and emphasizes that "the rock was Christ." After the singing of Alleluia comes the reading of the Gospel (Mk 1.9–11), which recounts Christ's baptism by John the Baptist in the Jordan.

After the readings, the deacon intones the Litany of Peace, expanded with special petitions:

- *That this water may be sanctified by the power, operation, and descent of the Holy Spirit;*

- *That there may come upon this water the purifying operation of the supersubstantial Trinity;*

- *That there may be granted unto them the grace of redemption, the blessing of Jordan, by the power, operation, and descent of the Holy Spirit;*

- *That Satan may quickly be crushed under our feet, and that every evil counsel direct against us may be bought to ruin;*

- *That the Lord God may deliver us from every attack and temptation of the adversary, and count us worthy of the good things that are promised;*

[82]Mateos, *Le Typikon de la Grande Église*, 1:182–183.

- *That we may be illumined with the illumination of understanding and piety, through the descent of the Holy Spirit;*

- *That the Lord God will send down the blessing of Jordan, and sanctify these waters;*

- *That this water may be a gift of sanctification, and a deliverance from sins, for the healing of soul and body, and for every good purpose;*

- *That this water may spring up unto life eternal;*

- *That it may be shown to be the averting of every snare of enemies, visible and invisible;*

- *For them that draw of it and take of it for the sanctification of their homes;*

- *That it may be to the cleansing of soul and body of all that with faith draw and partake of it;*

- *That we may be counted worthy to be filled with sanctification through the partaking of these waters, by the invisible manifestation of the Holy Spirit.*

During the Great Litany, the celebrant reads the sacerdotal prayer in a low voice, as mentioned in the Barberini *Euchologion*: *O Lord Jesus Christ, the only-begotten Son.*[83] And after the *Amen* at the end of the Litany, the priest begins the prayer attributed to Saint Sophronius of Jerusalem, in a loud voice: *Trinity beyond all being, beyond all goodness.* In the Greek practice, the prologue is said only on day of the feast itself, while it is not found in the Slavic euchologia. After completing this first part, he says thrice in a louder voice: *Great art thou, O Lord, and wondrous are thy works, and no word shall be sufficient to hymn thy wonders.* Then he continues the prayer: *For thou, by thy will, from nothingness hast brought all things into being . . .* And then he says thrice in a louder voice: *Do thou thyself, O King, the Lover of mankind, come now through the descent of thy Holy Spirit, and sanctify this water.* And he continues the prayer: *And give it the grace of redemption, the blessing of Jordan . . .* And then he says thrice in a louder voice: *And do thou thyself, O Master, sanctify this water by thy Holy Spirit.* And he continues the prayer: *And grant unto all them that touch it, and partake of it, and*

[83]*Barberini*, 133.

anoint themselves with it, sanctification, health, cleansing, and blessing. Then he commemorates the civil authorities, the ruling bishop, the whole order of presbyters, the diaconate in Christ, every rank of the clergy, the people present, and the brethren. Next he gives the peace and says the prayer of inclination: *Incline thine ear and hearken unto us, O Lord, who didst will to be baptized in the Jordan.*

Then the celebrant blesses the waters in the form of the cross, immersing the precious Cross, plunging it upright into the water and lifting it out again, while chanting the troparion of the feast, *When thou, O Lord, wast baptized in the Jordan.* Then he sprinkles the entire assembly with the newly blessed water. The faithful drink from the water and return to the church while chanting the idiomelon in Tone 6: *Let us sing, O faithful, the greatness of God's dispensation for us . . .* Then the chanters sing: *Blessed be the name of the Lord,* as usual at the end of the Divine Liturgy, and the usual dismissal follows.

3.3. The Small Blessing[84] of Water

Table 8.3: The Order of the Small Blessing of Waters

---

1. Opening blessing: *Blessed is our God*

2. Psalm 142: *O Lord, hear my prayer*

3. *God is the Lord,* and the troparion: *Let us who are lowly and sinful now diligently run to the Theotokos*

4. Psalm 50

5. Troparia in honor of the Theotokos

6. *For Holy art thou, O our God,* and troparia, Tone 8: *The time that sanctifieth all men,* etc., concluding with the Trisagion

7. Prokeimenon: *The Lord is my Light and my Savior*

8. Epistle (Hb 2.11–18)

9. Alleluia

10. Gospel (John 5.1–4)

11. Litany

12. Prayer: *O Lord our God, great in counsel and wondrous in deeds*

---

[84]The *Great Book of Needs,* 1:282, refers to this rite as the "Lesser Sanctification of Waters."

13. Prayer of inclination: *Incline thine ear and hearken unto us, O Lord who didst will to be baptized in the Jordan*
14. Troparion: *O Lord, save thy people and bless thine inheritance*
15. *Make us worthy of thy gifts, O Virgin Theotokos*
16. Troparion: *Having a fountain of healings, O holy Unmercenaries*
17. Litany
18. Dismissal.

The Small Blessing of Water may be served at any time throughout the year, whenever there is a need, and especially on the first day of each month, as well as on special feast days (such as the feast of the Procession of the Cross on August 1, the day of Mid-Pentecost, the patronal feast day of the church), and on other special occasions (blessing of a new house, beginning of the school year, etc.). Thus, it could be served anywhere. On a small table, the celebrant places the gospel book, a silver-bound wooden Cross, a censer, a bowl of water, two candlesticks with their candles, a few sprigs of basil, and a clean white towel.

The celebrant intones the opening blessing: *Blessed is our God. . . .* The reader reads Psalm 142: *O Lord, hear my prayer.* Then the chanters sing, in tone 4: *God is the Lord,* and the troparion: *Let us who are lowly and sinful now diligently run to the Theotokos,* and the theotokion. Psalm 50 is then read, followed by the singing of the troparia in honor of the Theotokos: *All-Holy Theotokos, guard, protect and keep thy servants*; *O Virgin who didst receive from the Angel the salutation "Rejoice"*; and the rest of the sequence. In his treatise on the seven sacraments, Job Hamartolos (13th c.) explains that the Small Blessing of Water is accomplished through the grace and intercession of the Theotokos,[85] and for this reason it begins with troparia invoking her, and concludes by the troparion asking her to make us worthy of her gifts, to disregard our transgressions, and to grant healing to those who, through faith, receive her blessings. When these troparia have been sung, the priest says the ecphonesis before the Trisagion: *For holy art thou, O God,* and then further troparia in honor of the Theotokos are sung before the Trisagion itself. As we have already noted, the singing of the Trisagion is a remnant of the stational liturgy of Constantinople.[86]

---

[85]Job Hamartolos, *On the Seven Mysteries of the Church*, in Chrysanthos of Jerusalem (Ed.), *Συνταγμάτιον*, 132.

[86]Cf. S. Janeras, "Le Trisagion: une formule brève en liturgie comparée," 496–499.

The readings are preceded by the prokeimenon: *The Lord is my Light and my Savior* (same as for the Great Blessing of the Waters). The Epistle (Hebrews (2.11–18), talks about him who sanctifies and those who are being sanctified, being all of One, and it is followed by the Alleluia and the reading of the Gospel (Jn 5.1–4), which mentions the pool called Bethesda by the Sheep Gate in Jerusalem, where the miracle occurred through the descent of the angel of the Lord.

After the readings, the deacon intones the Litany of Peace, expanded by special petitions:

- *That this water may be sanctified by the power, operation, and descent of the Holy Spirit;*

- *That there may come upon this water the purifying operation of the supersubstantial Trinity;*

- *That this water may be to the healing of soul and body, and to the banishing of every adverse power;*

- *That the Lord God may send down the blessing of Jordan, and sanctify this water; For all them that need help and protection from God;*

- *That we may be illumined by the illumination of understanding by the consubstantial Trinity;*

- *That the Lord God may show us to be sons and heirs of his kingdom, through partaking of this water, and through the sprinkling therewith.*

After the ecphonesis, the celebrant says the prayer: *O Lord our God, great in counsel and wondrous in deeds.* He gives the peace, and reads the prayer of inclination: *Incline thine ear and hearken unto us, O Lord*, as in the Great Blessing of the Waters. Then, taking up the venerable Cross, he dips it crosswise in the water thrice, while singing the troparion of the Cross: *O Lord, save thy people and bless thine inheritance.* Afterwards in the Greek practice he sprinkles the holy water with a bunch of basil in the form of the cross and sings the troparion in honor of the Theotokos: *Make us worthy of thy gifts, O Virgin Theotokos.* Then he kisses the precious Cross, and with the newly blessed water he blesses the entire assembly, sprinkling everyone, as well as the sanctuary and the entire church. Meanwhile the chanters sing the troparion in honour of the Holy Unmercenaries. The service ends with the litany and the dismissal.

Glossary

NB: Apart from titles and a few words transliterated from Greek or Slavonic, words in italics are also defined in this glossary, which generally omits terms well defined in the main text.

Altar table: The table in the *sanctuary* on which the Divine *Liturgy* is celebrated.

Acrostic: The initial letters of a series of *troparia* which, when combined, form a sentence.

Akolouthia: A term signifying the unfolding of a service. It can signify the prescribed order of an *office*, or the body of hymnography constituting an *office*.

Alleluia: A term literally meaning "Praise the Lord." 1) It can designate the *office* called "Alleluia," i.e., the office on fast days when *God is the Lord* is not sung at Matins, but instead Alleluia with psalm verses sung by the *canonarch*. 2) It can also refer to the doxology: "Alleluia, alleluia, alleluia, glory to you, O God."

Ambo: Originally, a raised platform in the center of the church where readings were done. In contemporary usage, the central part of the *solea* in front of the *holy doors*.

Ambo Prayer (also referred to as the Prayer behind the Ambo): The final prayer of the Divine Liturgy, recited by the priest, who in the Russian tradition stands facing the altar from the western side of the festal icon stand (which now stands where the ancient ambo was located), while in the Greek tradition he stands on the solea facing the icon of Christ in the icon screen; the prayer consists of a final intercession before the dismissal.

Anabathmoi: Graduals. *Antiphonal* hymns, distributed in the eight tones of the *Octoechos*, composed on the basis of the gradual psalms (Pss 119–133) and sung at festal Matins before the *prokeimenon* and the gospel reading. On Sundays, the anabathmoi are sung in the tone of the Sunday, while on feast days, the first *antiphon* of the anabathmoi in tone 4 is sung.

Analabos: A piece of fabric with the representation of the cross, worn as an apron.

Anaphora: The Eucharistic prayer of the Divine Liturgy.

Antidoron: A term literally meaning "instead of the gift." The bread distributed by the priest at the end of the Divine *Liturgy*, consisting of the remains of the *prosphora* used at the *proskomidē* (*proskomedia*).

Antimension: A term originally designating the cover of a tomb, later the altar erected over the tomb of a martyr, and finally the altar table. A silk or linen cloth, about 40 x 60 cm (approximately 16 x 24 inches), on which is represented the burial of Christ, consecrated and signed by the local bishop and containing a small relic, thus constituting a portable altar.

Antiphon: 1) Psalm (or group of hymns) appointed to be sung *antiphonally*. 2) One of the three sections constituting a *kathisma* and concluding with a doxology.

Antiphonally: Generally, with two *choirs*.

Aposticha: *Stichera* accompanied by psalm verses sung at the end of *Vespers* during the entire year and at the end of non-festal *Matins*.

Apostol: Liturgical book containing the Acts of the Apostles and the Epistles.

Archdeacon: An high diaconal rank.

Archieratikon: Liturgical book with services as celebrated by a bishop.

Archimandrite: The highest rank among monastic clergy.

Archpriest: An intermediate rank among non-monastic clergy.

Artophorion: A box, often shaped like a church, used to contain the consecrated Gifts reserved for the communion of the sick or for the *Presanctified Liturgy*.

Assembly: A term referring to all of those gathered for a divine service, both clergy and laity.

Autocephaly: The status of an Orthodox Church that elects its own primate without the need for confirmation by any other Church.

Automelon: A *sticheron* with its own rhythmic structure and its own melody, which serves as a model for other *stichera*.

Axios: Acclamation at an ordination.

Baptistery: The place, generally adjacent to the *narthex*, housing the baptismal font, where baptisms and the blessing of water are celebrated.

Beatitudes: Verses taken from the Sermon on the Mount (Mt 5.3–12) beginning with the word "Blessed," sung at the *Typika* and at the *Liturgy*, which are intercalated with *troparia* from the *Octoechos* (troparia of the Beatitudes) or *troparia* taken from the *canon* of festal *Matins*.

Canon: A hymnographic composition consisting of *heirmoi* and *troparia*. The latter were originally intercalated between the verses of the nine *biblical canticles*. This explains why the canons consist of nine *odes*, the second usually absent, because the second biblical canticle is sung only during *Great Lent*. Some canons, however, contain only four odes [tetra-ode], or three odes [tri-ode], or of two odes [di-ode]. The term also applies to regulations adopted and published by various councils or fathers.

Canonarch: The chanter appointed to chant (from the center of the church) certain psalm refrains and to proclaim their verses.

Canticles, biblical or of Moses: The nine biblical canticles constituting the structure of the *canon* of *Matins* and contained in the Palestinian *Psalter*: 1) the canticle of Moses (Ex 15.1–19; 2) the canticle of Moses (Dt 32.1–43); 3) the prayer of Hannah (1 Kgs 2.1–10); 4) the prayer of Habakkuk (Hab 3.1–19); 5) the prayer of Isaiah (Is 26.9–20); 6) the prayer of Jonah (Jonah 2.3–10); 7) the prayer of the three youths (Dan 3.26–56; 8) the canticle of the three youths (Dan 3.57–88); 9) The Magnificat and the Benedictus (Lk 1.46–55, 68–79). The Canticle of St Symeon the God-Receiver (Lk 2.29–32) is not used in Matins, but has its place in Vespers every day, and in certain other services.

Cathedra: In the Russian tradition, a raised platform in the center of the church where the bishop stands until the Little Entrance of the Divine Liturgy; in the greater Byzantine tradition, the throne on the nave side of the icon screen.

Chanter: The person leading the singing of the *choir*, or appointed to perform a reading (see *Reader* and *Canonarch*).

Cherubikon: The Hymn of the Cherubim, sung during the Great Entrance in the Divine *Liturgy*.

Choir: A term designating the place, to the left and right of the *iconostasis*, where the *chanters* stand during the *office*; also, the body of chanters or singers. A number of chants are performed "with two choirs," or "antiphonally," indicating that each of the choirs, in turn, sings a verse.

Diataxis: The prescribed order for a service; ordo.

Dismissal: The liturgical formula of dismissal at the conclusion of a service, consisting of the final blessing by the celebrating priest.

Diptychs: A book in which are inscribed the names of the living and the dead commemorated during the Divine *Liturgy*.

Diskos: A liturgical vessel, shaped like a plate with a pedestal, used to hold the holy bread (lamb); paten.

Doxastikon: *Sticheron* sung after "Glory to the Father. . . ."

Doxology, Great: Used in Matins, this exists in two redactions. The Palestinian monastic redaction is used at the end of weekday Matins, and is done in liturgical recitative; the Constantinopolitan redaction is used at the end of Sunday and festal Matins, and is rendered with melody.

Ecclesiarch: The person responsible to watch over the good order of the *offices* and often replacing the *hegoumen* of a monastery in his absence, or the rector of a parish if he is not available to serve.

Eisodikon: Psalm verse chanted during the Small Entrance at the Divine *Liturgy*.

Encolpion: A pectoral icon of the Theotokos with the infant Christ, worn by a bishop in place of or in addition to a pectoral cross.

Epiclesis: A prayer asking for the transformation of the Holy Gifts through the coming of the Holy Spirit.

Epigonation: A diamond-shaped piece of stiffened fabric worn by bishops (and as an award by certain priests), signifying the victory of Christ over sin through the resurrection. It is worn on the right side, at or just above the knee, where it is suspended from the wearer's left shoulder by a ribbon crossing chest and back, whose ends are joined at the upper corner of the epigonation.

Epimanikia: Decorative cuffs, usually of the same stuff as the rest of the celebrant's vestments, worn at the wrist by deacons, priests, and bishops.

Epitrachelion: A wide band of fabric worn by priests and bishops. The center is placed at the back of the neck, and the left and right portions fall almost to the ground in front; these are joined by stitching or buttons at several places along the length. It is essentially the deacon's or subdeacon's *orarion*, now worn in a different manner by the higher orders of the clergy.

Evlogetaria: *Troparia* in honor of the resurrection or in memory of the dead sung after Psalm 118, with the refrain "Blessed are you, O Lord, teach me your statutes" (Ps 118.12).

Exaposteilarion: Literally meaning "hymn of sending out" (from the Greek ἐξαποστέλλω, *exapostello*). This hymn gets its name from its content, not its place in the *office*. It alludes to the sending out of the apostles after the Resurrection (on Sunday) or of the light (during the week), and not to the dismissal of the community. The expression "Matins Exaposteilarion" designates one of the eleven hymns attributed to Emperor Constantine Porphyrogenitus and sung following the *canon* at Sunday *Matins*, accompanying the reading of one of the eleven resurrectional gospels.

Exclamation: A doxological formula, said aloud by the priest, which concludes a *litany*.

Fast: 1) An ascetical practice consisting of abstinence from certain kinds of food (meat, eggs and dairy products, fish, wine, and oil) or from all food. 2) A type of *office* celebrated on fast days and consisting of a large number of *prostrations*, the singing of *Alleluia* at the beginning of *Matins*, and the reading of the Prayer of St Ephrem, accompanied by prostrations, at the conclusion of each office, following a particular order. 3) A synonym of *Great Lent*.

God is the Lord: A selection of psalm verses from Psalm 117 sung by the *canonarch* at the beginning of *Matins*, with Psalm 117.26, 25, as the refrain. Generally speaking, this expression indicates the festal *office*, as distinct from what was once the usual *office*, kept today only on fast days and referred to as the *office* with *Alleluia*.

Hegoumen: The superior or abbot of a monastery.

Hieratikon: The service book containing the priest's and deacon's portions of the major services.

Heirmos (plural, in Greek: *heirmoi,* or in Slavonic: *irmosi*): A term that in Greek literally means a "link." The hymn opening each *ode* of the *canon*, thus creating the "link" between the biblical *canticle* and the hymnography.

Holy Doors: The central doors of the icon screen, leading to the *altar table.* These doors are not to be confused with the Royal Doors, the central doors between the narthex and the nave, reserved for the emperor in Constantinople's Church of the Holy Wisdom, although the terms are often confused in contemporary speech and writing.

Holy Table: see *altar table.*

Hour: An *office* composed of three psalms, hymns, and prayers, read at a particular time during the day. There exist the First Hour (Prime), the Third Hour (Terce), the Sixth Hour (Sext), and the Ninth Hour (None).

Iconostasis (also *icon screen*): Row(s) of icons separating the sanctuary from the nave. At the center of the iconostasis, the *holy doors* lead to the *holy table.*

Idiomelon: A *sticheron* with its own rhythmic structure and its own melody, which is not imitated by other stichera.

Ikos: Hymn following the *kontakion.*

Kamilavka, kamilavkion: A clerical hat; cylindrical in form, in the Russian tradition it is slightly flared from bottom to a flat top; in the greater Byzantine tradition, the sides are not flared, and the top is slightly raised in the middle.

Katavasia: The *heirmos* sung at the end of the third, sixth, eighth, and ninth odes of the *canon* at *Matins* (and at the end of each ode on feast days) as the conclusion of the ode. The term comes from the Greek καταβαίνω (*katabaino*) meaning "to go down," because, originally, the two *choirs* would go down from their places and come together in the center of the church to execute this chant.

Kathisma: One of the twenty sections of the Palestinian *Psalter*.

Koinonikon: Communion verse. Psalm verse sung at the Divine *Liturgy* while the members of the *assembly* partake of the consecrated holy gifts.

Kolyva: A platter of boiled wheat grains with honey, offered in memory of a saint or a dead person.

Kontakion: Hymn sung after the sixth *ode* of the *canon* at *Matins*.

Koukoulion: The headdress of a monk in the Great Schema; also of the Patriarch of Moscow.

Lent, Great: The period of fasting beginning on the seventh week before Pascha. Note that Holy Week is not, properly speaking, part of the forty-day Great Lent.

Litany: A collection of short sentences by which the deacon (or, in his absence, the priest) invites the *assembly* to pray for various intentions, and to which the *assembly* (or the *choir*) responds. The responses differ according to the litany intoned by the deacon (or priest): for example, in the Great Litany and the Small Litany, the major response is "Lord, have mercy"; in the Augmented Litany, it is a triple "Lord, have mercy"; in the Litany of Supplication it is "Grant it, O Lord." The litany to be intoned is part of the structure of the services. Other litanies with somewhat different responses are also used in various services.

Lity (Also litē or litiya): A procession, often including an intercessory litany. There is a lity at the end of Vespers at a Vigil. The *assembly* generally processes to the *narthex* while singing the lity *stichera*, after which the deacon recites the long *litany* of intercession. There can also be a lity at the end of *Matins*, and this is the time at which prayers are offered for the dead. Because of this, the term "lity" is often used to refer to a short office of intercession for the dead.

Liturgy: A term generally used to refer to the eucharistic Divine Liturgy.

Liturgy, full: An expression referring to the regular eucharistic Divine *Liturgy*, i.e., with the anaphora and the consecration of the Holy Gifts, as opposed to the *Presanctified Liturgy*.

Liturgy, vesperal: Divine Liturgy that begins with Vespers because of a strict fast day, as for example, on the eves of Christmas and Theophany, on Holy Thursday, and on Holy Saturday.

Lord, I call: An expression containing the first words of the evening psalms (Pss 140, 141, 129, and 116), sung daily at Vespers. The final verses of these psalms are intercalated with stichera.

Mandyas (also mantia/mantiya): A monastic garment, a sort of sleeveless cloak.

Matins: Morning *office*, celebrated after the Midnight Office, before the rising of the sun.

Menaion: The liturgical book for the fixed annual cycle. The word is derived from the Greek word μῆν (*mēn*), meaning "month," and the book contains the hymnography for each day of the month. There are twelve such volumes, one for each month of the year.

Miter: a crown-like headpiece worn by bishops and as an award by some priests.

Mnemosyno: In the Greek tradition, a short memorial service between the *Ambo Prayer* and the *Dismissal* at the *Divine Liturgy*.

Myron: Chrism.

Nabedrennik: A type of rectangular *epigonation*, worn on the right side by priests who have not been awarded the diamond-shaped *epigonation*, and on the left side by those who have received that reward. The Nabedrennik is not worn by bishops.

Narthex: The vestibule at the western end of the church, separated from the central nave by the royal doors. It is customarily here that the Midnight Office, the Hours, and Compline are read, and where the lity at Vigil is celebrated.

Nave: The body of the church where the *assembly* gathers for divine services, between the *narthex* and the *sanctuary*.

Octoechos: Book containing the hymnography for each day of the week in a cycle of eight weeks, each corresponding to one of the eight ecclesiastical musical tones or modes.

Ode: One of the divisions of the canon, consisting of an *heirmos* and *troparia*, originally accompanying the verses of a biblical canticle. NB: We often use the term "ode" for the hymnographic material, and the term "canticle" for the biblical material, even though this distinction does not exist in either Greek or Slavonic.

Office: A divine service; see *Akolouthia.*

Omophorion: The vestment proper only to bishops, it exists in two forms: The great omophorion is a long, broad strip of cloth draped over the bishop's shoulders, with one end falling in front and the other in back; the small omophorion is similarly broad, but shorter, and both ends fall in front.

Orarion: A wide band of fabric worn during services by subdeacons (crossed in front and back) and deacons (suspended from the left shoulder).

Orthros: See *Matins.*

Pannikhida: A memorial service.

Paramantion, paraman: A monastic garment, a piece of square fabric worn on the back with cords passing over both shoulders and tied in front.

Paramone: A Greek term literally meaning eve, vigil, urgent expectation. Used for the eves of the Nativity of Christ and Theophany, during which everyone fasts strictly while awaiting the feast.

Pedalion: A collection of church canons and commentaries on them, assembled by St Nicodemus of the Holy Mountain; also called *The Rudder.*

People: A term referring to the liturgical *assembly.*

Phelonion: The outer garment worn by priests when serving the Divine Liturgy and certain other services. In ancient times it was a sort of long pancho, with a hole in the center for the head; in contemporary use, the front is mostly made much shorter than the back, so the priest's arms and hands can move more freely.

Polyeleos: The singing of Pss 134 and 135, with the refrain "Alleluia" intercalated between the verses; it is sung at Matins on feast days and certain Sundays, thus constituting a third section of psalmody.

Prayer of Inclination: A prayer said by the priest after the deacon bids the members of the *assembly* to bow their heads to the Lord.

Presanctified Liturgy: An evening *office* with eucharistic communion, celebrated following Vespers on days of strict fasting, when the *full Liturgy* is not permitted. Communion is distributed from the Holy Gifts consecrated at the preceding Divine *Liturgy*, usually on the previous Sunday, hence the expression "presanctified."

Prokeimenon: Psalm refrain accompanied by psalm verses read by the *canonarch* or the *reader*, generally preceding a biblical reading.

Proskomidē (also Proskomedia or Prothesis): The first part of the Divine Liturgy, during which the priest prepares the eucharistic bread and wine and commemorates all the members of the Church, alive and dead.

Prosomion (pl. *prosomoia*): A hymn whose rhythm and melody are copied from an *automelon*.

Prosphora: Bread used for the Eucharist in the Divine Liturgy.

Prostration (also metanoia or metanie): A small metanoia is a prostration made by touching the floor with one's hand. A full prostration is one in which one's head touches the floor, implying a bending of the knees. We should note that the expression "three full prostrations" sometimes implies that they accompany the Prayer of St Ephrem.

Prothesis: See *Proskomide.*

Psalmody: The reading of a *kathisma* from the Psalter.

Psalter: The liturgical book containing the 150 psalms of the Septuagint, divided into twenty *kathismata* in the Palestinian Psalter; it contains also the nine *biblical canticles.*

Reader: The person appointed to carry out a *reading* or *readings.*

Readings: This term, in the singular, can also designate biblical, patristic, or hagiographic readings at the Vigil, at the end of Great Vespers ("Great reading"), after the Polyeleos, after the third and sixth odes of the canon, or at the end of Matins.

Riasophore: A monk in the first monastic rank.

Sanctuary: The eastern part of the church, separated from the *nave* by the *iconostasis*, where the *altar table* is found.

Savanon: A white apron with sleeves the covers and protects the vestments of a bishop when he is consecrating an altar.

Schema: The monastic garment of those in the middle and highest ranks of monastics, with a different form for each rank, Little Schema and Great Schema.

Sedalen: A *troparion* sung after a reading from the *Psalter*, or at certain places in the *canon*; also called a "kathisma hymn" or "sessional hymn."

Skevophylakion: Sacristy; the place, usually close to the *sanctuary*, where the sacred vessels and precious relics are kept.

Skufia, skoufos: a soft clerical hat, of varying construction according to the local church to which the wearer belongs.

Sluzhebnik: The liturgical book containing the prayers and litanies said by the priest (or deacon) at *Vespers, Matins,* and the three liturgies.

Solea: A raised area in front of the *iconostasis*.

Stasis: One of the three sections of a *kathisma*.

Station: In pre-iconoclast Constantinople, a place where a procession stopped for psalms and prayers on the way from one church to another.

Stavrophore: A monastic in the middle rank.

Sticharion: The first vestment put on by serving clergy, with different designs for subdeacons and deacons, priests, and bishops.

Sticheron (pl. *stichera*): A hymn intercalated between psalm verses.

Superior: A term used for the *hegumen* in a monastery, or the rector of a non-monastic church.

Synaxis: *Assembly.* 1) This term is generally used for the eucharistic assembly. Within anchorite monasticism, it is used to designate the moment when all the monks gather in the main church of the monastery on the occasion of an important feast to celebrate a *Vigil* and the Divine *Liturgy.* 2) This term is also used in reference to the day after a major feast, honoring the person whom God chose to serve in the accomplishment of his plan. For example, on the day after Christmas, the Church celebrates the Synaxis of the Most Holy Theotokos. 3) This term can also designate the feast of a group of saints, such as the synaxis of the twelve apostles, the synaxis of the seventy apostles, etc.

Theotokion: Hymn in honor of the Mother of God, concluding a series of *troparia* or *stichera.*

Theotokos: The ancient patristic title accorded to the Virgin Mary, approved at the Third Ecumenical Council (Ephesus, 431). It is often translated by the expression "Mother of God," and in older translations as "Birthgiver of God."

Trebnik: From the Slavonic word *treba* meaning "need": the liturgical book containing the services of various sacraments and blessings. Also called "The Great Book of Needs."

Triodion: 1) The liturgical book for the annual moveable cycle, containing hymnography for the preparatory period before Great Lent, starting on the Sunday of the Publican and the Pharisee (tenth Sunday before Pascha) to Cheese-Fare Sunday (seventh Sunday before Pascha), as well as all of Great Lent and Holy Week. This book gave its name to the whole period preceding Pascha, during which this type of canon (i.e., with three odes) is commonly used.

Trisagion: A term designating the prayer "Holy God, Holy Mighty, Holy Immortal, have mercy on us."

Troparion (pl. *troparia*): A hymn, generally brief.

Typika: This term generally designates the *office* which, originally in Palestine, accompanied individual communion in monastic cells. Later, it became a service substituting for the Divine Liturgy when the Eucharist could not be celebrated. The term is also used for Pss 102 and 145, which are chanted at the beginning of this *office.*

Typikon: The book that regulates the order of the services of the liturgical cycle and their proper execution.

Usual beginning prayers: Opening blessing; O Heavenly King (or Christ is risen, in Paschal season); Trisagion; All Holy Trinity; Lord have mercy, Glory; Our Father; Lord have mercy, Glory; O come let us worship.

Vespers: Evening *office,* celebrated at sunset.

Vigil, All-night Vigil: According to the Sabaite Typikon, the office of the *all-night Vigil*, consisting of *Great Vespers*, a reading, *Matins* with the *Polyeleos*, and the First *Hour*, celebrated on the eves of Sundays and great feasts.

Bibliography

Afanasieff, N. *Vstuplenie v klir*. Paris, 1968

Almazov, Alexander I. *Tainaya ispoved' v Provoslavnoi Vostochnoi Tserkvi. Opyt vneshnei istorii: Issledovanie preimushchestvenno po rukopisyam*. 3 volumes. Odessa, 1894.

Ambrose, Bp of Milan. *Epistola* 22. PL 16:1066. English in *Saint Ambrose: Letters*. Translated by Sister Mary Melchior Beyenka, O.P. Washington: The Catholic University of America Press, 1967, 1987, 2001.

Antoninus Placentius (otherwise the Piacenza Pilgrim). *Antonini Placentini Itinerarium*. CCSL 175:129–153.

Apostolic Constitutions. Les Constitutions apostoliques. Vol. 3. M. Metzger, ed. SC 336. Paris: Les Éditions du Cerf, 1987. English in *The Teaching of the Twelve Apostles*. ANF 7:369–509.

Archieratikon. Athens, 1994.

Arranz, Miguel. *L'Eucologio costantinopolitano agli inizi del secolo XI: hagiasmatarion & archieratikon (rituale pontificale): con l'aggiunta del Leiturgikon (messale)*. Rome: Pontificia Università Gregoriana, 1996.

_____. "Les formulaires de confession dans la tradition byzantine (Les sacrements de la restoration de l'ancien Euchologe constantinopolitain: II-3)." *OCP* 58 (1992): 426–31, *OCP* 59 (1993): 63–89, 357–86.

_____. "La liturgie des Présanctifiés de l'ancien Euchologue byzantin." *OCP* 47 (1981): 332–88.

_____. "Les prières pénitentielles de la tradition byzantine (Les sacrements de la restoration de l'ancien Euchologe constantinopolitain, II-2)." 1ère partie." *OCP* 57 (1991): 87–143; 2e partie: *OCP* 57 (1991) 309–329; 3e partie: *OCP* 58 (1992): 23–82.

_____. "Les prières presbytérales de la pannychis de l'ancien euchologe byzantin et la panikhida des défunts II." *OCP* 41 (1975): 119–139.

_____. "Les sacrements de l'ancien Euchologe constantinopolitain (3): II: Admission dans l'Eglise des enfants des familles chrétiennes (premier catéchuménat)." *OCP* 49 (1983): 284–302.

_____. "Les sacrements de l'ancien Euchologe constantinopolitain (4): III-a: Préparation au baptême : 1. Second catéchuménat." *OCP* 50 (1984): 43–64

_____. "Les sacrements de l'ancien Euchologe constantinopolitain (5): III-b: Préparation au baptême : 2. Renonciation à Satan et adhésion au Christ." *OCP* 50 (1984): 372–397.

_____. "Les sacrements de l'ancien Euchologe constantinopolitain (6): IV-a: L'illumination de la nuit de Pâques : 1-a. Bénédiction de l'eau et de l'huile baptismales." *OCP* 51 (1985): 60–86

_____. "Les sacrements de l'ancien Euchologe constantinopolitain (7): IV-b: L'illumination de la nuit de Pâques : 1-b. Bénédiction de l'eau et de l'huile baptismales (suite et fin)." *OCP* 52 (1986): 145–78.

_____. "Les sacrements de l'ancien Euchologe constantinopolitain (8): IV-c: L'illumination de la nuit de Pâques : 2. Onction pré-baptismale. 3. Immersion baptismale. 4. Onction post-baptismale. 5. Entrée dans le temple et liturgie. Appendice : Les autres jours de baptême." *OCP* 53 (1987): 59–106.

_____. "Les sacrements de l'ancien Euchologe constantinopolitain (9): IV-d: L'illumination de la nuit de Pâques: 6. Ablution et tonsure des néophytes." *OCP* 55 (1989): 33–62.

Brotherhood of St Tikhon of Zadonsk. *A Small Book of Needs*. Second edition revised and edited by Hierodeacon Herman and Vitaly Permiakov. South Canaan, PA: St Tikhon's Monastery Press, 2012.

Bruni, Vitaliano. *I funerali di un sacerdote nel rito bizantino secondo gli eucologi manoscritti di lingua greca*. Jeruaslem: Franciscan Printing House, 1972.

Cabrol, Fernand and Henri Leclercq, eds. *Dictionnaire d'Archéologie Chrétienne et de Liturgie*. Paris: Letouzey et Ane. Vol. 1, 1907; Vol. 2, 1910, 1925; Vol. 4, 1920.

Chinovnik. Vol. 2. Moscow, 1983.

Chronicon Pascale. PG 92:69–1028.

Chronz, T. *Die Feier des Heiligen Öles nach Jerusalemer Ordnung. Mit dem Text des slavischen Codex Hilferding 21 der Russischen Nationalbibliothek in Sankt Petersburg sowie gerorgischen Übersetzungen palästinischer und konstantino-politanischer Quellen. Einführung. Edition. Kommentar*. Jerusalemer Theologisches Forum, Vol. 18. Münster: Aschendorff Verlag, 2012.

Clement of Rome. *Clément de Rome. Épître aux Corinthiens*. A. Jaubert, ed. SC 167:98–204. Paris: Éditions du Cerf, 1971. English in *First Letter to the Corinthians*. ANF 9:229–248.

Conybeare, F. C. *Rituale Armenorum together with the Greek Rites of Baptism and Epiphany*. Oxford: Clarendon Press, 1905.

Constantine VII Porphyrogenius. *De ceremoniis aulae byzantinae (Book of Ceremonies)*. PG 112:73–824.

Cyprian of Carthage. *The Letters of St. Cyprian of Carthage, Letters 67–82*. Edited by Walter J. Burghardt and Thomas Comerford Lawler. Translated by G. W. Clarke. Ancient Christian Writers volume 4. New York; Mahwah, NJ: Newman Press, 1989.

Cyril of Jerusalem. *Mystagogical Catecheses*. Pages 84–137 in *St Cyril of Jerusalem: Lectures on the Christian Sacraments: The* Procatechesis *and the Five Mystagogical Catecheses Attributed to St Cyril of Jerusalem*. Greek original and English Translation. Maxwell E. Johnson, ed. PPS 57. Yonkers, NY: St Vladimir's Seminary Press, 2017.

――――. *Mystagogical Homilies. Cyrille de Jérusalem. Catéchèses mystagogiques*. Edited by P. Paris and A. Piedagnel. Sources chrétiennes 126. Paris: Les Éditions du Cerf, 1966. English in Cyril of Jerusalem. *Lectures on the Christian Sacraments: The* Procatechesis *and the Five Mystagogical Catecheses Ascribed to St Cyril of Jerusalem*. Trans. Maxwell Johnson. PPS 57. Yonkers, NY: St Vladimir's Seminary Press, 2017.

O. Delouis, "La profession de foi pour l'ordination des évêques (avec un formulaire inédit du patriarche Photius)." Pages 119–38 in *Le saint, le moine et le paysan. Mélanges d'histoire byzantine offerts à M. Kaplan*. Edited by S. Metivier and P. Pages. Byzantina Sorbonensia 29. Paris: Publications de la Sorbonne, 2016.

Denysenko, Nicholas. *The Blessing of Waters and Epiphany*. Farnham, Surrey: Ashgate, 2012.

Diadochos of Photiki. *On Spiritual Knowledge and Discrimination: One Hundred Texts*. English translation in *Philokalia*, edited by G. E. H. Palmer, Philip Sherrard, and Kallistos Ware. Vol. 1:253–296. London: Faber & Faber, 1983.

Didache. La Doctrine des douze apôtres (Didachè). W. Rodorf and A. Tuilier, eds. Second edition. Paris: Les Éditions du Cerf, 1998. English in *On the Two Ways: Life or Death, Light or Darkness: Foundational Texts in the Tradition*. Translated and edited, with an introduction by Alistair Stewart(-Sykes), 35–44. PPS 41. Yonkers, NY: St Vladimir's Seminary Press, 2011.

Dmitrievsky, A. "Bogosluzhenie v Russkoi Tserkvi za pervye pyat vekov." *Pravoslavnii sobesednik* 12.1–3 (1882).

――――. *Opisanie liturgicheskikh rukopisej khranyashchikhsya v bibliotekakh Pravoslavnogo Vostoka*. 3 vols. Kiev, 1895–1917.

Dositheos of Jerusalem. Dositheos of Jerusalem, *Confession of Faith*. Pages 110–181 in *The Acts and Decrees of the Synod of Jerusalem*. Translated by J. N. W. B. Robertson. London: Thomas Baker, 1899.

Dragas, G. D. "The Manner of Reception of Roman Catholic Converts into the Orthodox Church." *Greek Orthodox Theological Review* 44 (1999): 235–271.

Egeria. *Itinerarium. Égérie: Journal de voyage*. P. Maraval, ed. SC 296. Paris: Les Éditions du Cerf, 1982, 2002. English in *Egeria: Diary of a Pilgrimage*. Johannes Quasten, Walter J. Burghardt, and Thomas Comerford Lawler, eds. George E. Gingras, trans. Ancient Christian Writers vol. 38. New York; Mahwah, NJ: The Newman Press, 1970.

Ephrem of Syria. *Hymn 25 on Oil and the Olive*. In Sancti Ephraem Syri. *Hymni et sermones*. Edited by Thomas Joseph Lamy. Vol. 2. Malines: Dessain, 1886, columns 787–792.

Erickson, John H. "Reception of Non-Orthodox into the Orthodox Church: Contemporary Practice." *SVTQ* 41 (1997): 1–17.

————. "Penitential discipline in the Orthodox Canonical Tradition." Pages 23–28 in *The Challenge of our Past*. Crestwood, NY: St Vladimir's Seminary Press, 1991.

Eusebius of Caesarea. *The Life of Constantine*. PG 20:909–1230.

Filias, George N. *Les prières pour les malades et sur l'huile de l'onction dans l'Euchologe Barberini grec 336*. Athens, 1997.

Germanus of Constantinople. *Ecclesiastical History*. See next entry.

Germanus of Constantinople. *St Germanus of Constantinople On the Divine Liturgy*. Greek text with English translation. Edited and translated by Paul Meyendorff. PPS 8. Crestwood, NY: St Vladimir's Seminary Press, 1984.

Getcha, Job (Abp). "Confession and Spiritual Direction in the Orthodox Church." *SVTQ* 51 (2007): 203–20.

————. "La dédicace des églises dans le rite byzantin," *Les enjeux spirituels et théologiques de l'espace liturgiqu: Conférences Saint-Serge. 51ᵉ Semaine d'Études Liturgiques*. Rome, 2005.

————. "La liturgie de l'ordination épiscopale dans l'Église orthodoxe." Pages 160–174 in *Le concile Vatican II et l'Église orthodoxe*. Analecta Chambesiana 5. Chambésy, 2015. Also in Greek: "Ἡ Ἀκολουθία τῆς ἐπισκοπῆς χειροτονίας στὴν Ὀρθόδοξη Ἐκκλησία." *Θεολογία* 3 (2014): 7–23.

————. "La liturgie hagiopolite et l'origine de la Liturgie des Présanctifiés." Pages 163–178 in *Sion, mère des Églises: Mélanges liturgiques offerts au Père Charles Athanase Renoux*. Edited by Daniel Findikyan, Daniel Galadza, and André Lossky. Semaines d'études liturgiques Saint-Serge Subsidia 1. Münster: Aschendorff, 2016.

————. "Une prière pour ceux qui se confessent d'un Euchologe slave prémoghilien: Quelques implications théologiques." Pages 137–49 in *La prière liturgique. Conférences Saint-Serge. 47ᵉ Semaine d'Etudes Liturgiques*. Edited by Achille Triacca and Alessandro Pistoia. BEL Subsidia 115. Rome: CLV-Edizioni Liturgiche, 2001.

————. *La réforme liturgique du métropolite Cyprien de Kiev*. Patrimoines—Orthodoxie. Paris: Les Éditions du Cerf, 2010.

————. *The Typikon Decoded*. Orthodox Liturgy Series 3. Yonkers, NY: St Vladimir's Seminary Press, 2012.

Goar, Jacobus. *Euchologion sive Rituale Graecorum*. Paris: Simon Piget, 1647. Venice: Typographia Bartholomaei Javarina, 1730.

Golubtsov, A. "Ob obryadovoi storone tainstva eleosvyashcheniya." *Pribavleniya k izdaniyu tvorenii svyatykh ottsov v russkom perevode za 1888 god*. 42.3 (Moscow: Redaktsiya "Bogoslovsky vestnik," 1888): 113–30.

Gregory the Great. *Letters*. PL 77:441–1328.

Grumel, Venance. "L'auteur et la date de la composition du tropaire Ὁ Μονογενής." *EO* 22:132 (1923): 398–418.

Hanssens, Jean-Michel. *Institutiones liturgicae de ritibus orientalibus*. 3 vols. Rome: Pontificia Università Gregoriana. 1930–1932, repr. 1962.

Hawkes-Teeples, Steven. *The Liturgy of the Word*. Fairfax, VA: Eastern Christian Publications, 2016. A translation of Juan Mateos, *Le célébration de la parole dans la liturgie byzantine*.

Herman, E. "Il più antico penitenziale greco." *OCP* 19 (1933): 71–127.

Hippolytus. *Hippolytus: On the Apostolic Tradition*. Second edition. Alistair C. Stewart, tr. PPS 54. Yonkers, NY: St Vladimir's Seminary Press, 2018.

Ignatius of Antioch. *Ignatius of Antioch: The Letters*. Edited and translated by Alistair Stewart. PPS 49. Yonkers, NY: St Vladimir's Seminary Press, 2013.

Ionita, Viorel. *Towards the Holy and Great Synod of the Orthodox Church: The Decisions of the Pan-Orthodox Meetings since 1923 until 2009*. Studie Œcumenica Friburgensia 62. Basel: Friedrich Reinhardt Verlag, 2014.

Isidore of Seville. *De eccles. officiis*. PL 83:737–826.

Izzo, Januarius M. *The Antimension in the Liturgical and Canonical Tradition of the Byzantine and Latin Churches*. Rome: Pontificium Athenaeum Antonianum, 1975.

Jacob, A. "Où était récitée la prière de l'ambon?" *Byzantion* 51 (1981): 306–15.

Janeras, Sebastià. "Les Byzantins et le Trisagion christologique." *Miscellanea Liturgica in onore di Sua Eminenza il Cardinale Giacomo Lercaro*, vol. 2 (Rome: Desclée, 1967), 469–99.

———. "Le Trisagion: une formule brève en liturgie comparée." Pages 534–562 in *Acts of the International Congress of Comparative Liturgy. Fifty years after A. Baumstark (1872–1948)*. Edited by R. Taft and G. Winkler. OCA 265. Rome: Pontificium Institutum Orientalium Studiorum, 2001.

Janin, Raymond. "Les processions religieuses à Byzance." *REB* 24 (1966): 69–88.

Joannou, Périclès-Pierre. *Discipline générale antique (IVe–IXe s.)*. Volume 1.1. *Les canons des conciles oecuméniques*. Grottaferrata (Rome): Tipografia Italo-Orientale "S. Nilo," 1962.

———. *Discipline générale antique (IVe–IXe s.)*. Volume 1.2. *Les canons des Synodes Particuliers*. Grottaferrata (Rome): Tipografia Italo-Orientale "S. Nilo," 1962.

———. *Discipline générale antique (IVe–IXe s.)*. Volume 2. *Les canons des Pères Grecs*. Grottaferrata (Rome): Tipografia Italo-Orientale "S. Nilo," 1963.

Joasaph, Metropolitan of Ephesus. *Canonical Answers.* Edited by A. Almazov. Odessa, 1903.

Job Hamartolos. *On the Seven Mysteries of the Church.* Cod. 64 Supplementi graeci Parisiensis. Quoted in M. Jugie, *Theologica Dogmatica Christianorum Orientalium,* vol. 3 (see below).

John Chrysostom. *Homilies on Colossians.* PG 62:299–392. English: NPNF¹ 14:257–321.

————. *Homilies on Ephesians.* PG 62:9–176. English: NPNF¹ 14:50–172.

————. *Homily on the Captive Eutropius. In Eutropium.* PG 52:391–396. English: *On Eutropius, Patrician and Consul.* NPNF¹ 9:249–265.

————. *On the Baptism of Christ.* PG 49:363–372.

————. *On the Priesthood. De sacerdotio.* Edited by A. M. Malingrey. SC 272. English: St John Chrysostom. *Six Books on the Priesthood.* Translated by Graham Neville. PPS 1. Crestwood, NY: St Vladimir's Seminary Press, 1977.

John the Faster. *Penitential.* PG 88:1899–1918.

Johnson, M. *The Prayers of Sarapion of Thmuis: A Literary, Liturgical and Theological Analysis.* OCA 249. Rome: Pontificio Istituto Orientale, 1995.

Jugie, Martin. *Theologica Dogmatica Christianorum Orientalium.* Vol. 3. Paris: Letouzey et Ané, 1930. [Vol. 1: 1926; 2:1933; 4: 1931; 5:1935].

Justin Martyr. *First Apology.* Edited by C. Munier. SC 507. Paris: Cerf, 2006.

Karmiris, I. *Τὰ δογματικά καὶ συμβολικά μνημεία τῆς Ὀρθόδοξου Καθολικῆς Ἐκκλησίας,* vol. 2. Athens, 1953.

Katansky, A. L. "Ocherk istorii liturgii nashei Pravoslavnoi Tserkvi." *Khristianskoe chtenie* 2 (1868): 525–576.

Kokkinos, Philotheos. *Diataxis of the Divine Liturgy.* PG 154:745b–766b.

Kontouma, V. "Baptême et communion des jeunes enfants: la lettre de Jean d'Antioche à Théodore d'Éphèse (998/999)." *REB* 69 (2011): 185–204.

————. "La Définition des trois patriarches sur l'anabaptisme (1755/56)." *Annuaire de l'École pratique des hautes études (EPHE),* Section des sciences religieuses 121 (2014): 255–67.

L'Huillier, P. "Les divers modes de réception des catholiques-romains dans l'Orthodoxie." *Le Messager orthodoxe* 82 (1979): 15–23.

Larin, Vassa. *The Byzantine Hierarchical Divine Liturgy in Arsenij Suxanov's Proskinitarij: Text, Translation and Analysis of the Entrance Rites.* OCA 286. Rome: Pontificio Istituto Orientale, 2010.

Leclercq, Henri. "Autel." *DACL,* 1.2, columns 3155–3189.

Lisitsyn, Mikhail A. *Pervonachal'ny slavyano-russkii tipikon.* Saint Petersburg, 1911.

Lossky, A. "Les prières byzantines de confession: repentir et rémission des péchés par miséricorde divine." Pages 151–163 in *La prière liturgique: Conférences*

Saint-Serge: 47e Semaine d'Etudes Liturgiques. Edited by Achille Triacca and Alessandro Pistoia. BEL 115. Rome: CLV-Edizioni Liturgiche, 2001.

————. " 'Remettre les péchés': quelques aspects liturgiques et doctrinaux de la confession et de l'absolution." *Θυσία αἰνέσεως: Mélanges liturgiques offerts à la mémoire de l'archevêque Georges Wagner.* Edited by J. Getcha and A. Lossky. Analecta Sergiana 2. (Paris: Presses Saint-Serge, 2005), 173–85.

Mandalà, P. M. *La protesi della liturgia nel rito bizantino-greco.* Grottaferrata: Scuola Tipografica Italo-Orientale "S. Nilo." 1935, 1955.

Mateos, Juan. *La célébration de la parole dans la liturgie byzantine.* OCA 191. Rome: Pontificium Institutum Orientalium Studiorum, 1971. For an English translation, see Hawkes-Steeples, *The Liturgy of the Word.*

————. "Évolution historique de la liturgie de saint Jean Chrysostome. Première partie: De la bénédiction initiale au Trisagion." *OCP* 15 (1965): 333–351; *OCP* 16 (1966): 3–18; *OCP* 16 (1966): 133–161 = J. Mateos, *La célébration de la parole dans la liturgie byzantine.* OCA 191: 27–90.

————. *Le Typikon de la Grande Église: Ms. Sainte-Croix no. 40, Xe siècle.* Introduction, texte critique, traduction et notes par Juan Mateos, S.I. Vol. 1: *Le cycle des douze mois.* Orientalia Christiana Analecta 165. Rome: Pontificium Institutum Orientalium Studiorum, 1962.

————. *Le Typikon de la Grande Église: Ms. Sainte-Croix no. 40, Xe siècle.* Introduction, texte critique, traduction et notes par Juan Mateos, S.J. Vol. 2: *Le cycle des fêtes mobiles.* Orientalia Christiana Analecta 166. Rome: Pontificium Institutum Orientalium Studiorum, 1963.

Maximus the Confessor. *On the Ecclesiastical Mystagogy.* Greek text with Introduction, Translation, Notes, and Bibliography by Jonathan J. Armstrong, in collaboration with Shawn Fowler and Tim Wellings. PPS 59. Yonkers, NY: St Vladimir's Seminary Press, 2019.

————. *Quaestiones ad Thalassium.* PG 90:244–785. In English: St Maximos the Confessor, *On Difficulties in Sacred Scripture: The Responses to Thalassios,* trans. Maximos Constas. The Fathers of the Church 136. Washington, DC: The Catholic University of America Press, 2018.

Mazza, E. *The Celebration of the Eucharist: The Origin of the Rite and the Development of its Interpretation.* Collegeville, MN: The Liturgical Press, 1999.

Menevisoglou, P. *Τὸ Ἅγιον Μύρον ἐν τῇ Ὀρθοδόξῳ Ἀνατολικῇ Ἐκκλησίᾳ, ἰδίᾳ κατὰ τὰς πηγὰς καὶ τὴν πρᾶξιν τῶν νεωτέρων χρόνων τοῦ Οἰκουμενικοῦ Πατριαρχείου.* Ἀνάλεκτα Βλατάδων 14. Thessalonica, 1972.

Meyendorff, Paul. *The Anointing of the Sick.* Orthodox Liturgy Series 1. Crestwood, NY: St Vladimir's Seminary Press, 2009.

Migne, J.-P., ed. Patrologia Graeca, series secunda. 161 Volumes. Paris, 1857–66.

Miklosich, Franz, and Joseph Müller. *Acta et diplomata graeca medii aevi sacra et profana.* Six volumes. Vienna: Karl Gerold, 1860–1890.

Μικρὸν Εὐχολόγιον. Athens, 1974.

Μικρὸν Εὐχολόγιον. Athens, 1996.

Milgrom, Jacob. *Leviticus 1–16: A New Translation with Introduction and Commentary.* New Haven, CT : Yale University Press, 1998.

Milosevic, Nenad. *To Christ and the Church. The Divine Eucharist as the All-Encompassing Mystery of the Church.* Los Angeles: Sebastian Press, 2012.

Mingana, A. "Commentary of Theodore of Mopsuestia on the Lord's Prayer and on the Sacrament of Baptism and the Eucharist." *Woodbrook Studies* 6 (1933).

Miscellanea Liturgica in onore di Sua Eminenza il Cardinale Giacomo Lercaro, vol. 2 (Rome: Desclée, 1967), 469–99.

Moghila, Peter. *Eukhologion albo Molitvoslov, ili Trebnik.* Vol. 1. Kiev: Monastery of the Caves, 1646.

_____. *Sluzhebnik.* Kiev, 1639.

Moschus, John. *The Spiritual Meadow.* SC 12:65, 266. English translation: *The Spiritual Meadow: By John Moschos.* Introduction, translation, and notes by John Wortley. Cistercian Studies 139. Collegeville, MN: The Liturgical Press, 2008.

Neselovsky, A. *Chiny khirotesii i khirotonii.* Kamianets-Podol'sk, 1906.

Nicholas Cabasilas. *Commentary on the Divine Liturgy.* Tr. J. M. Hussey and P. A. McNulty. Crestwood, NY: St Vladimir's Seminary Press, 1998.

_____. *Explicatio divinae liturgiae.* R. Bornert, J. Gouillard, P. Périchon, and S. Salaville, eds. *Nicolas Cabasilas, Explication de la divine liturgie.* Sources chrétiennes 4-bis. Paris: Éditions du Cerf, 1967.

_____. *Vita in Christo.* Edited by M.-H. Congourdeau. Two volumes. SC 355, 361. Paris: Éditions du Cerf, 1989–1990. English in Nicholas Cabasilas. *The Life in Christ.* Translated by Carmino deCatanzaro. Introduction by Boris Bobrinskoy. Crestwood, NY: St Vladimir's Seminary Press, 1974.

Nicodemus of the Holy Mountain. *Concerning the Schema of Monks and their Garments.* Pages 156–163 in *Exomologetarion,* vol. 2. Athens, 1900. English translation: pages 129–140 in N. F. Robinson, *Monasticism in the Orthodox Churches.* London: Cope and Fenwick, 1916.

_____. *Πηδάλιον.* Thessalonica, 1998.

Nicodemus of the Holy Mountain and Makarios of Corinth, compilers. *The Philokalia: The Complete Text.* Translated from the Greek and edited by G. E. H. Palmer, Philip Sherrard, and Kallistos Ware. Four of five volumes. Vol. 1. London: Faber and Faber, 1979; Vol. 2, 1981; vol. 3, 1894; vol. 4, 1995; vol. 5, forthcoming.

Nicodemus the Hagiorite. *See* Nicodemus of the Holy Mountain.

Nikolsky, Konstantin. *Ob antiminsakh Pravoslavnoi Russkoi Tserkvi*. Saint Petersburg: Tipografia Yakova Treya, 1872.

Odintsov, N. *Poryadok obshchestvennogo i chastnogo bogosluzheniya v drevnei Rossii do XVI v.* St Petersburg, 1881.

Origen. *Homilies on Leviticus 1–16.* Translated by Gary Wayne Barkley. The Fathers of the Church Series 83. Washington, DC: Catholic University of America Press, 1990.

———. *Homilies on Luke, Fragments on Luke.* Translated by Joseph T. Lienhard, S.J. The Fathers of the Church Series 94. Washington, DC: Catholic University of America Press, 1996.

Parenti, Stefano and Elena Velkovska, eds. *L'Euchologio Barberini gr. 336.* Second, revised edition. Rome: CLV/Edizioni Liturgiche, 2000.

Pentkovsky, A. "Chinosledovaniya khirotonii v viznatiiskikh Evkhologiyakh VIII–XII vv." *Vizantiskii Vremenik* 61 [86] (2002): 127–30.

———. "Le cérémonial du mariage dans l'Euchologe byzantin." In *Le mariage: XLᵉ semaine d'études byzantines*, 259–288. BEL 77. Rome, 1994.

Petit, L. "Du pouvoir de consacrer le saint chrême." *Échos d'Orient* 3 (1899–1900): 1–7.

Pétridès, Sophrone. "Antimension." Columns 2319–2326 in *DACL* 1.2. Paris, 1907.

———. "L'antimension." *EO* 3 (1899–1900): 193–202.

Petrovsky, A. "Drevnii akt prinosheniya veshchestva dlya tainstva evkharistii i posledovanie proskomidii." *Khristianskoe chtenie* 84.3 (1904): 406–431.

Phidas, V. *L'institution de la pentarchie des patriarches* (in Greek). Vol. III. Athens, 2012.

———. "Τὸ κύρος τοῦ βαπτίσματος τῶν αἱρετικῶν καὶ τὸ ζήτημα τοῦ ἀναβαπτισμοῦ." *Orthodoxia* 11 (2004): 421–456.

Phountoulis, Ioannis M. Ἀκολουθία τοῦ εὐχελαίου. Κείμενα Λειτουργικῆς 15. Thessalonica, 1978.

———. Λειτουργική, Α´, εἰσαγωγή στη Θεία λατρεία. Thessalonica, 1993.

Prilutsky, Vasily D. *Chastnoe bogosluzhenie v Russkoi tserkvi v XVI v pervoi polovine XVII v.* Kiev: Petr Barsky, 1912.

Pseudo-Kodinos. *Traité des Offices.* Edited by Jean Verpeaux. Paris: Centre National de la Recherche Scientifique, 1996.

Puniet, Pierre de. "Bénédiction de l'eau en la fête de l'Épiphanie." *DACL* 2: 698–708.

———. "Dédicace des églises." *DACL* 4.1, columns 374–405.

Raes, A. "Antimension, tablit, tabot," *POC* 1 (1951): 65–70.

———. "Le consentement dans les rites orientaux." *Ephemerides Liturgicae* 47 (1933): 36–47, 249–259.

_____. "Les formulaires grecs du rite de pénitence." Pages 365–72 in *Mélanges en l'honneur de Mgr Michel Andrieu*. Strasbourg: Palais Universitaire, 1956.

Raquez, O. "Les confessions de foi de la chirotonie épiscopale des Églises grecques." *Traditio et progressio: Studi liturgici in onore del Prof. A. Nocent*. Studia Anselmiana 95. Rome: Pontificio Ateneo S. Anselmo, 1988.

Renaudot, Eusèbe. *Liturgiarum Orientalium Collectio*. 2 vols.. Paris: Coignard, 1716.

Rhalles, G. A. and M. Potles. *Syntagma*. Vol. 2. Athens, 1852; Vol. 4. Athens, 1854; Vol. 5. Athens, 1855.

Ritzer, K. *Le mariage dans les Églises chrétiennes du Ier au XIe siècle*. Paris: Les Éditions du Cerf, 1970.

Roberts, Alexander, James Donaldson, and A. Cleveland Coxe, eds. The Ante-Nicene Fathers: Translations of the Fathers down to AD 325. 10 vols. Buffalo, NY: Christian Literature Company, 1885–1896, many reprints.

Robinson, N. F. *Monasticism in the Orthodox Churches*. London: Cope and Fenwick, 1916.

Salaville, J. "Antimension." Columns 643–644 in *Catholicisme*. Volume 1. Paris, 1948.

Schmemann, Alexander. *Of Water and the Spirit*. Crestwood, NY: St Vladimir's Seminary Press, 1974.

_____. "Report to the Holy Synod of the Orthodox Church in America," https:// oca.org/holy-synod/encyclicals/on-confession-and-communion. Accessed May 12, 2020.

Socrates Scholasticus. *Historia ecclesiastica*. PG 67:33–842. In English: *Ecclesiastical History*. NPNF^2 2:1–178.

Soteriou, G. A. "Ἡ Πρόθεσις καὶ τὸ Διακονικὸν εν τῇ Ἀρχαίᾳ Ἐκκλησίᾳ." *Θεολογία* 1/18 (1940): 76–100.

St Tikhon's Monastery. *Great Book of Needs Expanded and Supplemented*. Translated from Church Slavonic with notes by St Tikhon's Monastery. Four vols. South Canaan, PA: St Tikhon's Seminary Press, 1998–99.

Stewart, Alistair, tr. and ed. *The Testament of the Lord*. An English Version. With Introduction and Notes by Alistair C. Stewart. PPS 58. Yonkers, NY: St Vladimir's Seminary Press, 2018.

Stewart(-Sykes), Alistair, tr. and ed. *On the Two Ways: Life or Death, Light or Darkness: Foundational Texts in the Tradition*. PPS 41. Yonkers, NY: St Vladimir's Seminary Press, 2011.

Stričević, D. "Dyakonikon i protezis u ranokhristsanskim tsrkvama." *Starinar* 9 (1958): 59–66.

Symeon of Thessalonica. *De sacra liturgia*. PG 155:253–304.

_____. *De Sacramentis*. PG 155:175–237.

_____. *De sacris ordinationibus*. PG 155:361–470.

_____. *De sancto euchelaeo*. PG 155:515–536.

_____. *Dialogus in Christo adversus omnes haereses*. PG 155:33–176.

_____. *The Liturgical Commentaries*. Edited and Translated by Steven Hawkes-Teeples. Studies and Texts 168. Toronto: Pontifical Institute of Mediaeval Studies, 2011.

Symeon the New Theologian. *Letter on Confession* 11. In *Enthusiasmus und Bussgewalt beim griechischen Mönchtum: Eine Studie zu Symeon dem Neuen Theologen*. Edited by Karl Holl. Leipzig: J. C. Hinrichs'sche Buchhandlung, 1898.

Taft, Robert. *The Communion, Thanksgiving and Concluding Rites*. OCA 281. Rome: Pontificio Istituto Orientale, 2008.

_____. *The Diptychs*. OCA 238. Rome: Pontificio Istituto Orientale, 1991.

_____. *The Great Entrance*. OCA 200. Rome: Pontificio Istituto Orientale, 1978.

_____. *The Pre-Communion Rites*. OCA 261. Rome: Pontifico Istituto Orientale, 2000.

_____. "Water into Wine. The Twice-mixed Chalice in the Byzantine Eucharist." *Le Muséon* 100 (1987): 323–42.

Taft, Robert, and G. Winkler, eds. *Acts of the International Congress of Comparative Liturgy: Fifty years after A. Baumstark*. OCA 265. Rome: Pontificium Institutum Orientalium Studiorum, 2001.

Thedore the Lector. *Historia ecclesiastica*. PG 86a:165–216.

Theodore of Andida. *Protheoria*. PG 140:417a–468d.

Theodore of Mopsuestia. *Les homélies catechétiques de Théodore de Mopsueste*. Edited by Raymond-M. Tonneau and Robert Devresse. Vatican City: Biblioteca Apostolica Vaticana, 1949.

Trebnik, vol. 1. Moscow, 1991.

Trebnik. Moscow: Sretensky Monastery, 2000.

Trempelas, Panagiotis N. "L'Audition de l'anaphore par le peuple." In *L'Église et les Églises*, vol. 2. Chevetogne, 1954; 207–220.

_____. *Μικρὸν Εὐχολόγιον*. Vol 1. Athens, 1950.

_____. *Αἱ τρεῖς λειτοθργίαι*. Athens: Ekdoseis tes megales patriarkhikes epistemonikes, 1935.

Tsypin, Vladislav. *Tserkovnoe pravo*. Moscow, 1994.

Uspensky, Nicholas. "The Collision of Two Theologies in the Revision of Russian Liturgical Books in the Seventeenth Century." Pages 191–240 in his *Evening Worship in the Orthodox Church*. Crestwood, NY: St Vladimir's Seminary Press, 1985.

_____. *Evening Worship in the Orthodox Church*. Crestwood, NY: St Vladimir's Seminary Press, 1985.

———. "Liturgiya prezhdeosvyashchennykh darov: Istoriko-liturgicheskii ocherk." *Bogosluzhebnie Trudy* 15 (1976): 146–84.

———. "The Liturgy of the Presanctified Gifts: History and Practice." Pages 156–162 in *Evening Worship in the Orthodox Church*. Crestwood, NY: St Vladimir's Seminary Press, 1985.

Vidalis, M. "La bénédiction des eaux de la fête de l'Épiphanie." Pages 237–257 in *La prière liturgique: Conférences Saint-Serge: XLVIIe Semaine d'Études Liturgiques*. BEL Subsidia 115. Rome: CLV/Edizioni Liturgiche, 2001.

Vogel, C. "La discipline pénitentielle dans l'Église orthodoxe de Grèce." *Revue des Sciences Religieuses* 27 (1953): 374–99.

Wagner, Georges. "La consécration du myron." *La liturgie, expérience de l'Église*. Analecta Sergiana 1. Paris: Presses Saint-Serge, 2003: 148–149.

———. "Penitential discipline in the Oriental Tradition." In German. Pages 251–64 in *Liturgie et rémission des péchés*. Conférences Saint-Serge. 20e Semaine d'Etudes Liturgiques. Edited by Alessandro Triacca. Rome, 1975. Also: "La discipline pénitentielle dans la tradition orientale," in *La liturgie, expérience de l'Eglise. Études liturgiques*. Analecta Sergiana 1. Paris: Presses Saint-Serge, 2003: 67–80.

Wenger, A. "Les influences du rituel de Paul V sur le *Trebnik* de Pierre Moghila." *Mélanges en l'honneur de Mgr Michel Andrieu*. Strasbourg: Palais Universitaire, 1956. Pages 477–99.

Widok, N. "Christian Family as Domestic Church in the Writings of St. John Chrysostom." *Studia Ceranea* 3 (2013): 167–175.

Woodfin, W. *The Embodied Icon: Liturgical Vestments and Sacramental Power in Byzantium*. Oxford: Oxford University Press, 2012.

Zheltov, M. S., and I. O. Popov. "Antimins." Pages 489–492 in *Pravoslavnaya Entsiklopediya*. Volume 2. Moscow, 2001.

Index of Manuscripts

Index of Selected Authors

253

Index of Subjects